Tour Climbs

Tour Climbs

THE COMPLETE GUIDE TO EVERY
TOUR DE FRANCE MOUNTAIN CLIMB

Chris Sidwells

Collins

First published in 2008 by

Collins, an imprint of
HarperCollins Publishers
77–85 Fulham Palace Road
Hammersmith, London W6 8JB

www.collins.co.uk

First published 2008

Reprinted in paperback with updates and corrections 2009
5 4 3 2 1
2010 2009

A catalogue record for this book is available from the
British Library

ISBN: 978 0 00 731521 5

Publisher: Myles Archibald
Designer: Heike Schüssler
Production: Chris Gurney

Printed in China by Leo Paper Products Ltd

Contents

The Tour de France

The Tour de France is the biggest annual sporting event in the world. For three weeks it has priority over a nation's roads. As long ago as the 1960's a French writer said that President De Gaulle might run the country for eleven months but in July, France was ruled by the Tour.

A social scientist could probably come up with clever reasons as to why a bike race has captured the hearts of a nation. But I think that one reason could be the setting. France is a beautiful country, and any sporting event run off against a backdrop of such stunning scenery is onto a winner.

Another reason could be that July is holiday time in France. People associate the Tour with being away from the everyday, being free and having fun. To see how true this is, you only have to visit any village when the Tour passes through. On a flat stage the riders stream past in seconds, but in each village an all-day party will be held.

Then there are the riders themselves. The Tour de France is hard, maybe the hardest sporting event in the world. There are flat days of superfast racing – a painful crash in the tight pack of 200 riders is only a moment's inattention away. In contrast the mountains draw the race out, with every rider having to fight their own battle against nature.

The race forges heroes, it creates colourful characters. Hard workers who people identify with. You don't fluke the Tour de France. Simply finishing is a triumph – but winning places a man in the pantheon of champions. The race has its faults. Some riders want to win too much and have cheated. But the Tour de France is fighting that, and the race has somehow become nobler because of it.

The Tour de France

'ITS MEN AND ITS MOUNTAINS'

The Tour de France is a stretch of anyone's imagination. It is the biggest annual sporting event in the world; 15 million spectators line the road to watch it pass by, while many more sit glued to a thousand hours of television beamed during its three weeks to all four corners of the world. The Tour is long and gruelling, its course is spectacular, its infrastructure huge. And mountain climbs have been part of the Tour de France almost since it began.

The race was born out of a turn of the 20th century battle to increase newspaper circulation. Count de Dion was the fiery tempered owner of a magazine called *Le Velo*, but when its editor criticised De Dion's stance over the Dreyfus Affair, a case that rocked France where a Jewish army officer was wrongly accused of spying, he withdrew his cash and set up a new magazine that he called *L'Auto*.

Bicycle racing had been going in France since 1867, encouraged by manufacturers who set up works teams to compete in long races that were the perfect stage on which to demonstrate the durability of their machines. Something about the struggle that the competitors had with the elements, and the speed with which they ate kilometre after kilometre of dreadful roads, struck a chord with French people, and the sport became hugely popular.

It's no surprise then that the editor of a new sports magazine should turn to bike racing as a way of boosting his sales figures. And even less of a surprise given that the editor of *L'Auto*, Henri Desgrange, had been a professional racer in his youth.

However, although he is known as the 'Father of the Tour,' it wasn't Desgrange who first thought up the Tour de France. That was *L'Auto*'s chief cycling reporter, Geo Lefevre, who had the mad idea of a bike race around the whole of France – indeed at first Desgrange deeply sceptical.

There were several long races already in existence. Paris-Brest-Paris for example, a trip of well over 1000 kilometres in one go from the French capital to the tip of the Breton peninsula and back again. But this? The race Lefevre was proposing was 2500 kilometres long and would take its competitors to all six corners of France. As well as a sporting challenge it was a going to be a logistics nightmare.

The race takes shape

But the more Desgrange thought about it, the more he liked the idea. Break the distance down into stages, and the race begins to seem possible. So it was, on 1 July 1903, at the Café du Réveil du Matin in the village of Montgeron, now a suburb of Paris, the Tour de France departed for the first time.

Sixty men, some of them full time professionals but most self-financed amateurs, lined up to ride the first stage of 467 kilometres from Paris to Lyon.

Above: The Eagle of Toledo, Frederico Bahamontes

Strong of arm and leg, sound of body, men with tough minds and even tougher handlebar moustaches, these modern-day knights of the road pedalled their heavy machines into history.

A Parisian chimney sweep called Maurice Garin won the first Tour de France. It was 2428 kilometres long and split into six stages. Paris to Lyon, Lyon to Marseille, Marseille to Toulouse then on to Bordeaux, Nantes and back to Paris. Garin's prize was 6,125 gold francs, and his victory margin over second-placed Louis Pothier was getting on for three hours. Interest in the race was huge – France had fallen for the Tour

The race has changed much since 1903, but its basic template was laid down in that very first edition. No matter how many stages there are, or how many a rider wins, the Tour de France winner is the man who completes the whole route in the least time. So it's possible to win the race without winning a single stage. And it's been done, although not very often. But one thing was missing from the first event – the mountains. But once the organisers saw that racing around France was possible, they decided to make it harder. And to do that they headed for the hills.

Going into the mountains

France has four mountainous areas: in order of increasing height, the Vosges, the Massif Central, the huge peaks of the Pyrenees and the giant Alps. In order to see how cyclists would fare, the organisers decided to include a stage through the Vosges in the 1905 race, and to visit the very edge of the Alps.

Competitors had climbed the Col de la Republique during the first Tour, but that is only a pass over the low shoulder of a mountain range, and there was no way around it. Now though, the riders would take on a real mountain, virtually crossing its summit – and its name was the Ballon d'Alsace.

In his editorial before the race, Desgrange predicted that no competitor would be able to ride all the way to the top. They would have to dismount and walk for at least part of it, he thought. But René Pottier proved him wrong. He was the only one to do it, but Pottier pedalled all the way to the top. He even overtook Desgrange, who was riding in the lead motor vehicle at the head of the race.

Pottier's effort destroyed his chances of winning. He was caught by other more prudent riders on the descent and later forced to retire from the stage through exhaustion. But as the riders pedalled on to the stage finish in Besancon, right on the edge of the Jura, Pottier had made a point to Desgrange

On the next but one stage the race climbed the Col de Bayard, while travelling from the Alpine gateway city of Grenoble to Toulon on the Mediterranean coast. Everyone wanted to know if the riders would beat the stage coach that went over the climb from Grenoble and south to Gap. The coach was drawn by six horses on the flat and ten on the climbs, but the riders beat it by hours, and then carried on to Toulon.

Before the first Tour de France the daily circulation of *L'Auto* was 140,000. By 1910 the race had grabbed people's interest to the point where Desgrange was selling 300,000 copies a day. But he wasn't satisfied with that. The mountains were a big success. The pedalling heroes could conquer them, so in 1910 the Father of the Tour planned an epic stage, a stage to top all others, a stage that would capture the imaginations of everyone in France.

It was 326 kilometres long, it ran east to west from Luchon to Bayonne and crossed some of the most famous mountain passes in the Pyrenees; the Col de

Peyresourde, Col d'Aspin, Col du Tourmalet and Col d'Aubisque. Almost no one had climbed these passes on a bike, and certainly no one had climbed them one after the other on a single ride. In 1910 they were routes generally used by mountain people to get from one valley to the next, and not much more than rutted tracks.

It was a big adventure, and one guaranteed to make *L'Auto* the number one sports publication in France, but the thought of the challenge that lay ahead of the riders filled Desgrange and his staff with great trepidation. Desgrange wasn't any more at ease when he drove to the top of the Peyresourde to see the riders on the first climb.

He had an anxious wait. It was the first time that Desgrange had seen the climb. All he had to go on before the race were reports from his staff, who had visited the Pyrenees to see if the stage was possible. That morning he had learned of reports of bear attacks in the area. The news didn't make him feel any better as he waited

Then he saw a dishevelled figure trudging towards him pushing a bike. It was a Tour de France rider, but Desgrange couldn't identify him as he was covered in mud and he refused to speak to the race organiser. The next rider was easy to identify, and had a little more to say. He was Octave Lapize, a great rider and one of the favourites to win the 1910 Tour. Desgrange asked him what had happened to the others, but Lapize looked straight through him and spat out a single word: "Murderer!"

Desgrange loved that. He once said that his perfect Tour de France would have only one finisher, one hero who had battled through it all to the end. Lapize won the first Pyrenean stage at an average speed of 23 kph, and over 40 riders managed to haul themselves over the mountains, the last three admittedly over seven hours behind the winner. Every rider hated Desgrange, but no one had died. His race was now the most important and most popular sporting event in France – and the mountains would be part of it for ever.

The yellow jersey

The First World War called a halt to the Tour shortly after the 1914 race, but as soon as was humanly possible, Desgrange and the Tour were back. In 1919 the riders raced across the bombed out battlefields of northern France, a symbol of hope in a rubble-strewn wasteland.

But the colour of the 1919 Tour de France was yellow. Desgrange always looked for ways to improve his race. One criticism he'd heard was that spectators could never tell which of the riders was the overall race leader when they pedalled by, so Desgrange decided that the Tour leader should wear a distinctive jersey. The legend goes that yellow was chosen because it was the colour of *L'Auto*'s pages.

However, it is also said that yellow was the only colour left in suitable numbers when Desgrange needed the jerseys in a hurry.

The Tour became established as the number one international cycling event between the World Wars. Cycle road racing was now a very popular sport in many European countries and in 1909 the Tour had its first foreign winner: François Faber of Luxembourg. The Tour of Italy was born in the same year. Odile Defraye of Belgium won the 1912 Tour de France, and his countrymen followed him to victory in the next six editions of the race.

Ottavio Bottecchia was the first Italian to win, in 1924, and he did it again in 1925. Then in 1949 the Tour de France was won by cycling's first really big international superstar, a compatriot of Bottecchia's, Fausto Coppi. Coppi could win every kind of race, he was a superb athlete, and his fame soon surpassed his own sport.

Media stars

The media had grown by 1949. Fans could read about Coppi, and they could see films of him racing, as well as watch by the roadside. He had more coverage than any other cyclist before him. This made Coppi a celebrity, and a controversial celebrity at that.

Coppi earned more money than any other cyclist had before him, and money gave him a lifestyle to be envied – and also one that fascinated his fans too. He fell in love with the beautiful wife of his doctor. He left his own wife to live with her. They had a son, and Coppi was excommunicated from the Catholic church.

Coppi won the Tour de France again in 1952, before Frenchman Louison Bobet became the first man to win the race three times in a row. Bobet was another rider who made a lot of money from cycling, so much infact that he often piloted his own aircraft to races. Cycling had come of age, its top riders were wealthy men, and even though it was, and still is, a brutal struggle to succeed, professional cycling now carried with it the gloss of glamour.

In the 1960s the sport was dominated by Jacques Anquetil, a Frenchman, who from humble beginnings as a strawberry grower's son in Normandy, became the first five-times winner of the Tour, the first French winner of the Tour of Italy, and when he won the Tour of Spain, which had started up in 1935, Anquetil became the first cyclist ever to win all three major stage races.

New management

The Tour de France saw a change of direction after the Second World War. When the race started up again in 1947, Henri Desgrange had fallen ill and his place was taken by Jacques Goddet, the son of *L'Auto*'s first company accountant. Goddet was a well-educated man who had spent part of his youth in England, and who spoke several languages.

Going global

L'Auto was shut down by the allies when they liberated Paris in 1945, but Goddet just upped sticks and set up a new newspaper across the road. He called it *L'Equipe* – to this day, one of the biggest and best known daily sports newspapers in the world.

Goddet took the Tour de France with him, and *L'Equipe* owned the race until they sold it to the Amaury Sport Organisation in the mid-1980s. Amaury are still the company behind the Tour de France, and the whole thing, along with a number of other international bike races and other sporting events, are run from a modern office block in the Paris suburb of Issy-les-Molineux.

The Tour prospered under Goddet. He was quite modern – though he didn't look it, especially when the race was in the hot south of France when Goddet used to wear his tropical gear of pith helmet, shorts, long socks and a Safari shirt. Goddet had a shrewd assistant called Felix Levitan, who looked after the commercial side of the race. Between them they ruled with a rod of iron, and despite there being official referees and judges on the race, Goddet and Levitan's word on everything was final.

An Australian team raced in the Tour de France of 1928, but in general up until the mid-1950s Tour competitors were almost exclusively from mainland Europe. Then in 1955 a British team, sponsored by a bike manufacturer called Hercules, raced the event. Only two of their riders, Brian Robinson and Tony Hoar, finished, but Robinson graduated into mainstream European pro racing and won stages in the 1958 and 1959 Tours.

More Britons followed Robinson. Tom Simpson wore the leader's Yellow Jersey in 1962, and Barry Hoban won eight Tour stages during his long pro career. Robert Millar then became the Britain's most successful Tour de France rider ever when he finished fourth overall and won the King of the Mountains competition in 1984.

While this was going, on Australians, Irish, Americans and Canadians continued to swell the English-speaking presence on the Tour. Other nations joined in too, most notably the Colombians and Scandinavians began to write themselves into Tour history. The Tour de France was going global.

Its fame and appeal exploded in 1986 when an American, Greg Lemond won the Tour. His victory was followed by that of Stephen Roche from Ireland in 1987. New interest in the race from all over the world meant a flood of new sponsors. Major names like Coca Cola wanted a piece of the Tour. An American, Lance Armstrong set a record in 2005 with seven consecutive victories in the Tour, and a Frenchman hasn't won since 1985.

Twenty-first century Tour

Today the Tour de France is huge. London paid £1.5 million to host the start of the race in 2007, but got far more than that back from the visitors who came to watch. The prize pot for the race totals €3 million, with €400,000 going to the winner. Not that he sees any of it. Traditionally he splits it among his team, because the winner of the Tour de France automatically becomes the highest earner in the sport. Lance Armstrong is reputed to have earned $17 million in product endorsements alone during 2005.

The Tour de France has its own motorcycle police force and a travelling bank, the only one allowed by law to open on the nation's Bastille Day holiday. Each year there are 2,300 accredited journalists on the race, 1,100 technicians and chauffeurs (many of them ex-competitors who drive race officials and guests). On top of that, 1,500 vehicles accompany the riders on the road in the form of a publicity cavalcade that companies pay dearly to be part of. Another 4,500 support staff work on the Tour, either in race routing, hospitality or assembling and taking down the temporary Tour village that moves from town to town between the stages.

At the heart of all this activity are the riders. As many as 200 of the world's best pro road racers start the Tour – although every year there are a good few that don't make it to the finish. Like the race, the riders personal statistics are prodigious. For example, it's reckoned that a competitor will burn around 123,000 calories if he gets through to the end of the race. He will make getting on for 500,000 pedal revolutions, wear out three bicycle chains, and every year the whole field gets through 700 ultra light racing tyres.

How it works

The Tour de France is big, and it's getting bigger with a prosperous and exciting future ahead of it, but it is a race that is firmly rooted in tradition. It has always been what in cycling is called a stage race. That is, a race decided on total time to complete the whole course, but with the course broken up into individual stages. The rider who completes the whole course in the least time is the overall winner, and at any given point after the first stage the race has an overall leader who wears the yellow jersey.

Most of the stages are straightforward races. They are referred to as road stages, where all the riders start together and the first over the line wins the stage. A few stages are time trials; riders start individually at intervals and the one who covers the course on his own in the fastest time wins the stage. Team time trials work on the same principle, but the individual teams complete the course together and their times are added to each team member's overall time for the race.

Soon after the first editions were run, the Tour de France settled into a

Above: The Alpe d'Huez all day Tour party

pattern that is preserved today. It usually occupies the first three weeks of July, which covers the time that French people traditionally take their summer holidays. Since 1967 it has started with a short prologue time trial, which provides some order for the first few stages. The prologue winner wears the yellow jersey on the first road stage.

Most years see the first few stages run off over flat to undulating countryside, giving riders who don't shine in the mountains the chance for some glory. A longish time trial comes after this first phase, and then the mountains. To win the Tour de France a rider must be good at the time trials, but he must also excel in the mountains. He certainly can't be a specialist in one to the exclusion of the other, although many Tour winners have leant towards one or other speciality.

Since they were first visited, the Alps and Pyrenees have been included in every race and the Tour tries to visit the Vosges and Massif Central whenever it can. The race always finishes in Paris, and the others stage towns and cities are decided by geography and by the various municipalities pitching to be hosts. Many places, including towns and cities in neighbouring countries, want to be visited by the Tour. Each year the organisers have a notional idea of where they would like to go, what climbs they would like to include, then they look at who wants the race and come up with a route.

The first long time trial and the first day in the mountains are when the Tour de France begins to take shape each year. The riders and pundits say that while you cannot tell who will win in Paris after the first mountain stage, you can always tell who will not. A number of favourites invariably fall out of the running on this crucial day.

The importance of mountain climbs

Why should this be? Why are mountain climbs so important in shaping the outcome of the Tour de France? Part of the reason is to do with wind resistance. As a cyclist's speed increases linearly, the air resistance that cyclist has to overcome increases exponentially. So bike racers have to overcome far more air resistance to increase their speed by one mile per hour when travelling at 25 mph than they do when travelling at 10 mph. This means that when they are travelling fairly fast, on a flat stage for example, the riders find it very difficult to break away from each other. The whole field can slipstream each other, saving energy, and will often finish virtually together.

Going uphill though, involves a different set of physics. It's the force of gravity rather than air resistance that has to be overcome. No cyclist can travel faster uphill than on the flat, so the reduced speeds mean that air resistance and

The King's story

slipstreaming have less of an effect when climbing. In the mountains a rider has to fight against his own weight, thus the mountains favour riders with the highest power-to-weight ratio.

But that isn't the whole story. Cycling is a complicated sport, and long stage races like the Tour de France are its most complex arena. A good mountain climber might have a phenomenally high power-to-weight ratio, but that could be because he is incredibly light and his absolute power is quite low, which is a limiting factor in a time trial. So although a Tour de France winner must excel in the mountains, and climbing specialists have won the race, he must still be able to ride a fair time trial. In fact, broadly speaking, there are two kinds of Tour winners; time trial specialists who can limit their losses in the mountains, and climbers who can do the same in a time trial.

There are also differences in the way overall contenders go about racing uphill. Some riders, the ones who are good at time trials and can climb well, favour setting a high average pace in an attempt to slowly burn off all the others. Whereas climbing specialists will make violent changes of pace, attacking and being caught before attacking again until their rivals are exhausted by chasing them. These are the riders who win the King of the Mountains title in the Tour de France.

The King of the Mountains competition started in the 1933 Tour, and is based on points awarded for the first riders over each climb. The number of points and how far down the field they go depends on the severity of the climb. They are ranked from third category for hills and small passes, to first category for bigger climbs. Then there is a category the French call Hors Categorie, or beyond category, for the real giants.

The leader of the King of the Mountains competition wears a distinctive red and white polka-dot jersey. The design for that came from the fact that when it was first awarded as the symbol of leadership in this section of the race, the sponsor of the mountains competition was a chocolate manufacturer, whose wrappers were white with red polka-dots on them.

A Spaniard called Vicente Trueba, who was nicknamed the Torrelavega Flea because he was so slight, was the first winner of the King of the Mountains title. Many great climbers and Tour winners have gone on to win the title, including the Italians Gino Bartali and Fausto Coppi, but in the mid-1950s the title was taken by two of the greatest climbers the Tour de France has ever seen, Frederico Bahamontes of Spain and Luxembourg's Charly Gaul.

Bahamontes, who journalists christened the Eagle of Toledo, and Gaul, who they referred to as the Angel of the Mountains, both went on to win the Tour de France overall, and Bahamontes was six times the King of the Mountains champion. They were both capable of attacking early on a mountain stage and decimating the field. That was how they won their Tours.

Bahamontes might have won the Tour more than once, but for the fact that his career overlapped that of Jacques Anquetil, and their battles were a classic confrontation of a time trial specialist who could climb against a pure climber. Anquetil was the time trial specialist and was content to limit his losses on the climbs, but on occasions, and especially against Bahamontes, he had to climb incredibly well to do that.

Their battles came to a head in the 1963 Tour de France on the Col de la Forclaz. Bahamontes, in the yellow jersey, was determined to destroy Anquetil that day and win his second Tour de France, but Anquetil knew that he couldn't allow him any more of a lead. He had to stay with the Spanish climbing star, and he had to summon all of his strength to do it. Anquetil suffered, but he clung on to the Spaniard, surviving all his attacks. He even beat Bahamontes to the line at the end of the stage. Later, Anquetil won the final time trial and his fourth Tour de France.

The best ever

There have been many such epic contests over the years – but who is the best Tour de France climber of all time? There are many candidates, but I'll go for the man who Bahamontes says is best. After all, can there be a better judge? His name is Lucien Van Impe. He is from the flat fields of Flanders in Belgium, but no one could accelerate uphill like Van Impe.

A short man, light but not a featherweight, he won the King of the Mountains six times, but always says he backed off winning a seventh out of respect for Bahamontes. Van Impe also won the Tour overall in 1976. He often said that climbing mountains was an art rather than a science, and spent weeks each year before the Tour de France training in the Alps or Pyrenees in an effort to discover his climbing rhythm.

The Tour de France still throws up great climbers. Lucho Herrera from Colombia and Claudio Chiappucci of Italy were two of the best. In 2004 Frenchman Richard Virenque completed a record seven King of the Mountains titles, which he usually won by attacking early on the first day in the mountains to get a strangle hold on the competition, then chasing every point on offer after that. Marco Pantani never was King of the Mountains, although he was a climber who won the Tour overall for Italy in 1998. The Tour winner in 2007, Alberto Contador of Spain, is an excellent climber (maybe one of the best), and the winner of the 2007 mountains title, Colombian Mauricio Soler, looks to have a good future ahead of him.

Above: A cyclist's eye view of the start of a Tour climb

Blueprint For a Tour

Every year the Tour de France plays out to a pattern. After the first range of mountains, which in some years are the Pyrenees and in others the Alps, there are usually some flattish stages. On these the sprinters in the race, who never have a good time when the roads go upwards, fight for the stage victories, while the overall contenders try to stay out of trouble and conserve their energy for the next set of mountains. These stages are called transition stages, and they are often in the south of France, so are characterised by sun and warm weather and the compelling picture of glittering bikes and bright colours streaming through a patchwork of vineyards, sunflowers and lavender fields.

The second major mountain range often decides the winner of the Tour de France. Most years there are a number of riders who still have a chance at the beginning of this part of the race, but coming out of the second set of mountains there is often just one man left with a commanding lead. On the occasions where that doesn't happen, a time trial held on the penultimate or even last day of the race will decide the outcome.

Many things can cause a riders to come unstuck in the second set of big mountain stages. Riders who are strong in the Alps can find the Pyrenees less to their liking, because the climbs of the two ranges are different. Alpine climbs tend to have uniform gradients, the Pyrenees don't, and even the weather can be different. Another problem is cumulative fatigue. Most pro riders perform well for two weeks, but only the best are strong in the third week of the Tour de France.

The mountains are crucial to the Tour. Their evocative names; the Galibier, Alpe d'Huez, Mont Ventoux, the Tourmalet and Peyresourde are mentioned in the sporting press for months before and after each race. They roll from the tongue as fans argue about who will be strong and where. Fathers tell their children stories about these places, and old men look back at when they raced and dreamed of conquering their lofty peaks.

The mountains are a theatre in which the drama of the Tour de France is played out in front of its most dedicated fans. On the biggest peaks the diehards will arrive with their tents and camper vans up to three days before the race is due to pass. On the day there can be as many as half a million people on one climb, all cheering, drinking, eating and sharing the moment in a big party.

The mountains are where the greatest battles of this historic race have been enacted – and where its tragedies unfold. In the heat of competition they are fearsome places to be, but away from that, taken at whatever pace you decide, conquering their slopes is something that any reasonably fit cyclist with the proper equipment can do. I hope that this book will inspire you to take on some of the Tour climbs yourself.

Above: Lucien Van Impe – simply the best

The mountains of the Tour de France

The mountains of France have been the Tour's theatre – where it's dramas, it's successes, failures and tragedies have all been played out.

Anyone with designs on winning the race has to master the mountains, has to be able to soar upwards in defiance of gravity. To see some of the great climbers of the Tour is to witness a combination of brute force and ballet. Such men appear to have wings on their feet as they dance effortlessly upwards.

Of course the reality is not like that at all. It takes years of hard work and application, natural talent, supreme physical fitness and sometimes shear bravery to take on these giant climbs at race pace.

But the bike is a truly beautiful machine. While the racers of this world will use theirs to force their way up the gradients, set records, break personal bests and punish the opposition, others prefer to shift down a gear and take their time.

The mountains belong to both – to all of us really. If you enjoy cycling you can enjoy climbing the mountains of the Tour de France in your own way – and what a lot there is waiting for you.

From the intimacy of the Vosges, through the dark and rugged Massif Central, to the unpredictable Pyrenees and the off-the-scale splendour of the Alps – all of the French mountains are accessible to cyclists. A bit of training, a bit of application, a bit of know how, a sound bike and the mountains are yours for ever. Enjoy!

The mountains of the Tour de France

'HOW TO RIDE THEM'

Climb every mountain, or so the song goes. And with the right equipment, preparation, a bit of technique and the correct mental approach you can do just that. You can climb every mountain of the Tour de France.

The mountains are a huge challenge in a race, they separate the champions from the very best in the sport, but any averagely fit person who has done a bit of training can get to the top of them, too. Slower yes, much slower in many cases, but that's not the point. Mountain climbs are a personal challenge and all that matters is that you enjoy your journey to the top.

So what is needed to take on the mountains of the Tour de France? The first answer is obviously a bike. But just any bike? Well, basically yes. The pros in the Tour de France ride on road-race bikes made from the latest space-age materials at a cost of thousands of pounds a piece, but you can climb the Tour de France mountains on a road bike, a mountain bike or a hybrid bike. The latter being a bike with some of the features of both road and mountain bikes. All these bikes are suitable for climbing mountains, although you might want to swap some of the equipment on yours to make life a bit easier when you do.

Road bikes

Road bikes have dropped handlebars, thin tyres and multiple gears. Entry level models cost about £400 and the amount you pay, as with most things in life, will reflect the quality and sophistication of the machine. However, you don't have to break the bank to buy a good bike. What you are looking for in a road bike suitable for climbing mountains are lightness and gear ratios low enough to allow you to pedal up the climbs in a seated position, and at a reasonably high cadence.

This is the crux of climbing up mountains. You can muscle your way up a short hill by climbing out of the saddle to put more power into the pedals, but you can't climb the mountains of the Tour de France like that. Not even the pros can. The Tour de France climbs are long, and sometimes they are long and steep. You have to take your time with them. You have to gear down and ride within yourself.

There are two options that give you the low gear ratios you need for climbing Tour de France mountains, triple or compact chainsets. Chainsets are the part of a bike's drive train that the pedals are attached to. Gear ratios are determined by the size of the chainring on a chainset and the size of the teethed sprockets on the rear wheel. Small chainrings and large sprockets give you low gears, so on a

Above: What goes up must come down

triple chainset there is an extra-small chainring, and on compact chainsets both chainrings are smaller than standard.

The best system is the compact system because it is the simplest to use, and it's lighter. You don't loose high gears either, because most road bikes now have nine or ten sprockets on the rear wheel, more than enough to provide a wide range of gear ratios.

You can buy bikes with triple or compact chainsets, but it's quite a simple procedure to fit one and adapt almost any road bike to work with them. A good bike shop will advise you on the swap, and happily take on the job if you don't want to do it yourself.

Touring bikes and cyclo-cross bikes are similar to road bikes. These come equipped with low gears already, so there is no problem in using either of them to climb mountains. However, cyclo-cross bike have tyres with heavy knobbly treads to give you grip when riding on loose or muddy cross-country surfaces. You should swap these tyres for smooth road tyres if you want to use a cyclo-cross bike in the mountains.

Mountain bikes

Mountain bikes have triple chainsets and very low gears, but their tyres are designed to grip in even worse conditions than cyclo-cross tyres, so they are especially heavy and will cause excessive drag on the hard surfaced roads of the mountain climbs.

You need to swap these for what mountain bikers call slicks. They are the same diameter as normal mountain bike tyres, but come in a number of widths. As a general point wider tyres are more comfortable to ride on than narrow ones, but no mountain bike slicks are so narrow that this becomes an issue. Go for the narrowest you can get.

Otherwise your mountain bike is excellent for climbing mountains, and especially good for descending them. Mountain bikes have a low centre of gravity and they are longer than the equivalent sized road bike, so they are very secure when cornering.

Hybrid bikes

In many respects these are a best of both worlds bike. They have the flat handlebars of a mountain bike, a wide range of gear ratios provided by triple chainsets. And if you get a more street oriented hybrid bike, which most new ones are today, it will have slick tyres on it already.

Pedals

Bikes have three sorts of pedals. Flat pedals on which you just place your feet and push down. Pedals with toe clips and straps, where your feet can pull up on the clips as well as push down on the pedals. And by far the best system for climbing mountains, clipless pedals.

These work by inserting a cleat, which is fixed to the sole of a specialist cycling shoe, into a spring loaded retaining mechanism on the pedal. Once engaged your foot is always in contact with the pedal, and the muscles of your legs can input power throughout the whole 360 degrees of every pedal revolution. All you do to disengage your foot from the pedal is twist it sideways. They take a bit of practice to get used to but are very efficient and totally safe.

Bike preparation

No matter how light and sophisticated your bike is, it needs to be well maintained at all times, and it will need some extra close attention before you venture into the mountains. But before that it pays to get into the habit of going through some basic safety checks before every ride.

Check your bike's frame for cracks. Apply each brake in turn while pushing your bike forward. With the front brake on the front wheel should not turn. The same goes for the rear brake with the rear wheel. Check all brake cables and

Above: Elbows out, shoulders relaxed and breath deeply

housings for signs of wear, and replace them if you see any. Check your tyres, replacing them if you find any excessive wear, cuts or bulges. Finally shift through all the gears and make sure that they mesh properly and that the chain doesn't jump around.

Do a more detailed check whenever you clean your bike, which is something you should do regularly anyway. You must also carry out a regular service on your bike. There are many good bike maintenance books available to help you, but most bike shops will look after your bike if you don't want to do it yourself.

Before a ride check that your tyres are pumped up to the recommended pressures that are usually printed on the tyre. Make sure anything you have fastened onto the bike, like a drinking bottle, a bag or a tyre inflator is safe. And always have another shift through all your gears while riding on the flat somewhere before you start to climb. If you can't get bottom gear the whole experience might be ruined.

Physical preparation

Climbing some of the easier Tour de France mountains is within the scope of almost any reasonably fit and healthy person, given a bike that is in good condition, is fitted with low enough gears – and provided the rider takes his or her time. However, some of the bigger climbs, the most famous ones in fact, do require some physical training. And in any case, the fitter you are the more enjoyable the whole experience will be.

Without trying to state the obvious, the best way to get fit for cycling is to ride your bike regularly, but that doesn't mean that other physical exercise is of no use. One of the biggest factors that will impact how quickly you can ride a bike uphill is your body weight, or more particularly your power to weight ratio.

There is no doubt that being active helps to keep your weight down, so any activity is good activity as far as this is concerned. Linked with a varied diet of good wholesome food, and perhaps a little restraint with regard to eating the classic weight gaining foods like cakes and chocolate, plenty of varied physical activity is a good foundation on which to build some specific cycling fitness.

If possible you should add some form of resistance training to your varied programme, concentrating on your leg muscles. This helps to build up the power side of the power to weight equation. Then if you include three or more bike riding sessions a week for about two months before tackling the mountain climbs, you should be ready. The bike sessions don't all have to be on the road, although at least one should be. You can use a gym fitness bike or put your own bike on a turbo trainer and ride indoors.

Once you are riding regularly you should start to seek out some hills in your neighbourhood. The longer these are the more benefit they will have on your ability to master the Tour de France climbs. You can also simulate long climbs on indoor bikes by upping the resistance on the machine you are using.

Whatever way you choose to begin your specific mountain climbing preparation, try to ride all the uphill parts on your routes by sitting on your saddle and spinning your legs in a low gear. Concentrate on relaxing your upper body and breathing deeply and rhythmically. Occasionally you should ride a hill in a little higher gear, both in the seated position and out of the saddle, to help build up some functional muscular strength. And there is nothing wrong with riding up a hill, turning around carefully at the top, descending and doing it again.

All the advice in the last paragraph comes from the man who many recognise as the best mountain racer ever, Lucien Van Impe of Belgium. He says: "I spent weeks before every Tour de France learning to spin my legs quickly on the

Above: Sit up to breath easy – 2007 King of the Mountains Mauricio Soler shows how

Climbing technique

climbs. I would try to match my breathing with the rhythm of my legs. When I was a pro rider I practiced in the Pyrenees, but when I was a young amateur I trained near where I live in the north of Belgium. There are no mountains there, so I would ride up and down the same hill maybe ten times."

When Van Impe arrived at the foot of a mountain in the Tour de France he says: "I shifted to a gear that was lower than really necessary for the first part of the climb. I did this so I could concentrate on gaining control of my breathing at the start. If you don't do that, if you go straight into a higher gear and attack a long climb, you will go into oxygen debt."

If you can keep once piece of advice in your mind when climbing the Tour de France mountains it should be that piece. It is crucial to control your breathing. You can be the strongest cyclist in the world, but if you don't get oxygen into your muscles you will have to slow down to recover. And if you slow down too much when going uphill, gravity makes you grind to a halt.

Start each climb conservatively. After cycling for only a short time you learn instinctively what gear ratio you need on a particular day for a particular slope and in particular conditions. But at the beginning of a long climb you should use a lower ratio than the one you think you need until you are breathing deeply and rhythmically and until your legs get used to the effort.

Then you can shift to the gear that you feel allows you to make comfortable progress. But still ere on the side of caution, Mont Ventoux for example takes an averagely fit club cyclist around two hours to climb, the Télégraphe and Galibier combination takes more than three. If you are inexperienced you could be climbing for much longer. It is essential then that you start every climb conservatively.

The more upright you sit on your bike, the easier it is to breath. Mountain and hybrid bikes are set up to give their rider an upright position, but the dropped handlebars on road bikes are designed with the aerodynamics of speed in mind. Hold dropped handle bars on the flat upper part with your hands close to where the handlebars begin to bend.

Don't grip the handlebars too tightly, as that wastes energy. Relax your shoulders, try to keep you back as straight as possible, but without straining to do so, and point your elbows out slightly. This all facilitates deep, unrestricted breathing. If you tuck in your elbows, tense your shoulders or arch your back excessively, you will restrict the space in which your lungs can move to inhale and exhale air. The same also goes for crouching too low .

When pedalling comfortably in a low gear you should just be supporting yourself on the handlebars. But for short steep stretches you might have to pull with your arms as you make more powerful pedal strokes. That's ok, but don't get bogged down doing this for a long time. Shift to a lower gear on long steep stretches, don't try to muscle your way over them.

Riding out of the saddle should be kept to a minimum on long climbs, although it's ok to do it for a few metres to keep your momentum on a steep bit of the climb. Shifting to a slightly higher gear and getting out of the saddle on long stretches of the same gradient brings other muscles into play, preventing them from stiffening up. It also takes some of the strain off the muscles you have been using constantly on the climb. Push down slightly harder as you get out of the saddle to keep your upward progress smooth. And when you do climb out of the saddle, still try not to tense your upper body.

Drink plenty while you are climbing, especially in hot weather. Water or well diluted energy drinks are the best. Dilute them more than the manufacturers instructions recommend in hot weather. When it's hot Tour de France riders pour water over their heads to cool down, which is ok if you have a plentiful supply. If water is limited it will do more good inside you.

It's best to carry two specialist cycling drinking bottles on your bike, one with your diluted energy drink in it and the other full of water. There are usually plenty of cafes or shops near to the mountains of the Tour de France to buy more water. Don't fill bottles from springs or mountain streams. You never know what might be contaminating them further up the mountain, and even the purest streams might have microbes in them that you aren't used to. For long rides in remote areas, like some parts of the Pyrenees and the southern Alps, augment your bottles with one of those hydration systems that you carry on your back.

It's difficult to eat while your are climbing simply because you are breathing too hard. If you are riding up one climb then eat a solid meal about two hours before you start, so your stomach isn't overburdened while you are climbing. Make your meal bigger, and maybe leave a little longer to digest it, if you are doing several climbs in one day. Eat solid food like cakes or energy bars on the flat bits between climbs, using carbohydrate gels to top up your fuel requirements on the climbs themselves. And always follow a gel with a drink of water to dilute it.

Use cycling specific clothing. Cycling shorts have a padded seat that won't cause chaffing in delicate areas. They also transport sweat away from your body, as do cycling specific tops. The best tops for mountain climbing are ones with full zips so you can undo them and get some cooling air flowing over your skin. Cycling tops also have pockets in the back of them for carrying food and other essentials. Wear thin cycling socks and cycling specific shoes.

Short fingered gloves called track mitts provide extra grip and soak up sweat. They also offer protection to your hands in case of a fall. You should wear a cycling helmet. Modern ones have plenty of ventilation, so you won't overheat.

You can get very hot climbing mountains, even though the air temperature on some of the tops can be quite low. If you have no one in a motor vehicle supporting your attempt on a given climb, then it is wise to carry a thin windproof sleeved top and a pair of thin windproof gloves for the descents. They make the descents comfortable and safer, because cold hands aren't good at applying brakes. These two items roll up and will fit in the pockets of a cycling top, or in a small bag that you can secure under your saddle.

You should also carry at least one spare inner tube and some tyre levers in that bag. Plus a mobile phone in case of emergencies. And always take a serviceable bike pump with you.

Descending technique

What goes up must come down – but coming down a Tour de France mountain isn't just a question of letting gravity take over. There are certain rules you must follow. The first is to do with braking.

Speed is great, you get a real feeling of exhilaration when descending a Tour de France mountain. But speed must be controlled. Go into a corner too fast and you are going to crash, the laws of physics say so. The same will happen if you leave your braking until the corner, it must be done well before. And with the rim brakes fitted to road bikes and some mountain and hybrid bikes, there is an added complication. Excessive braking causes the wheel rims to heat up. This causes the air inside your tyres to expand and can result in a disastrous tyre blowout. The best way to avoid problems is to not let excessive speed build up in the first place.

When descending, a road bike is easier to control if you hold the bottoms of the dropped handlebars. You also get a more powerful pull on your brake levers in that position. Your arms should be slightly flexed to absorb any road bumps. However, to stop excessive speed building up you should straighten your arms occasionally so that your body is raised and acts as an air brake.

It also pays on long straights to do a bit of braking now and again just to stop speed building up to high. Don't apply your brakes on and off in a jerky way. Just

Above: Approach the bend a little out and cut the apex

gently pull on the levers, front before the rear, and let the brakes scrub off a bit of speed now and again. That way you won't have as much speed to take off with hard braking before a corner.

As you approach a corner, begin to slow down in plenty of time. If you can't see how tight the bend is then ere on the side of caution and take off a lot of speed. In any case all your braking should be done before you make the turn. A wheel under braking could lock and skid, and it tends to track straight. Either way your bike is not under control and you risk crashing.

For a right-hand bend in France, if road conditions allow, move slightly out towards the middle of the road, having checked for traffic behind and in front of you first. Then turn in across the apex of the corner and end the bend slightly out towards the middle of the road again. For a left-hand bend you start fully over on the right and cut in a bit towards the apex and end up out on the right again.

These are the most efficient ways of cornering. They cut down on your braking and allow you to carry some speed through a corner, but you should only use them if the road conditions, surfaces and other traffic allow you to. You must never move out more than halfway towards the middle of the road in any case, even if it is empty. And if there is any other traffic near you, the road surface is loose or wet, or you can't see right around a bend, you must slow right down and take each bend fully over on your own side of the road.

Mountain bikes and hybrid bikes fitted with disc brakes have a big advantage on descents. You can use these brakes exactly when you need to and don't have to worry about them overheating your tyres. They are also much more powerful than rim brakes, although that in itself can cause a wheel to lock up. So even with these brakes, anticipation is the key. Always brake smoothly and in a straight line. Never snatch at your brake levers, and always apply your brakes gradually.

Your body position is also important when cornering at speed. Crouching lower than your normal riding position lowers your centre of gravity and reduces the forces trying to push you outwards in a corner. Pointing the knee that is on the inside of the corner out slightly, and lowering your inside shoulder, helps to guide you through a corner. At the same time pressing down with your outside leg helps stabilize you. If this sounds complicated look at some picture of Tour de France riders taking corners on mountain descents. The shifts of position and the angles of their knees and shoulder are subtle, but they can be seen.

The most important thing to remember though is caution. Descend and corner at a speed that you are comfortable with and build up your skills slowly. There are a number of good cycling instruction books that will help.

Above: Good cornering technique is essential for safety

Eastern ✪ Pyrenees

The Eastern Pyrenees run from Bagnères-de-Brigorre nearly to Perpignan on the Mediteranean coast of France. They can be sub-divided further by their geology. Most of the Eastern Pyrenees are like the rest of the range and made from ancient igneous rocks that are resistant to erosion and are responsible for the rounder, more permanent look of the Pyrenees when compared to the Alps. However, the Ariège Pyrenees, which run in an ever-widening triangle with an apex near Andorra, are formed of limestone – this is a land of deep gorges and light-grey cliffs.

But even the igneous mountains are different in character. The climbs south of the town of St Girons, like the Col de Menté or the Portet d'Aspet, are lower than those in the East and in Andorra. This means that they are generally covered in trees or pasture, whereas the far eastern climbs are topped with straggly grass or bare rock.

The towns of Andorra La Vella or Font Romeu make good bases for the far eastern climbs, and here you will come across plenty of examples of the Occitan language that is close in origin to Catalan Spanish and was spoken in this region in times gone by. Best base for the Ariège Pyrenees are Ax-les-Thermes or Tarascon-sur-Ariège and Foix.

A number of the climbs that have been used by the Tour de France in this region are wholly in Spain – these offer another aspect of this region to be enjoyed. The Spanish climbs, especially the Collado del Canto and Port de la Bonaigua, are in lonely and quite sparsely populated areas, where you can ride for miles without seeing a soul.

Arcalis   'ANDORRA'S PRIDE'

⊙⊙ 2 STARS

Length: 20 km.

Altitude: 2240 metres.

Height gain: 1298 metres.

Average gradient: 4.7%.

Maximum gradient: 10%.

WHAT TO EXPECT

➤ **Wild wonders.** Arcalis is remote. The mountains that surround it are at least 2500 metres high and some scrape 3000 metres. Few people live up here, and most visiting skiers are Andorrans or Spanish who drive up on day trips or for the weekend. Arcalis really is a wild mountain wonder.

➤ **Link up.** As well as the Col d'Ordino and Pal, try the climb to Arsinal. The Tour hasn't been there but it's really steep in places.

➤ **Three countries.** Arcalis is close to the French border. The Col de la Botella, which is a continuation of the Pal climb ends at the Spanish border. All three countries meet ten kilometres north of there at the Pic de Médécourbe (2914 metres).

Arcalis is a ski resort with a difference. It's publicly owned, quite remote and it doesn't have a purpose-built ski village with the high rises and cuckoo clock wooden chalet's you find in some resorts. Andorrans are justifiably proud of it.

It is part of the Vallnord group of ski resorts that are divided into the Pal, Arsinal and Arcalis sectors, of which Arcalis is the most northerly. It has 24 kilometres of downhill and 12 kilometres of prepared ski pistes, and is very popular with ecologically switched-on skiers. Nice touches in the resort include a permanent display of sculptures.

The climb starts in Ordino, where the altitude is already 1200 metres. The beginning is easy enough, climbing the Valira del Nord watercourse that flows straight out of the snows of the French border mountains.

After eight kilometres you arrive at the village of El Serrat, where there is a very steep descent followed by a short stretch of ten percent climbing. Then the road starts to twist and turn to find the easiest way up the steepening mountainside as you enter the Cercle d'Arcalis where the ski slopes are located.

Keep going until the end of the road, even though the Tour stage finished just short of it. The road goes to the Port du Rat, which is an old crossing into France over which a track still passes.

If you've got plenty of energy left, descend to Ordino and climb the Col d'Ordino.

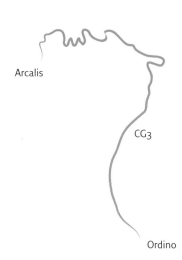

Arcalis

CG3

Ordino

Left: Road into Andorra from France   **Above:** Andorran mountains

And if you return to Ordino once more you are only two kilometres from the start of another Tour de France climb, the one up to the ski resort of Pal.

Andorra La Vella has plenty of hotels, as do the ski resorts, and with the famous climbs of the Port d'Envalira on hand, as well as the chance to explore some climbs that the Tour hasn't visited yet, that makes the town an ideal place to stay on a visit to this tiny and remote country.

WHICH WAY?

Ordino is eight kilometres north-east of Andorra La Vella. Head for the suburb of Escaldes-Engordany and follow the CG4 north, then turn right on the CG 3 to Ordino. Once there continue on this road to Arcalis.

MOUNTAIN MOMENTS

➤ The Tour has only climbed Arcalis once when it was the finish of a stage in 1997 and the German rider Jan Ullrich beat top mountain climber Richard Virenque to win it. Ullrich, who was born in 1973 and won his first bike race at nine years old, was sucked into the giant East German sports system and only able to become a pro rider after the fall of the Berlin Wall.

When he won at Arcalis he was riding only his second Tour de France, but he went on to win overall. Next year though, Ullrich was beaten by Marco Pantani and after that he never got on terms with Lance Armstrong, even though some thought that Ullrich was physically more gifted than Armstrong.

Port d'Envalira 'GATEWAY TO ANDORRA'

✪✪ 2 STARS

Length: 27,5 km.
Altitude: 2408 metres.
Height gain: 1378 metres.
Average gradient: 5%.
Maximum gradient: 7%.

WHAT TO EXPECT

➤ **Traffic.** The French side is very busy but the Andorran side gets it's fair share of traffic too. The road is well surfaced and wide though.

➤ **Duty-free.** Andorra is famous as a place for bargains, especially electrical goods. Make sure you know the customs regulations of the country you are taking stuff back to.

➤ **Altitude.** At 2408 metres the Port d'Envalira is the highest major road in Europe. It can be cold at the top, even in summer.

The Port d'Envalira isn't a particularly hard climb, although it is long. The road up it can get very busy with traffic, but it deserves its ranking as a major climb because it was where the first five times winner of the Tour de France, Jacques Anquetil nearly lost one of his Tours. The Frenchman was really in trouble on the Envalira, and had to dig deep into his store of courage to save the day

The Tour de France has climbed the Port d'Envalira seven times from both the Andorran and the French sides. The first time was in 1964, when Spaniard Julio Jiménez was first to the top. I have picked the Andorran side because it was where the Anquetil incident happened, and because the French side isn't very attractive.

One thing that detracts from the French side is the Pas de la Casa, a ski resort that looks like a moon base and doubles as a shopping complex. It is just over the Andorran border from France, but is on the French side of the climb. Bargain hunters flock up here to buy duty-free items, and on Saturdays in particular there is a procession of cars driving up the French side of the Envalira.

The good thing about the Pas de la Casa is that it leaves the climb from Andorra la Vella, which is the capital of Andorra, less busy than it would otherwise be. The climb starts in Andorra la Vella and at first it is very gentle. It starts to bite at the village of Canillo, and a few kilometres after a place called Soldeu it gets quite steep as you climb a wonderful series of *lacets* up to the summit. 'Lacet' is the French term for hairpin bends.

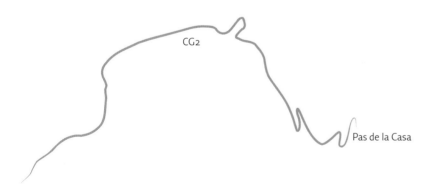

CG2

Pas de la Casa

Andorra La Vella

The top part, with the lacets, has much less traffic on it nowadays due to the opening in 2002 of the Envalira tunnel. At nearly three kilometres in length, and at an altitude of 2000 metres, its construction was quite a feat of engineering.

The Ariège river, which gives its name to a whole department of France, begins just over the French side of the Envalira summit. A trickle in summer, this stream has carved out a remote valley that has long been refuge for wildlife and for people. It's an Ariège boast that they have always been free thinkers who are a long way from central government.

WHICH WAY?

Andorra sits at the bottom of the Andorran side of the Port d'Envalira on the CG2 road. The city is 47 kilometres south-west of Ax-les-Thermes on the N20, after turning right onto the N22 at the entrance to the Puymorens tunnel. This road then changes into the CG2 at the Andorran border. You can either carry on through Pas de la Casa and go over the top of the Envalira or use the Envalira tunnel to descend into Andorra La Vella

MOUNTAIN MOMENTS

> Jacques Anquetil was a one-off, with his own ideas about what was good for him. There are two rest days during the Tour de France and wisdom has it that the riders have to ride their bikes during the breaks, or else seize up. One of the 1964 Tour rest days was in Andorra and while his rivals dutifully rode their bikes then rested, Anquetil went to a party. "Let the others ride on their holidays," he said as he dug into the barbeque and knocked back a few glasses of champagne. Next day the stage started with the Port d'Envalira and immediately Anquetil was in trouble. He was left behind and in a very bad way. A team mate rallied him, and on the descent they chased like lunatics. In front of him the favourites raced away because they thought they'd got rid of Anquetil. It took him 140 kilometres to catch them, but catch them he did and he even managed to gain time on some of his rivals. Anquetil was *sans pareil*.

Left: Mist rolling over the Envalira

Above: The Pas de la Casa

Guzet-Neige 'MILLAR'S MASTERPIECE'

⊛⊛ 2 STARS

Length: 11,5 km.

Altitude: 1480 metres.

Height gain: 820 metres.

Average gradient: 7%.

Maximum gradient: 10%.

WHAT TO EXPECT

➤ **Constant climbing.** Once you leave the Ustou valley there is no respite, and with plenty of gradient changes you gear shifters will get a lot of use.

➤ **Climbing warm-up.** The road from Oust to the start of the Guzet-Neige climbs slowly, rising about 600 metres in 12 kilometres. It is well worth doing as a warm-up and for the beauty of the countryside that surrounds it.

➤ **Circuit training.** Once you've completed Guzet-Neige, why not do the Col de Latrape? Go back down to the D8-D68 junction and turn right onto the D8. You then descend for a bit, before a short climb takes you over the Col de Latrape. You can then go down and up that climb to tick it off, or just descend and continue on to Oust for a nice mountain circuit of 60 kilometres. Or you could do both.

Le Trein d'Ustou

D8

D68   Guzet Neige

This is a climb to a winter sports resort called Guzet-Neige that is located at the base of the Pic de Freychet (2061 metres) about 43 kilometres south-east of St Girons. The approach to it is a particularly beautiful bike ride along the Gorges de Ribaouto to the small town of Oust.

Guzet-Neige can be reached in two ways from Oust; up the Garbet valley and over the Col de Latrape, or by following the river Alet, which is the most direct way and the way that the Tour de France climbs.

The climb starts in the Ustou valley at a place called Le Trein d'Ustou. You cross a small bridge and leave the valley by a series of lacets that start at Serac. This section

Left: Towards Guzet from the Col de la Core   **Above:** The Spanish border mountains

is quite hard – another reason why a nice ride along the valley before you begin the climb is a good idea. It will ensure that you are fully warmed up.

The road then straightens, dips into and out of the forest that covers much of the lower part of the climb, and the gradient eases slightly up to where the road from the Col de Latrape joins it at a very tight hairpin bend. From there the gradient steepens again and a couple of lacets take you up to the steepest pitch of the climb, which comes just before you enter Guzet-Neige and start to see the ski lifts.

The climb isn't over yet and the last stretch through the streets of the ski resort is still hard. It's a nice resort, a place of tasteful, well-made chalets that are dotted amid the pines. It all blends together quite naturally.

At the top of the climb you can ride a bit further on a road that branches to the right and leads to the Col d'Escot. There you get good views of the mountains that form a circle around the resort, including in the far distance and to the south-east, the Estats (3144 metres) and Montcalm (3077 metres), the two highest peaks of the Ariège.

WHICH WAY?

St Girons on the northern edge of the Pyrenees is the nearest big town to Guzet-Neige. Take the D618 south out of St Girons, then turn right onto the D3 to Oust. In Oust continue on the D3 (Guzet-Neige is also signposted in Oust on the D32, but that takes you over the Col de Latrape first). At the Pont de la Taule turn left onto the D8. At the Col de Latrape junction follow the D68 to the summit.

MOUNTAIN MOMENTS

➤ The British rider Robert Millar was the first Tour man to the top of Guzet-Neige when it was introduced to the race in 1984. He won the stage by leaving his companions in a breakaway group on the slopes of the climb. That day he also put on the polka dot jersey of the King of the Mountains, a title he still held when the race finished in Paris, where Millar was fourth overall. This remains the highest overall placing by a British rider in the Tour de France, and Millar is also the only Brit to have won one of the race classifications. Millar also won a Tour stage in 1983, and he finished second in the Tours of Spain and Italy, as well as winning the Italian Tour's mountains title. He is Britain's most successful ever stage racer.

Col de Menté *'OCAÑA'S DOWNFALL'*

⭐⭐⭐ 3 STARS

Length: 11.1 km.

Altitude: 1349 metres.

Height gain: 754 metres.

Average gradient: 6.8%.

Maximum gradient: 11%.

WHAT TO EXPECT

➤ **Peace and quiet.** With not many population centres near it and even fewer people needing to use it, the Col de Menté is a haven of peace for cyclists.

➤ **Memorials.** At the top of the climb there is a memorial to a local Tour de France rider from the 1970s, Serge Lapebie. Serge was from a cycling family. His father, Guy was an Olympic gold medallist on the track and his uncle, Roger won the 1937 Tour de France. On the descent you will also find a memorial to Luis Ocaña on the spot where he crashed in 1971.

➤ **Full Menté.** For an extra challenge follow the D85 before switching to the D44 and going for the top of the Menté. This road takes you over the Col d'Artigastou, which has never been climbed by the Tour, and down to the N125. It's just 3 kilometres along this road to the Spanish border.

D8

D85

Col de la Mente

Starting at the foot of the Col de Portet d'Aspet, the Col de Menté has had a long involvement with the Tour de France. It's a classic climb, full of history. Not a long one, nor that high, but it has a sinuous, secluded feel that is typical of the Pyrenees.It has an air of peace, allowing you to really appreciate where you are.

The climb starts at the Pont de l'Oule, and it is easy to miss if you are riding via the descent of the Portet d'Aspet. You are looking for a sharp left turn about two kilometres after the Casartelli memorial. Coming in the other direction it is much easier to see the signpost to the climb.

The first part of the climb is through a dense forest that grows along the sides of the Ger valley, which is especially beautiful in Autumn. The first two kilometres climb at less than four percent, but then there is an 500 metre section of eleven

Left: Waterfall on the descent   **Above:** Lacets on the Col de Mente   **Above:** Where Ocana fell in 1971

percent that eases slightly to just under ten for the next kilometre. After that comes a short descent, then the climb starts properly.

It's fairly unrelenting now until the top. The road breaks from the forest and climbs a set of lacets, then spears eastwards in a straight line. This is a specially beautiful part of the climb as it traverses crazily angled fields that are studded with wild flowers in spring and early summer. Traffic is rare because there are quicker ways into the upper Garonne valley than going by the Col de Menté.

More lacets take you to a junction with an old forest road, the Col de Clin, and from there the climb goes more or less straight to the top, where a road heads off to the left through a dense pine forest to the ski station of Mourtis. The ski station has hosted two stage finishes of the Tour de France. There is a café at the top, if you need refreshing.

The Col de Menté is the location for one of the world's toughest duathlon races. It comprises a nine-kilometre run, an 85-kilometre bike ride that includes two ascents of the Menté, and a 16-kilometre run to finish. It's usually held at the end of July, so it's hot as well as hard.

WHICH WAY?

There aren't many big towns close to the Col de Menté. St Gaudens is 25 kilometres away but a good base. Head south-east on the D5 until you see the right turn along the D85 signposted to the col. Follow the D85, then the D44 to the top. Otherwise you could climb the Col de Portet d'Aspet from St Girons and turn left for the Col de Menté at the end of the descent.

MOUNTAIN MOMENTS

➤ The Col de Menté made its first Tour appearance in 1966. A Spaniard, Manuel Galera was the first to the top, and since that day the Tour has been back 14 times.

➤ The most turbulent visit was in 1971 when Eddy Merckx was fighting Luis Ocaña for overall victory. Ocaña had humbled Merckx on the stage to the Alpine climb of Orcieres-Merlette, and taken the lead by a huge margin. Merckx attacked every day after that and was clawing back time, but it didn't look like it would be enough. He threw everything he had at Ocaña on the Menté. Ocaña resisted Merckx, but then nature stepped in. They descended the Menté in torrential rain and Ocaña, trying to stay with Merckx, crashed. His injuries were too bad for the Spaniard to continue and Merckx won the Tour, but he was lucky.

Plateau de Beille *'ARMSTRONG'S FAVOURITE'*

✪✪✪ 3 STARS

Length: 15.8 km.
Altitude: 1780 metres.
Height gain: 1255 metres.
Average gradient: 7.9%.
Maximum gradient: 10.8%.

WHAT TO EXPECT

➤ **Outdoor activities.** These thrive in the Ariège valley. You can do rafting and kayaking on the river. Rock climbing and mountain biking are also very big here. For a more reflective trip try one of the cave tours, where you can see cave paintings done by the prehistoric people who used to live here.

➤ **Shady first half.** The first part of the climb runs through a forest, but shortly after the Henry IV fountain you break clear of the trees and you'll feel the sun – if it's out.

➤ **Wild boar.** They live all over France, but are plentiful here. Watch out for the big ones, they can be a bit tetchy. Best to back off and let them cross in front of you if they want to.

➤ **Cross-country skiing.** The Plateau de la Beille is famous for it and has 70 kilometres of tracks in the winter.

Pont des Clarans

D527

Les Cabannes

This shelf of land high above the Ariège valley is a relatively new climb to the Tour de France, but it's severity has made it a favourite with the organisers. Since its first visit in 1998 the race has been back three times.

It starts in the pretty village of Les Cabannes, and after a fairly easy first kilometre the climb gets very un-Pyrenean and the gradient remains quite constant around six percent for the next ten kilometres.

Then the climb seems to remember where it is, and all of a sudden you come across an absolutely flat stretch of 300 metres. After which the gradient rears up to 10.8 percent for the next kilometre, before slowly easing off to the summit.

Les Cabannes, like many of the settlements along the bottom of the Ariège valley, owes its development to the minerals that were mined there and processed in local forges – and to the railway, which was established in 1888. In 1929 the railway linked up with Spain through the Puymorens tunnel. Les Cabannes has always been a thriving place, although much of the economy today is based around tourism.

The first part of the climb uses regular and well-constructed lacets to gain height, and you get fantastic views between the trees of the Ariège river and over one of its tributary valley, the Aston. The rock faces you can see are limestone, and it is limestone that gives the Ariège it's distinctive look. The rest of the Eastern Pyrenees are granite or gneiss, and are consequently not so easily eroded into the gorges that you find in the Ariège. To the north-east you might be able to spot the Trimouns quarry, which the biggest talc quarry in Europe

There is a restaurant, a refuge and a large car park at the top of the climb, where the Quioules stream joins the Aston. The high mountains directly to the south of you are the French border with Andorra.

WHICH WAY?

Les Cabannes is 20 kilometres south-east of Foix on the N20. The road to the Plateau de Beille is the D527, which becomes the D522 and it is on your right just as you enter Les Cabannes on the N20. It is clearly signposted.

 **MOUNTAIN MOMENTS**

➤ Marco Pantani was the first winner on Plateau de Beille in 1998. The Tour has been back three times since.

➤ Lance Armstrong won twice here, the first time in 2002 and the second in 2004. The Plateau de Beille is a bit like Alpe d'Huez, another climb on which Armstrong excelled and liked a lot. There was something about its regularity that suited him. Of the 21 Tour de France stages the American won, 11 were in the mountains but only five were in the Pyrenees.

➤ Spain's Alberto Contador won here in 2007. It was his first Tour stage win and it set the foundations for his overall victory in the race at the age of 24, which is young for a Tour de France winner. Contador is in the same team as Armstrong was, which meant his victory was their eighth in nine years.

Left: Half way up the climb   **Above:** Rear of the 2007 Tour field climbs the Plateau

Plateau de Bonascre

'RISING ABOVE THE THERMALS'

⊙⊙ 2 STARS

Length: 7.8 km.

Altitude: 1380 metres.

Height gain: 670 metres.

Average gradient: 8.6%.

Maximum gradient: 11.6%.

WHAT TO EXPECT

➤ **Real climbing.** The twists and turns, changes of gradient and steepness make the Plateau de Bonascre into what pro racers call a climber's climb. Climbs that are more regular lend themselves to all rounders, like the Plateau de Beille did for Lance Armstrong, but climbs like the Bonascre are for the lightly built climbing specialists, as its list of winners prove.

➤ **360 degree views.** This climb doesn't follow a valley, so for much of it the land drops away on either side, which gives you great views. At the top you don't just see the usual mountains that circle a ski station, but get great views of the Ariège and Orlu valleys as well. The Orlu is well worth a visit, it's really quiet and ends in a extensive mountain bike trail. If you are interested in wildlife there is also a wolf reserve up there.

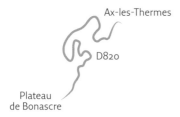

This climbs starts in the busy resort of Ax-les-Thermes, a place that was established as a hospital in 1260 by St Louis to treat soldiers wounded in the Crusades. The hospital grew as more people tried the cures of the sulphurous thermal water that comes from deep beneath the town. It later fell from popularity and all that is left of the hospital today is the Bassin des Ladres, which is across the road from St Vincent's church. It's still nice to dangle your feet in the warm pool though.

Today Ax-les-Thermes is famous for skiing, and Plateau de Bonascre is one of the local areas in which this winter activity takes place. The resort on the Plateau is called Ax-3Domaines, which can be a bit confusing when you look at the Tour de France history books, because the Tour has included this climb three times, once calling it the Plateau de Bonascre and on the other two occasions referring to it as Ax-3Domaines. They are the same climb.

Plateau de Bonascre starts just at the point where the road turns away from the Aiège river and after a relatively easy first two and a half kilometres the next

Above: First bend of the climb

three are the hardest of the climb as they fluctuate between just under ten percent and just over eleven percent. After that the gradient eases to five percent for one kilometre before getting steep, easing and steepening again to the top. The road is also full of twists and turns, which makes it hard to find a good climbing rhythm.

The Plateau is a wide open space bordered by a circle of mountains and dissected into an elongated strip of high country by the Savignac and Ariège valleys. It's also a sporting paradise with tennis courts, jogging and walking routes, mountain bike tracks, and of course loads of ski pistes in winter.

For the road rider though, the finish of the climb is as far as you can go. However, the Tour climbs of the Col de Chioula and the Port de Pailhères both start in Ax-les-Thermes and climb the opposite side of the valley. So off you go and try them.

WHICH WAY?

Ax-les-Thermes is 36 kilometres south-east of Foix on the N20. The road to Plateau de Bonascre is the D820 and it is on your right just as you enter Ax-les-Thermes from the direction of Foix. The climb is signposted from the main road too. Ax-les-Thermes is 15 kilometres south-east of Les Cabannes, so this climb can be combined with the Plateau de Beille.

Above: The Tour is over 100 years old

Above: You're on your way up

⛰ **MOUNTAIN MOMENTS**

➤ Plateau de Bonascre has hosted a stage finish in the Tour de France three times. The first was in 2001 when a Colombian rider, Felix Cardenas won.
➤ The Spanish winner of the 2008 Tour, Carlos Sastre, won here in 2003. When he crossed the line in Paris, Sastre stuck a baby's dummy in his mouth, which was meant as a greeting to his newly born daughter. Victory celebrations in cycling often have references to what is going on in a racer's life.

Above: Enthusiastic Spaniards swell the crowds in the Pyrenees

Col de Port   'THE HISTORY CLIMB'

✪✪ 2 STARS

Length: 17 km.

Altitude: 1250 metres.

Height gain: 777 metres.

Average gradient: 4.6%.

Maximum gradient: 9%.

WHAT TO EXPECT

➤ **A good introduction.** The Col de Port makes a great introduction to the Pyrenees for an inexperienced climber. It has a good dollop of Pyrenean character without any horrendously steep sections that other famous climbs in the range have.

➤ **Don't be put off.** The northern approach to Tarascon does not show the town to its advantage. All you can see is a tangle of cement works, railway sidings and the local sewage plant. That the graffiti on the town sign reads, "Welcome to the perfumed air of Tarascon," says it all really. Don't be put off, the town is quite nice really and the Eastern Pyrenees are beautiful. Trust me.

➤ **Round trips.** Try climbing the Port, descend to Massat, turn left on the D15 to climb the Port de Lers and descend to Tarascon for a round trip of 74 kilometres.

Not particularly long or steep, the Col de Port is a major climb because of its long history in the Tour de France. First included in the 1910 event, the Col de Port has been climbed nine times by the Tour since 1947 alone.

But the Col de Port has a connection with history that goes much further back. The caves in this part of the Ariège valley are some of the oldest inhabited places in the world, and there is a very interesting prehistoric park at the foot of the climb that attempts to depict what life was like here in those far off days.

The climb links the towns of Tarascon-sur-Ariège and Massat over the Arize massif, and it has been climbed from both sides by the Tour. I've picked the Tarascon side because that is the way the race went when it was the first climbed on the stage in 2007 from Foix to Loudenvielle. This was also the stage picked for the Etape du Tour that year, so a lot of cyclo-sportive riders will be familiar with the Col de Port.

The Col de Port's name is very strange, because port in French means the same as port in English, a harbour, and there are no harbours in the Pyrenees. In fact the name is tautological as port means pass in the Catalan-influenced Occitan dialect that used to be spoken in this part of France. So as col means pass in French, the Col de Port translates into English as the Pass Pass.

The climb starts shortly after the roundabout where the D618 leaves the N20,

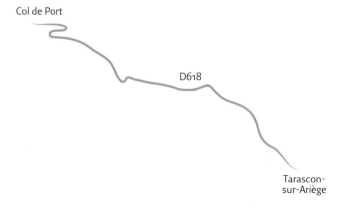

Col de Port

D618

Tarascon-
sur-Ariège

Above: Near the top, looking east

Above: The Pic des Trois Seigneurs   **Right:** This small peak marks the start of the climb   **Right below:** Scenery around the summit

just on the north-west edge of Tarascon-sur-Ariège. The start is quite easy as the first half of the climb meanders up the Saurat valley, gaining and loosing a little height as it goes, but never getting very steep.

Its character changes at the first bend after quite a long straight run. For the next four kilometres the road rises at an average of eight percent, but in keeping with the Col de Port's Pyrenean character constantly oscillates between seven and nine. The gradient eases towards the top, but the descent to Massat is equally unpredictable and irregular.

WHICH WAY?

Tarascon-sur-Ariège is ten kilometres south of Foix, which is 80 kilometres south of Toulouse on the A61, A66 and N20, and is considered one of the gateways to the Eastern Pyrenees. Leave Tarascon by going north to the N20-D618 junction and take the D816 over the Col de Port.

MOUNTAIN MOMENTS

➤ The first Tour de France rider to climb the Col de Port was Octave Lapize in 1910. Lapize won the Tour that year.
➤ Rik Van Looy from Belgium was the best single-day racer of his generation. He is the only rider in history to have won every one of the races that cycling calls the Classics, but he wanted to win the Tour de France as well. In the mid-1960s he thought he could do it, even though he was just too heavily built for success in the really high mountains. He tried though, and was first over the Col de Port in 1965.
➤ Juan-Manuel Gárate was first to the top of the Col de Port in 2007.

Port de Pailhères 'THE TOUGH EDGE'

✪✪✪ 3 STARS

Length: 16.8 km.

Altitude: 2001 metres.

Height gain: 1300 metres.

Average gradient: 7.7%.

Maximum gradient: 12%.

WHAT TO EXPECT

➤ **Uneven gradients.** The Port de Pailhères is another climber's climb. The hairpin bends it uses are more natural than constructed, so they are a bit unpredictable too, both in their tightness and gradients.

➤ **Sunny weather.** This part of the Pyrenees is protected from rain by the rest of the range, so the sun is southern-Europe strong. Use plenty of sun protection.

➤ **Part shelter.** The middle part of the climb skirts the northern edge of the Hares forest, so there is some shelter from the trees, especially in the afternoon.

➤ **Side shoots.** The Col du Pradel starts three-quarters of the way down the Pailhères descent towards Ax-les-Thermes. It's not a Tour climb, but very quiet and attractive with lots of off-shoots on its own descent to explore.

Right on the eastern edge of the Pyrenees, the Col de Pailhères is a tough but typical introduction to the rest of the range. It's a relatively new climb to the Tour that starts in Usson-les-Bains and runs partly along the edge of the Hares forest over to Ax-les-Thermes in anything but predictable steps.

The first kilometre is quite easy, although route finding at this stage is quite complicated as a maze of roads split off and rejoin the road to the top. Soon the way up becomes much clearer and, unfortunately, the gradient gets much steeper. After an easy first one-and-half kilometres the next thirteen average eight percent, but they constantly switch from just under seven to ten, eleven and even twelve percent for a short stretch.

The hardest bit of the climb comes at a set of lacets shortly before the final run at the summit, which at 6.4 percent for two kilometres is far easier than the rest of the climb.

Usson-les-Bains

The Port de Pailhères

D25

Left: Tour riders in the Pyrenees   **Above left:** Lake on the descent of the Pailheres   **Above right:** All the information you need

The summit touches on the border between the Midi-Pyrenées and Languedoc-Roussillon regions of France, although the whole of the climb is in the Ariège so is therefore in the Midi-Pyrenées .

The views from the top, over the Hares forest are a delight, and the descent to Ax-les-Thermes is even better. Watch out for the first hairpins. You arrive at them quickly because the descent is steep and straight just before. There are signs warning you of their existence in good time, so do your braking in good time.

The Port de Pailhères climb from Ax-les-Thermes isn't quite as hard as from Usson-les-Bains, and that side hasn't been climbed by the Tour de France yet. However, climbing from Ax-Les-Thermes might be more practical if you are combining this climb with the Plateaux de Beille or Bonascre, or with the Col de Chioula, which shares its first three and a half kilometres with the Pailhères when climbed from Ax-les-Thermes.

WHICH WAY?

Usson-les-Bains is on the D118, 19 kilometres south-west of the town of Axat, which is 51 kilometres west of the city of Perpignan on the D117. If approaching from Axat, turn right in Usson-les-Bains onto the D16 in the direction of Mijanès. In Mijanès turn left onto the D25 and follow this road to the top of the climb.

MOUNTAIN MOMENTS

➤ The first Tour rider over the Port de Pailhères was the Spanish rider Juan-Manuel Mercado in 2003.
➤ An Austrian, Georg Totschnig was first on the Pailhères in 2005. He used the climb to distance himself from two breakaway companions, flew down into Ax-les-Thermes and stormed up the Plateau de Bonascre to win the stage. Totschnig's performance was remarkable in that he held off Lance Armstrong, who was chasing him up the final climb, and because he was the first rider from his country to win since a Tour stage since Max Bulla in 1931.
➤ First on the climb in 2007 was a young Spanish rider, Ruben Plaza. He couldn't hang on, like Totschnig did, to win the stage at Plateau de Beille, but Plaza finished 50th overall in his first Tour, so might be a name for the future.

Portet d'Aspet 'CASARTELLI'S MEMORIAL'

●● **2 STARS**

Length: 18.1 km.
Altitude: 1089 metres.
Height gain: 586 metres.
Average gradient: 3.6%.
Maximum gradient: 10.8%.

WHAT TO EXPECT

➤ **The worst is last.** The last two kilometres of this climb are the hardest.

➤ **Difficult descent.** There are some very steep down gradients on the twisty descent, and the road is not wide. Take extra special care, particularly when you see the 17% signs.

➤ **Hard the other way.** The western side of the Portet d'Aspet is a harder climb than the eastern side. The 17% part is quite long and you will need very low gears for it.

➤ **Linking up.** The Col de Menté starts exactly at the point where the western descent of the Portet d'Aspet ends. Just before the turn there is a stone building and a low stone wall on your right. The road bends sharply right over a bridge and the Menté road is on your left at the apex of this bend.

A very tough climb from either side, since 1995 the Portet d'Aspet has been connected with one of the three tragic deaths in Tour de France history, when an Italian rider, Fabio Casartelli crashed and was killed on the descent of the western side of the climb.

Actually, in an event where men throw themselves into tumultuous sprint finishes, flog their tired bodies up incredible mountains and hurtle down the others sides at impossible speeds, it's amazing that there haven't been more deaths than those of Francisco Cepeda in 1935, Tom Simpson in 1967 and Casartelli in 1995.

Aside from its tragic connection, the Portet d'Aspet is a real Pyrenean gem. It starts easily, even if some short descents on the way up keep losing you what little height you gain in the first two-thirds of the climb.

After 12 kilometres you have still only risen about 200 metres, so with 389 metres left to be climbed in just six kilometres you know what is in store for you. The sense of foreboding won't be dispelled by the fact that the next two kilometres only averages a five percent gradient either.

Yes, you've guessed it, the last two kilometres are a brutal slog of ten percent and more as you climb the lacets that spin giddily upwards after the hamlet of Aspet. The one good thing about the top of the climb is that you are still in the shade of the trees that shelter you all the way up and down this climb.

The descent down the western side is very steep, twisty and has an irregular gradient that shifts between five and nine percent – then there is a stretch of 17 percent. It was just after this that Casartelli came to grief in 1995. He crashed and slid across the

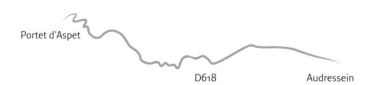

Portet d'Aspet

D618   Audressein

Left: Summit of the Portet d'Aspet **Above:** Beginning of the descent, it's a tricky one

**road, smashing his head against one of the square blocks that are placed to stop
vehicles plunging over the edge. Since his death some of the blocks have been replaced,
especially close to where he fell, but not all. Be very careful.**

WHICH WAY?

**The eastern side of the climb starts in Audressein, a tiny village that is 12
kilometres south-west of St Girons on the D618. St Girons is 30 kilometres south-
east of junction 20 of the A64 Autoroute on the D117. Continue through Audressein
on the D618 to the top of the climb.**

MOUNTAIN MOMENTS

➤ The Portet d'Aspet was first climbed in the Tour by
Octave Lapize in 1910. Since then the race has
visited the climb regularly, 27 time since 1947 alone.
Two famous Spanish climbers, Frederico
Bahamontes and Julio Jiménez share the record by
crossing the Portet d'Aspet in first place three times.
➤ A beautiful stone and marble memorial to Fabio
Casartelli has been built on the spot where he died.
It records his Olympic road race title in 1992 and
there is a sundial on it. There is also a hole drilled
through the base of the stone. Each year, at exactly
the time when Casartelli died the sun shines
through this hole and illuminates figures engraved
on the other face of the stone. The figures record
the date of his birth, the date he won Olympic Gold
and the date that he died.

Above left: The Fabio Casartelli memorial **Above right:** The marble comes from Casartelli's home region

Col du Puymorens 'THE CATALAN GATEWAY'

⭐ 1 STAR

Length: 18.2 km.
Altitude: 1920 metres.
Height gain: 670 metres.
Average gradient: 3.6%.
Maximum gradient: 5.3%.

WHAT TO EXPECT

➤ **Busy first bit.** All heavy goods vehicles must go through the Puymorens tunnel after five kilometres of the climb and a lot of other traffic follows them too.

➤ **Closed in.** Approaching the Puymorens tunnel entrance you enter the Défile de Fau, which can feel a bit claustrophobic, but soon after the tunnel you begin the hairpin sections that snake out onto the wide open mountainside.

➤ **Great view.** From the summit of the pass the Carol valley and it's tributaries look spectacular. You also get good views of the Pics Font Négre to the south.

➤ **Confusing descent.** There is a spaghetti tangle of roads on the descent to Ax-les-Thermes where the Puymorens tunnel emerges.

➤ **Open all year.** Even though it is high the Col de Puymorens is open all year.

Col de Puymorens

D618

Carol

This climb looks more impressive than it is. At the top you are high up, quite close to 2000 metres of altitude, and looking down at the climb's south-western side, which is the nicest to climb, the way up looks steep – but looks can be deceptive. This climb is already quite high when it starts, and it only gains 670 metres in 18 kilometres.

So why have I made it a major climb? First, because of it's history – the Puymorens had its first Tour de France visit in 1913 and has been used a number of times since. Second, the south-west side of the climb is just a beautiful place to be.

The climb starts at Carol, which is on the N20 main road, but inside the Catalan Pyrenees national park. This is the part of the eastern Pyrenees that is most heavily influence by associations with Spain. Apart from a period between 1463 and 1493 this area was ruled by the kings of Aragon then by the Spanish kingdom until 1659, and it is here that the Occitan language that you can still see in Pyrenean place names was born.

The climb is easy at first, up the Carol river valley with the towering Carlit massif on your right and the Pic Orientaux de Font Négre on your left. Don't worry if the road is busy at this point, because after five kilometres you get to the entrance of the Puymorens tunnel and much of the traffic leaves you here.

The true character of this climb emerges after the tunnel, when you begin to climb what is essentially the side of the Pic Pédrous (2842 metres) by means of a series

Left: The Col du Puymorens with the Carlit Massif behind it   **Above:** Clouds around the summit

of hairpin bends with steeper straights of around five percent gradient between them. The valley that the first hairpin loops into is formed by the stream that issues from a huge lake up at nearly 2000 metres altitude called the Étang de Lanous.

From the top of the climb you can descend down the Ariège valley to Ax-les-Thermes, which is where the ascent of the other side of Puymorens starts, or you can climb a bit of the French side of the Port d'Envalira and drop into Andorra. Both of these roads are very busy with traffic though.

WHICH WAY?

Carol is on the N20 10 kilometres north-west of the Spanish border town of Puigcerdà and 40 kilometres west of Font Romeu, which is in France and has plenty of hotels. Take the D618 south-west out of Font Romeu and turn right after 17 kilometres at the junction with the N20. Continue on the N20 to Carol and follow this road to the top of the Col de Puymorens

MOUNTAIN MOMENTS

➤ The first crossing of the Col de Puymorens by a Tour rider was Michel Buysse of Belgium in 1913. One of three brothers who all raced in the Tour de France, Michel won the race in 1926.
➤ The Tour has climbed the Col de Puymorens from both sides, and visited many times before the Second World War. However, since then the climb has been used only six times, the last was in 1993. Best man on the Puymorens in 1964 was Julio Jiménez, another Spaniard who is considered to have been one of the greatest climbers. He was very lightly built and never looked under any stress as he danced his way uphill. A British Tour rider of the sixties Vin Denson says that Jiménez seemed to climb just by fluttering his eyelids.

Col d'Agnes

Length: 17.6 km.
Altitude: 1570 metres.
Height gain: 921 metres.
Average gradient: 5.2%.
Maximum gradient: 8.2%.

Part of a complex group of climbs that join each other at various stages along their length, the Col d'Agnes links the Arac and Garbet river valleys with each other, and by means of the Port de Lers, the two valleys with the town of Vicdessos.

The Tour first climbed the Agnes in 1988 when Robert Millar was first to the top, no doubt trying to repeat his 1984 stage victory at Guzet-Neige because the 1988 stage finished there too.

The climb starts in the town of Massat and runs more or less straight up the course of a stream for its first few kilometres. The gradient is anything but straightforward. For the whole climb there is hardly 500 metres where it is the same, although there is nothing really vicious about the Col d'Agnes. That is if you don't count the short trick it plays on you by having a descent at 13 kilometres. Those lost metres then have to be made up.

The rest of the climb twists and turns to trace the contours of the easiest way up through the lush woodlands that cover most of the mountains in this part of the Pyrenees. The road from the Port de Lers that climbs from Vicdessos joins this route about four kilometres before the top of the climb.

The descents to Aulus-les-Bains is exciting as it's just as serpentine as the last section of the road you've climbed. For a really pretty circuit turn right in Aulus and head down the D32 until Ercé, where a right turn will take you over the Col du Saraillé, which hasn't been in the Tour de France yet, and back to Massat.

WHICH WAY? Massat is 25 kilometres south-east of St Girons on the D618. Turn right into the town centre and follow the D18 and D8 to the top of the climb. The right turn for the Col du Saraillé in Ecré is the D132, you then turn right again onto the D17 to cross that climb.

Port de le Bonaigua

Length: 23 km.
Altitude: 2072 metres.
Height gain: 1122 metres.
Average gradient: 4.8%.
Maximum gradient: 8%.

This climb is wholly in Spain, which might prove a problem if you want to be a purist and climb it in the direction the Tour has always climbed, because you'll have to climb it then descend, then turn around and ride back up again.

It's been used twice in the Tour de France. Once in 1974 when Spanish climbing ace, Domingo Perurena was first to the top, and again in 1993 when Tony Rominger of Switzerland was the best. On both occasions the riders climbed from the village of Esterri d'Àneu.

You could choose Andorra as a base for doing the climb, but it's well over a 100-kilometre trek to the start. Or you could climb from the Spanish town of Vielha, which is only 16 kilometres from Bossost, where the Col de Portillon starts.

From Vielha the climb of the Port de le Bonaigua is 23 kilometres long, gains 1102 metres in height, has an average gradient of 4.8 percent and some stretches of eight percent. So the climbs are very similar in terms of length and severity.

The Port de le Bonaigua is well up in the contenders for the location of wittiest piece of graffiti painted on the road by a bike fan. Usually these are messages to the painter's cycling hero, exhorting him to greater efforts or counselling against getting discouraged, but this one, picked out clearly by the TV helicopter in 1993, read, "Hello mum, what do you mean I never write?"

WHICH WAY? From Andorra take the NA145 south to Seo de Urgel, then the N260 south-west. Turn first right on the N260 to Sort, then right again on the C13 to Esterri d'Àneu. The road to the top of the climb is the C1412 From Bossost go south-east on the N230 to Vielha and turn left on the C26 for the top of the Bonaigua.

Collado del Canto

Length: 26.3 km.

Altitude: 1725 metres.

Height gain: 110 metres.

Average gradient: 4.2%.

Maximum gradient: 7%.

Another climb that is totally on the Spanish side of the Pyrenees, the Collado del Canto has made two appearances in the Tour, the first being in 1974 when Domingo Perurena was the first to conquer it.

The climb links the Spanish town of Seo de Urgel, which is just south of Andorra, with the Aneu valley, which is also in Spain. In turn, the Aneu leads to the Val d'Aran over the Port de la Bonaigua climb. The Collado del Canto has been used in two stages that started in Seo de Urgel or Andorra and go through the Val d'Aran to cross into France and finish at Pla d'Adet. On both occasions the riders attacked the Collado del Canto from the Seo de Urgel side.

The climb starts from Ardal. There are no steep gradients, very little traffic and the road winds its lonely way westwards in a series of well-constructed bends. The whole climb makes a very nice bike ride, and there are a couple of interesting little off-shoots to explore if you like.

The descent is shorter than the climb, and the last part is quite technical with some steeper gradients and a couple of tight hairpin bends. The descent ends in Sort and from there it is 36 kilometres to the start of the Port de la Bonaigua. That's a really nice ride too.

WHICH WAY? Go south on the N260 out of Seo de Urgel and turn right onto the N260 for the climb.

Col de la Chioula

Length: 9.7 km.

Altitude: 1450 metres.

Height gain: 771 metres.

Average gradient: 7.9%.

Maximum gradient: 10.7%.

A real Pyrenean toughie, the Col de la Chioula has been climbed four times since the Italian, Luciano Pezzi was the first Tour rider to scale it in 1955. It has also been climbed from both directions, but I've chosen the side from Ax-les-Thermes because it is especially tough, and it's easier to link it with other climbs in the same area from that side.

The first 3.5 kilometres are up a series of lacets, but already the character of the climb will have made itself felt as an easy first kilometre leads to a gradient that switches between seven and nine percent every few hundred metres. If you are climbing the Port de Pailhères from Ax-les-Thermes this section of road is the same for both climbs.

The two routes part at Ascou, where a really tight left-hand hairpin sets you on your way to the top of the Chioula. The hairpin is the prelude to some stiff climbing, with a long section of concerted effort required to get you over the six kilometre crux of this climb ending in a stretch of nearly eleven percent.

From the top you can descend then climb the Col des Sept Frères and the Col de

Pradel and return to Ax-Les-Thermes. Or you can continue after the Sept Frères towards Mazuby, Aunat and the D118. Turn right on the D118 to Usson les Bains and climb the Port de Pailhères before descending to Ax-les-Thermes.

WHICH WAY? Ax-les-Thermes is 36 kilometres south-east of Foix. Take the D613 north out of Ax-les-Thermes and turn left at Ascou to follow the D613 to the top of the Chioula. For the Sept Frères-Pradel circuit turn right at the top of the Sept-Frères onto the D20 and right again onto the D107.

Col de la Core

Length: 17.5 km.
Altitude: 1395 metres.
Height gain: 885 metres.
Average gradient: 5.1%.
Maximum gradient: 8%.

The Col de la Core links the Bourgane and Salat river valleys, and has been climbed five times by the Tour de France. You can start in Audressein in the Bourgane valley, which is to the west of the climb and where the Portet d'Aspet also starts, or from Seix in the Salat valley, which is to the east

The Tour has climbed the Col de la Core from both sides, but in its five visits since 1984 it seems to prefer the west, so that's the one I've gone for. Like all the climbs that surround it, such as the Portet d'Aspet and Col de Menté, the slopes of the Core are heavily wooded and the gradients irregular. Jean-René Bernaudeau of France was the first Tour de France rider over the Col de la Core

It climbs very gently for two kilometres, but a further two kilometres into the Bethmale valley sees the gradients increase and get steadily harder towards the top of the climb. There's a great view back down the Bethmale after the second of a series of hairpins that characterize the last four kilometres of the climb.

The Bethmale is a rural place of old customs, one of which is the gift of pointed shoes by a man to his fiancé at Christmas. The shoes, called *sabots*, have their toes shaped like a crescent moon. The length of the crescent is said to be a measure of the man's love for his intended.

WHICH WAY? Audressein is 12 kilometres south-west of St Girons on the D618. From Audressein head south on the D4 to Castillon-en-Couserans. At Les Bordes turn left onto the D17 and continue to the top of the Col de La Core.

Col de Jau

Length: 13.6 km.
Altitude: 1506 metres.
Height gain: 806 metres.
Average gradient: 5.9%.
Maximum gradient: 8.3%.

This is the most easterly of the Pyrenean Tour de France climbs. It was first visited by the Tour de France in 1976, and the race has been back twice. The leader over the Col de Jau in 1976 was a Frenchman, Raymond Delisle.

Delisle was a good but not great rider, who wore the yellow jersey for two days in 1976 before dropping back to fourth overall by the end of the ace. It was Delisle's best Tour finish, although he also won two stages in his 12 appearances in the race, and he was the French national champion in 1969.

Delisle has been far more successful since his racing career ended. He owns a beautiful château hotel near St Lô, deep in the Normandy countryside, called the Château de la Roque. He can be found there most nights regaling his guests with Tour de France stories around one of the château's huge open fires.

The Col de Jau starts in Mosset and winds its way upwards through a beautiful area of the Catalan Pyrenees national park. The twists and turns towards the top are a real treat with great views, but just like most Pyrenean climbs the gradient is ever changing and your gear shifters will be working overtime.

If you descend the other side of the Jau and climb two smaller passes, the Col de Garavel and Col de Moulis, you come out on the D118 five kilometres south of Usson-les-Bains and the start of the Port de Pailhères.

WHICH WAY? Mosset is seven kilometres north-west of Prades, a town on the N116 that is 30 kilometres west of Perpignan. Take the D619 north out of Prades, signposted Moltig-les-Bains. This road becomes the D14 and you follow it to Mosset, then continue to the top of the Col de Jau.

Port de Lers

Length: 11.5 km.
Altitude: 1517 metres.
Height gain: 807 metres.
Average gradient: 7%.
Maximum gradient: 10.9%.

Starting in Vicdessos, the Port de Lers climbs up through the Suc et Sentenac forest to join the road to the Col d'Agnes. Its first Tour de France visit was in 1995 when Marco Pantani blasted up the climb on his way to winning a stage at Guzet-Neige. The Tour visited the climb again in 2001, but did so from the other side.

The area of the Pyrenees in which this climb and the others around it are located is known as the Couserans and it is one of the most unspoilt parts, and certainly one of the most sparsely populated, of the whole of France. According to the 1999 census there are only 18 inhabitants per square kilometres living in this area. It makes for some very peaceful riding, and you will meet very few cars, as the ones that are here are quickly absorbed by an extensive network of tiny back roads.

The climb is up a fairly straight road which is interrupted occasionally by hairpins to help it climb the steepest slopes. The gradient doesn't fluctuate much above or below its average, but there are two shorts stretches of ten percent. One comes after two kilometres, and the other is about three kilometres from the top. There is a short descent to the road that goes over the Col d'Agnes.

WHICH WAY? Vicdessos is 15 kilometres south-west of Tarascon-sur-Ariège on the D8.Turn right off the D8 onto the D18, which turns into the D15 and is the road over the climb. If you desnd the Col d'Agnes on the D18 to Massat and turn right onto the D618 you can climb the Col de Port and complete a circuit in Tarascon-sur-Ariege that is 85 kilometres long.

Col de Latrape

Length: 5.9 km.
Altitude: 1112 metres.
Height gain: 424 metres.
Average gradient: 7.2%.
Maximum gradient: 14.7%.

Proving that a climb doesn't need to be long to be hard, the Col de Latrape is the shortest but toughest of the Tour de France climbs in the Pyrenees. It starts easily, but even the first kilometre ends with a stretch of seven percent. The gradient eases for one kilometre, then comes 500 metres of 13.7 percent.

After that there is a flat bit, good job too as the next kilometre is mostly 14.7 percent, easing as it ends to just over ten. The road then fluctuates between six and nine percent until it eases for the last 100 or so metres to the top.

The climb starts in Sérac, and uses some of the lacets of the Guzet-Neige climb before the road heads off to he summit of the Latrape in a straight line, which makes the steepest part even more excruciating because you can see exactly what's looming up in front of you.

The Col de Latrape has been visited five times by the Tour de France since 1984 when Jean-René Bernaudeau won the race to the top on the day that Robert Millar won his stage in Guzet-Neige. Today Bernaudeau is the manager of one of the French teams that take part in the Tour de France.

WHICH WAY? Serac is on the D8, 15 kilometres south-east of Oust, which is 13 kilometres south of St Girons. Follow the D8 in a south-easterly direction, ignoring the right hand turn off on the D68 to Guzet-Neige.

Col d'Ordino

Length: 10 km.

Altitude: 1981 metres.

Height gain: 691 metres.

Average gradient: 6.9%.

Maximum gradient: 7.8%.

A really pleasant climb in the tiny country of Andorra, the Col d'Ordino meanders lazily up from the town of Ordino over a ridge in the Vall d'Andorra that leads to the Pic de Casamanya (2742 metres). There aren't any really steep parts to this climb, and the gradient is fairly constant. Added to the valley views, this makes the Ordino a great climb for beginners.

The first Tour de France climber to get over the Col d'Ordino was Oliviero Rincon in 1993. Rincon was a great climber, who said his ability to accelerate uphill came from his riding a 20 kilogram bike to deliver 30 kilograms of newspapers every day in his mountainous home in Duitama, Colombia when he was a child.

WHICH WAY? Ordino is eight kilometres north-east of Escaldes, which is a suburb of the Andorran capital, Andorra La Vella, on the CG 4 and CG 3 roads. The climb is signposted in Ordino and the road to the top is the CS 240. If you carry on and descend the Ordino to the CG2 you can turn left onto that road and climb the Col d'Envalira.

Col de Pal

Length: 6 km.

Altitude: 1870 metres.

Height gain: 544 metres.

Average gradient: 9%.

Maximum gradient: 11%.

Another short but tough climb to one of the ski resorts of the Vallnord in Andorra, Pal has only had one Tour de France visit when Oliviero Rincon won a stage there in 1993. What makes this climb extra interesting though is the road after the ski resort that goes up to 2300 metres via the Coll de la Botella.

The climb starts in La Massana, which is already at 1326 metres and on the route that runs from Escaldes to Ordino. At first the road is straight as it climbs through quite an extensive built up area in the Arinsal valley, but at Erts the road bends to the left and the buildings fall away leaving you on your own to tackle the stretches of eleven percent up to Pal.

This is where the Tour stage ended, but the road continues upwards in a wide left and right sweep to the Col de la Botella. There is a short stretch of twelve percent just before the top of this climb. Next comes a short descent from the top of the pass then a really lonely bit up to 2300 metres, where the road abruptly changes into a track. This is the border between Andorra and Spain and it is mountain bike terrain. The track continues over the border and ends in a tiny hamlet called Tor, from which it is possible to descend a rough road into the Vall Ferrera.

WHICH WAY? La Massana is six kilometres north of Escaldes on the CG4. Continue on that road and turn left at Erts to Pal. For the Coll de la Botella continue on this road. The CG4 ends at the Andorran-Spanish border.

Col de Toses

Length: 21.8 km.

Altitude: 1800 metres.

Height gain: 710 metres.

Average gradient: 3.3%.

Maximum gradient: 8%.

This climb starts just over the Spanish border in Urtx near to Puigcerda and is totally within Spain. It's a very attractive climb with lots of twists, turns and gradients changes, but it is a main road so can be quite busy. The average gradient is not steep, but there are two stretches of eight percent going up and, infuriatingly, one stretch that descends.

The Col de Toses has only been visted by the Tour de France twice, once in 1957 when Jean Bourlès triumphed, and again in 1965 when the winer was a Spaniard called José Pérez-Francés.

Bourlès was a very talented French rider who won the 16th stage of the 1957 Tour de France, but was only a pro rider for three full years, despite legend having it that he was one of the best three bike riders that Brittany has ever produced. The thing was that Bourlès didn't like travelling, and cycling was so popular in his home region that he could earn enough money just from racing there as a semi-pro rider.

The Col de Toses also has its own legend. Some academics claim that there is evidence of a prehistoric tribe of people living there that were much shorter than other people of the same era and had red hair.

WHICH WAY? Urtx is seven kilometres south of Puigcerda on the N152. Puigcerda is about 30 kilometres south-east of the top of the Col de Puymorens on the N20 and 65 kilometres west of Perpignan on the N116. Continue on the N152 to the top of the Col de Toses.

Western
Pyrenees

The Western Pyrenees run from the region around the town of Oloron-Ste-Marie, south-east to start of the Col du Péyresourde just to the west of Bagnères de Luchon, which if not the geographic absolute middle of the whole range is certainly a convenient place to draw the line.

Like the rest of the range, the Western Pyrenees are far more unpredictable in their gradients and direction than the Alps. The roads, even the scenery, have a less engineered feel to them.

The Pyrenees are generally greener then the Alps. They are lower and they are further south so the tree line is higher – but the main reason for this verdancy is that they see more rain than the Alps. And that is certainly true of the Western Pyrenees, which get the full effect of frontal rain coming in off the Atlantic Ocean.

Oloron-Ste-Marie is ideal for exploring the misty soft folds of countryside and climbs around the far west of this region. Lourdes has the giant, Hautecam and the Col d'Aubisque almost on its doorstep. Tarbes or Bagnères-de-Brigorre are perfect for launching yourself at the rugged challenge of the Col du Tourmalet, and Bagnères-de-Luchon is the place for the ski station climbs like Superbagnères or the Péyresourde.

Col d'Aspin 'PYRENEAN PERFECTION'

✪✪✪ 3 STARS

Length: 11.9 km.

Altitude: 1489 metres.

Height gain: 670 metres.

Average gradient: 3.6%.

Maximum gradient: 5.3%.

WHAT TO EXPECT

➤ **Mountain view.** From the summit you can see some of the highest peaks in the Pyrenees. L'Arbizon (2831 metres) is almost due south and the Pic du Midi de Bigorre (2872 metres) with its observatory on top is to the west. To the left of that is the Col du Tourmalet.

➤ **Mountain bikers.** There are plenty of tracks for suitable off-road bikes in the Aspin area.

➤ **Green scenery.** Because of the warm temperatures of the south, the high annual rainfall, and relatively low altitude, the Aspin is a very green and pleasant place. Even it's summit is covered in grass.

Not too long, not too high and not too steep. The Aspin is a great place to start mountain climbing in the Pyrenees. It's no push over and it has a great Tour de France history, but the Aspin is fairly unique in the Pyrenees in that it climbs the mountain on well-engineered roads with plenty of hairpins to break the ascent into manageable bits.

There's a little taste of true Pyrenean character just after halfway, where the bends stop and the road is thrown straight at the climb's steepest part. It is a ten percent gradient here, steep and exposed if there is any wind, but this stretch doesn't last for long before another sweeping hairpin takes you up to the gently rounded summit.

The town of Arreau, which is a key settlement in the Aure valley with a castle and a museum of local life, nestles at the foot of the Aspin. It's squeezed into a thin ribbon by the mountains that surround it, and its houses are tall and grey. Most of

Col d'Aspin

D918

Arreau

Left: Village on the Aspin descent   **Above:** Lush landscape indicates high rainfall

them are topped with steeply-pitched roofs, an indication of the quantity of rain they get in this region.

The rain makes this area good for farming. Not for crops but cattle, which graze on the slopes of the Aspin. On the descent there is a herd of big cream-coloured animals, which also tend to roam freely on the roads. They don't look or care what's coming down the mountain, so be careful when you see them. They will walk out in front of you.

The descent isn't steep, so once you've survived the wandering cattle take time to look for the quarries, from which the green marble was extracted to build the Palace of Versailles, the Opera in Paris and many other monuments all across France. Once at the bottom your are at the foot of the Col du Tourmalet.

WHICH WAY?

Arreau is on the D929 with the towns of Lannemezan to the north and San Lary-Soulan to the south. From the north turn right, and south left, onto the D918 to begin the Aspin.

MOUNTAIN MOMENTS

➤ The Aspin was first used in the Tour de France in 1910, so is one of the longest-serving mountains on the Tour. First to the top was a Frenchman, Octave Lapize.

➤ In 1947, the first post-war Tour de France, the Breton Jean Robic laid the foundations of his eventual victory on the Col d'Aspin. A brilliant but mercurial rider, Robic dropped his breakaway companion Pierre Brambilla on the Péyresourde and climbed the Aspin alone. He stayed that way for 190 kilometres, eventually winning the stage in Pau by over ten minutes.

➤ The points that Richard Virenque of France won for crossing the Aspin in fourth place during the 2003 Tour sealed his record-equalling sixth win in the King of the Mountains. In 2004 Virenque took the record for himself by winning a seventh mountains title.

Col d'Aubisque 'THE TWO IN ONE CLIMB'

●●● 3 STARS

Length: 29.1 km.

Altitude: 1709 metres.

Height gain: 1365 metres.

Average gradient: 5.2%.

Maximum gradient: 10%.

WHAT TO EXPECT

➤ **Gradient changes.** The Aubisque presents a good case for being the most Pyrenean of Pyrenean climbs. You'll be shifting gear all the way up, and it's important not to spend too much of your energy on the steep first part of the Soulor

➤ **Sunshine.** The lower slopes of the Soulor get more than the Western Pyrenees average of sun each year.

➤ **Weather changes.** The top of the Aubisque sees a distinct climate change. The effects of the Atlantic are felt here and it is wetter than the southern and eastern side.

➤ **Four-legged friends.** As well as wild horses on the Aubisque there is a herd of donkeys at the top of the Soulor. I'm not sure if they are wild – but I know that they are friendly.

➤ **Botanic name.** The Aubisque is named after a local term, for a kind of sedge that grows on its slopes, particularly on the western side.

The Aubisque is two climbs in one. The first part is called the Col du Soulor, then there is a short descent before the final eight kilometres to the top of the Aubisque. It's an infuriating drop if you dwell on the metres you've just gained, but one typical of Pyrenean climbs.

The climb starts in the attractive town of Argelès-Gazost. Watch out for the slightly bewildering one-way system though. Once you have threaded your way out of town you hit the hardest part of the climb. The road rises at an average of seven percent with one or two stretches of ten.

At the end of this first stretch you leave the Azun valley to enter a wide open space of fertile fields surrounded by mountains before entering the village of Aucun. Here the climb gets serious again with several kilometres of seven to eight percent in front of you.

This continues to the top of the Col du Soulor, where its worth stopping to glance at the Pic du Midi towering over the valley behind you, and at the rock wall of sharp crests that ring the southern side of the Soulor.

The road descends now for two kilometres, where it looks like it has been cut into the wall of the Pic Gazibos (2692 metres). On this stretch you also cross the departmental border between the Haute-Pyrenees and the Pyrenees-Atlantique.

Then the climbing starts again, slowly racking up from two to seven percent by the top of the Aubisque. This last part is a wild-looking place of sharp grey rock

Argelès-Gazost

Col d'Aubisque

D918

and sparse grass that supports a colony of wild horses. They don't look at all out of place up here.

WHICH WAY?

Argelès-Gazost is 15 kilometres south of Lourdes on the D81. There is plenty of accommodation in both places, or in nearby Tarbes, so they are all good bases for exploring the Western Pyrenees. The Col de Soulor and Aubsique are both signposted from the centre of Argelès-Gazost, but the road up both climbs is the D918, the same one that traces the backbone of much of the Pyrenees.

MOUNTAIN MOMENTS

➤ The Aubisque first appeared in the Tour de France in 1910 on the legendary first day in the Pyrenees, when a Basque rider, Lafourcade was first to the top. The organisers breathed a sigh of relief when none of the riders died, so you can be sure they didn't expect the race would return to the Aubisque another 70 times.

➤ In 1985 the summit was the finish of a short stage of just over 52 kilometres from Luz-St Sauveur. The hugely talented Irish rider, Stephen Roche was determined to make his mark that day and lined up at the start in an aerodynamic one-piece outfit that riders use in time trials. A journalist asked Roche, "What are you doing, this isn't a time trial? To which Roche replied, "Want to bet," and attacked from the start and rode alone to victory.

Left: Jagged rocks of the Grand Gabizos **Above:** The Azun valley

Lourdes-Hautacam   'THE PILGRIMS WATCHTOWER'

✪✪✪✪ 4 STARS

Length: 15.5 km.
Altitude: 1616 metres.
Height gain: 1136 metres.
Average gradient: 7.3%.
Maximum gradient: 11%.

WHAT TO EXPECT

➤ **Twists and turns.** The road wriggles around as it climbs, trying to find the route of least resistance.

➤ **Great views.** The first part of the climb overlooks the Lac des Gaves, and the second part gives great views up towards the Gorge de Luz and the Pic de Viscos (2141 metres). There's a viewing point at a sharp bend called La Pene de Sereres where you get the best views.

➤ **Family rides.** A cycle path runs from Lourdes through Argelès-Gazost and almost to Cauterets on what was an old railway line. It's perfect for family bike rides.

➤ **Off-road riding.** The slopes of Hautacam mountain are laced with brilliant tracks for mountain biking.

Towering above Lourdes, Hautacam is a relatively recent addition to the Tour de France but its tough reputation has already made it a place of pilgrimage for cyclists. It is quite a brute with a tough first quarter, a bit of an easy passage, then the final two-thirds just get harder and harder, throwing constant changes of gradient at you. The climb has been the finish of three stages now, and they have all seen some epic racing.

The road to Hautacam follows what used to known as the Col de Tramassel. It is called Hautacam now to publicise the ski station there of the same name. The ski station took its name from the highest mountain of those ringing the southern edge of Lourdes.

The start is in Argelès-Gazost and the climb scales the opposite side of the valley to the Col du Soulor. The road really twists around to climb the slopes of Hautacam, and it passes through several villages on the way up.

The hardest part of the climb comes just after Artelans, with getting on for three kilometres of ten-percent climbing. It eases a little after this, but don't attack too hard yet because there is a very tough stretch of eleven percent to come just before the finish.

The last kilometre is a relatively easy six percent, and the finish of the climb is at the entrance to a huge car park at the ski station. If you want to go as far as the road goes there is an extra bit of climb up to the Col de Tramassel. Then if you are still in the mood for exploration, and you have thick tyres on your bike, there is a short length of rough track that leads to a group of lakes.

The lakes are a peaceful place set in a green bowl – home to many kilometres of cross-country ski routes in the winter. It's nice that cycling and cross-country skiing share this place as there are a lot of physiological similarities between the demands of the two sports, and many exponents of both often use the other sport as training.

WHICH WAY?

Argelès-Gazost is 15 kilometres south-west of Lourdes on the D821. The road to the ski resort is indicated in town, but coming from Lourdes you turn left onto the D913 and left again on the D100 and follow that road to the summit.

Argelès-Gazost

D100

Col de Tramassel

Above: Waiting for the Tour **Below:** The Hautecam range from the Col d'Aubisqueun valley

MOUNTAIN MOMENTS

> The first Tour rider to climb Hautacam was the Frenchman, Luc Leblanc in 1994. After him, Bjarne Riis of Denmark won a stage there in 1996.
In 2000 a young Spanish rider called Javier Ochoa was the winner. Ochoa looked to have a great future in pro cycling, but in February of the following year he and his twin brother, Ricardo were both hit by a car while out on a training ride. Ricardo was killed instantly, while Javier fell into a deep coma, where he stayed for almost a month. When he regained consciousness, Javier was severely handicapped but he started cycling again. What is more he began racing and in 2004 he won gold and silver medals at the Paralympic Games. In 2007 Javier Ochoa became world Paralympics road race champion.

Luz Ardiden *'TWISTS AND TURN'*

⊗⊗⊗⊗ **4 STARS**

Length: 13.4 km.
Altitude: 1720 metres.
Height gain: 1036 metres.
Average gradient: 7.7%.
Maximum gradient: 12%.

WHAT TO EXPECT

➤ **A thriving town.** Luz-Saint-Sauveur buzzes with activity. It's not a leisurely old spa town, but a big centre for outdoor activities like climbing, rafting and paragliding. If you've never tried it there is a Via Ferrata near Luz. These are an Italian idea and literally means 'Iron Road', but they are actually footpaths that use natural ledges and fixed metal ladders to scale rock faces. You get a rock climbing thrill without having to have a rock climber's skill.

➤ **Spanish influence.** The border is only 25 kilometres away, although it's a high altitude trek on foot to cross it. Still, Spain influences this part of France right down to the music on local radio.

➤ **Combining climbs.** They are so near that it's very easy to combine a climb of Luz Ardiden with Cauterets, or maybe the west side of the Tourmalet.

This climb isn't quite as tough a proposition as Hautacam because its gradient is much more regular, but to achieve that regularity the road builders created a series of twists, turns and tight lacets to overcome the gradient of the valley side from Luz-Saint-Sauveur to the top.

Luz-Saint-Sauveur is an attractive town that sits in the Gorge de Luz at the bottom of the west side of the Tourmalet at the junction of the Barèges and Gavarnie valleys. It is famous for its thermal baths, which promise cures for many ailments, but is also a great centre for exploring the Western Pyrenees. As well as having the Tourmalet, Luz Ardiden and other Tour climbs on its doorstep, it's worth riding to the head of the valley to see the Cirque de Gavarnie, the ridge of 3000-metre peaks that are the border with Spain.

Luz Ardiden

D100

Luz-Saint-Sauveur

Left: Towards Luz Ardiden from the Gorge de Luz   **Above:** Pyrenean sunset

This climb actually starts with a short descent, but as you pass the Solferino chapel the climbing begins. It's a leisurely three percent at first, the famous thermal baths are on your right on this section, but soon increases to eight percent on leaving the village of Sazos. After that you have to negotiate a series of steep lacets with pitches of twelve percent that only slowly give way to lesser gradients. It's tough more or less to the top.

But at least the gradient is constant. You can pick your gear ratio, pick your cadence, pick your climbing style and settle into it. Towards the top you leave the pastures and are in real mountain country of bare rock and waterfalls, surrounded by the high peaks such as Viscos (2141 metres) to the north, and Ardiden (2988 metres) to the south.

Like Hautacam the climb ends at car park situated at the furthest end of the ski resort, but unlike Hautacam there is nowhere else to go. You have to turn around and go back down the way you came. If you do want an alternative route down, turn left after three and a half kilometres and descend the Viscos road. It ends up in the valley about five kilometres north of Luz-St-Sauveur.

WHICH WAY?

Luz-Saint-Sauveur is 18 kilometres south-east of Argeles-Gazost on the D921. Luz Ardiden is clearly signposted in town, and the road to the top is the D12. The Viscos road that also leads from the D921 nearly to Luz Ardiden is called the Col de Riou.

MOUNTAIN MOMENTS

➤ Luz Ardiden first appeared on the Tour in 1985 when Spaniard Pedro Delgado won. The race organisers found the climb was so photogenic that they have included it six times since.
➤ Spaniards have won four out of the seven finishes on Luz Ardiden, but in 1987 it was a Norwegian rider who triumphed. Dag-Otto Lauritzen was a young military policeman when he was injured in a parachuting accident. His doctor prescribed cycling as rehabilitation, and Dag-Otto found he had a flair for it that saw him end up racing in the Tour de France.
➤ The winner on Luz Ardiden in 2003 was Lance Armstrong on his way to the record-equalling fifth Tour victory.

Col de Marie-Blanque 'WAY OUT WEST'

✪✪✪✪ 4 STARS

Length: 19.6 km.

Altitude: 1035 metres.

Height gain: 700 metres.

Average gradient: 3.6%.

Maximum gradient: 12%.

WHAT TO EXPECT

➤ **Damp conditions.** Rainfall is quite high in this part of France. Moist air blows in off the Atlantic and the mountains here get most of the precipitation. It leads to humid conditions, which means that even if it's not raining you get a lot of mist at the top of the Marie-Blanque.

➤ **Save something.** It can't be stressed too strongly how hard the top three-and-a-half kilometres of the Marie-Blanque are. This stretch is a bit like the kind of hill you find in the Welsh Mountains or North Yorkshire.

➤ **Bears.** They used to be quite common in the Pyrenees but were thought to be extinct, so some Slovenian bears were introduced in the Aspe valley. They thrived, and there are apparently fourteen of them living here now.

Linking the Aspe and Ossau valleys, the Marie-Blanque is the furthest west of the big Tour de France climbs. It's also a toughie. Not long and with an easy start, but the second half of the climb is really hard and includes one kilometre of constant twelve-percent climbing.

The Tour de France has climbed the Marie-Blanque twelve times and from both sides, but the western approach is harder and slightly more attractive. However, according to one legend, how the mountain got its name is a bit grim. Marie-Blanque is reputed to have been a professional mourner in the district who was famous for the singing of laments.

The climb starts in the village of Escot, a village that marks the beginning of the Béarn district, where the name Béarnaise sauce comes from. The climb is up the Barescou valley, a wide place of green pastures and lazy grazing cattle, and the first five kilometres are a joyful experience of easy climbing and great views.

But when you get to the barrier that closes the pass in winter, the real climbing starts and it's tough – very tough. For three and a half kilometres you have to scale a veritable wall of between ten and twelve percent that culminates in a short section

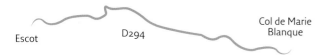

Escot   D294   Col de Marie Blanque

Above: View west towards Marie-Blanque from the Aubisque

that is even steeper. Have courage though, because when you get to this point you are nearly at the top.

On a clear day you can see the Pic Roumendarès (1964 metres) and Pic de l'Ourlene (1813 metres) from the top, and a few metres below on the descent is the wide open grassy Plateau de Benou, a big area in the winter for cross-country skiing. There are also a number of cairns dotted around the summit and plateau, but no one knows by whom or when they were built.

The descent is not nearly as steep as the route you've just climbed. It's still a test of skill though, as the road down into the Ossau valley has lots of twists and turns before it reaches the village of Bielle.

WHICH WAY?

The Marie Blanque starts in the village of Escot, which is on the N134 road that runs from Pau into Spain through the Somport tunnel. The nearest town to Escot is Oloron-Ste-Marie, which is 32 kilometres south-west of Pau, and Escot is 15 kilometres south of Oloron. Turn left off the N134, got through the village and follow the D294 to the top of the Marie-Blanque.

MOUNTAIN MOMENTS

➤ The Marie-Blanque was first climbed in the 1978 Tour by Michele Pollentier of Belgium.
➤ The happiest man to ever pass over the Marie-Blanque in first place was the Frenchman, Gilbert Duclos-Lassalle in 1987. He wasn't a lightweight climber at all, and was far better at the flat one-day races of northern Europe. He won the cobbled Classic, Paris-Roubaix twice. But Duclos, as his fans call him, lives just up the road in Oloron-Ste-Marie and had climbed the Marie-Blanque hundreds of times in training.
➤ In 1996 an Australian, Neil Stephens was first over the Marie-Blanque. He was trying to win the stage that finished in Pamplona, Spain, which is where he'd made his European home.

Above: The Tour de France in the Pyrenees

Col de Péyresourde *'FIELDS OF GREEN'*

⭐⭐⭐ **3 STARS**

Length: 14.3 km.

Altitude: 1569 metres.

Height gain: 944 metres.

Average gradient: 6.6%.

Maximum gradient: 10%.

WHAT TO EXPECT

➤ **Company**. The Péyresourde is a classic climb with lots of Tour de France history, so it's very popular with cyclists.

➤ **Gradient changes**. The road never goes up for long at the same rate, especially during the second half of this climb. Expect to make frequent gear changes.

➤ **Wind speed**. The wide open valley and straight roads mean that the Péyresourde offers little shelter from the wind. If its blowing strongly you will feel it, especially after the village of Garin.

➤ **Other valleys**. If you have time there are plenty of off-shoot valleys to explore from the Péyresourde. The Neste d'Oueil and Neste d'Oô are particularly beautiful. There is also a narrow road at St-Averin that joins the climb of Superbagnères at the point where it leaves the Pique valley.

This climb links the Aure and the Louron valleys and the top of the Péyresourde is the departmental border between Haute-Garonne and Hautes-Pyrenees. It starts gently enough in a Spa town, Bagnères-de-Luchon, which is twinned with Harrogate in England.

The first part scales a geological formation called a moraine. These are formed from detritus left behind by melting glaciers when they recede from their furthest point down a valley. This glacier formed the valley on your left, which is topped by the Pic des Spijoles (3085 metres) and Pic Lézat (3107 metres). There is still a small Spijoles glacier up at the head of the valley today.

After clambering up the moraine the road straightens and a long stretch of eight percent gradient begins. This takes you to the village of Garin, aptly named for a Tour de France route since the first ever winner of the race was called Maurice Garin.

Garin is a farming village, and the whole climb so far has a lovely pastoral feel to it, a feel that is created by the gently sloping wide valley that surrounds it. As the climb continues though, the grass becomes much sparser.

Col de
Péyresourde

D618

Bagnères-
de-Luchon

Above: Trace the road to the summit gap   **Right:** Just above Garin

The final part of the climb is up some well-engineered lacets that you can see for many kilometres before you reach them. The top is also clearly visible as a notch in the rock wall through which vehicles climbing the lacets suddenly disappear.

There's a small restaurant at the top, and a little pine glade that is nice for picnics. There is also a short road to a small ski resort. Before you lies the Louron valley and the whole of the Western Pyrenees.

WHICH WAY?

From Bagnères-de-Luchon take the D618 signposted Arreau and Col de Péyresourde. Bagnères is also at the start of the Superbagnères climb and at the bottom of the western side of the Col du Portillon, so it's a great place to stay, especially if you fancy a short trip into Spain.

MOUNTAIN MOMENTS

➤ First climbed on the eventful day in 1910 when the Tour first ventured into the Pyrenees and Octave Lapize was the winner. The race has returned 55 times since to the Péyresourde.

➤ The last time was in 2007 when Kazakhstan's Alexandre Vinokourov was first over the summit before plummeting down to Loudenvielle to win the day's stage. It looked a remarkable performance, early in the Tour Vinokourov had crashed badly and ended up with many stitches in his body. He slowly recovered and miraculously won this stage, but then the real reason for the miracle emerged. Vinokourov's blood test showed evidence of doping and he was stripped of the stage and eliminated from the Tour.

Pla d'Adet   'POULIDOR'S LAST STAND'

★★★★ 4 STARS

Length: 11.6 km.
Altitude: 1683 metres.
Height gain: 870 metres.
Average gradient: 8.2%.
Maximum gradient: 12%.

WHAT TO EXPECT

➤ **Adverse wind.** This climb goes up one side of the valley, turns around and continues to climb up the other, so the wind will be against you at some point.

➤ **Don't be cowed.** As you ride through St Lary you can see Pla d'Adet towering high above you. Tour de France riders who aren't good climbers say that this is the most demoralising aspect of the climb.

➤ **The no sweat way.** There's a téléphérique that goes from St Lary de Soulan to Pla d'Adet in five minutes flat.

➤ **Go high.** After the summit of Pla d'Adet descend to where the climb does the 180 and turn left to climb the old Col de Portet. It's not a Tour climb, but the road rises to 2215 metres and provides some spectacular mountain scenery.

D123

Pla d'Adet   St-Lary-Soulon

This is a tough one. It's the second last offshoot of the Aure valley before the Bielsa tunnel into Spain and it's full of Pyrenean menace. Its gradient changes constantly, but it still has a fierce average of 8 percent, because of several stretches of double digit climbing. Pla d'Adet is a climber's climb and many of the best have boosted their reputations on it since its inclusion in the 1974 Tour.

That day saw France's number one cycling hero of all time, Raymond Poulidor inflict a defeat on the great Eddy Merckx at the height of his powers. Poulidor is said to have been the unluckiest man in Tour history, because despite being a favourite for 15 years he never won the Tour or even wore the yellow jersey. His career coincided with those of Jacques Anquetil then Eddy Merckx, and in between Poulidor crashed or was beset by other misfortune.

Above left: Towards Pla d'Adet from the Aspin   **Above right:** King of the Mountains 1988, Steve Rooks after the Etape du Tour 2007 in the Pyrenees.

Poulidor's Pla d'Adet victory came ten years after beating Anquetil on the Puy de Dôme. He had Merckx in all kinds of trouble, just as he had Anquetil, but Poulidor didn't have the confidence to press his advantage early enough on either occasion, and that, more than bad luck, is why he twice finished second and took five third places in the Tour de France.

Pla d'Adet starts with one kilometre of six percent, a warm up for a brutal bit of twelve percent that eases to eight then increases again to eleven. This comes just after the first hairpin, where the road begins to climb one side of the valley that leads to an old way over the mountains called the Col de Portet.

The going is tough and it stays tough through the village of Soulan until the road does a full 180 degree turn and begins to climb the other side of the valley. This means that while you are climbing the tough bit you can see Pla d'Adet on top of the opposite valley side. Don't look though, because it's a lot higher than you are and you'll get demoralised. Once you've negotiated the sharp bend the gradient eases a bit and the run to the top is quite straightforward.

WHICH WAY?

St-Lary-Soulon is on the D929, 33 kilometres south of Lannemezan and the A64 Autoroute. It's a big town and ideal for Pla d'Adet, Piau Engaly, the Péyresourde, Aspin and even Tourmalet. Pla d'Adet is signposted in the town, follow the D123 to the top.

MOUNTAIN MOMENTS

➤ The Tour has visited Pla d'Adet nine times since 1974. The most interesting winner is Beat Breu, who took his victory in 1982. Breu is Swiss, but that is about all you can categorise him with. He has represented his country at road, off-road and track cycling, as well as winning stages in the Tour de France. He was one of the first climbers to experiment with very light bike equipment, even refusing to put tape on the handlebars of his climbing bike to save weight. After he retired, Breu did the usual ex-pro sportsman thing and started up a business, but he also developed a stand-up comedy routine and has appeared several times on Swiss TV to do his act.

Left: The 2007 King of the Mountains, Mauricio Soler

Col du Portillon 'THE STRAIN FROM SPAIN'

⭐⭐ 2 STARS

Length: 8.3 km.

Altitude: 1293 metres.

Height gain: 521 metres.

Average gradient: 7.2%.

Maximum gradient: 8.2%.

WHAT TO EXPECT

➤ **Regular riding.** The Col de Portillon has a regular gradient. Settle into a gear ratio that you know you can maintain to the top, concentrate on getting a good rhythm going and leave your mind free to enjoy the view.

➤ **Narrow descent.** The road up is wide and regular, but the descent is much narrower and has some very tight bends.

➤ **Forty eight springs.** That's how many thermal water sources there are in Bagnères-de-Luchon. There is evidence of bathing here dating back to Roman times, and one underground pool goes back over 1600 metres under the Superbagnères mountain.

➤ **Brown bears.** There used to be lots of these living in the mountains around here, and there are rumours that a few still exist.

This climb has appeared many times in the Tour and has been climbed from both sides. I chose the Spanish side because it is slightly different to most Pyrenean climbs, and it's harder than climbing from the French side.

The climb starts in Bossost, ten kilometres south of the Spanish border on the N230 in what is called the Val d'Aran. Vielha is the nearest Spanish town, about 16 kilometres to the south-east of Bossost. The nearest French town is Bagnères-de-Luchon, which is where the Col de Portillon leads to.

It's not a long climb and the road up it is well engineered with a constant gradient, a rarity in the Pyrenees. But just over eight kilometres of eight percent is still no joke, although this climb is recommended for less experienced climbers as the plentiful trees along the route offer plenty of shelter from wind and from the sun on hot days.

There is an incredible viewing point about three quarters of the way up, offering extensive views over the Val d'Aran and a great opportunity for photography. The rest of the journey to the summit is a bit more Pyrenean in that the road's bends are less regular – but the gradient still stays the same.

At the top all you can see of the border crossing is a metal barrier rusted into the raised position and a couple of signposts. There are some great views to be had on the Portillon descent of the Superbagnères ski station towering above Luchon, and there are several large waterfalls to admire. Just remember to stop before admiring them, because the Portillon's descent is quite tricky and will require all of your attention.

Col du Portillon — N230 — N141

Left: Hairpin on the descent **Above:** The Val d'Aran

WHICH WAY?

The N230 road is the Spanish designation for the N125, and Bossost sits on this road 26 kilometres south of the descent of the Col de Menté and St-Béat. The road over the Col is the N141 and it is clearly signposted in Bossost. The road becomes the D618 at the summit border with France.

> The first Tour de France rider over the Portillon was a Belgian, Désiré Keteleer in 1957. One of the most famous winners was a Spaniard, José-Manuel Fuente. Fuente was a climber of the old school – short, slight and the possessor of a killing turn of speed who seemed to have wings on his feet. His nickname was Tarrangu , an Asturian dialect word that means 'full of character'. Fuente certainly had plenty of fight, and his devastating climbing ability threatened to win him the Tour of France in the 1970s. Unfortunately he couldn't race like Eddy Merckx or Felice Gimondi on the flat stages, and was no match for either in a time trial. Fuente still managed to win the Tour of Spain twice though, plus two stages of the Tour de France and six in the Tour of Italy, all of them in the mountains.

Superbagnères *'FIRST BRITISH YELLOW JERSEY'*

⊕⊕⊛ 3 STARS

Length: 19.3 km.

Altitude: 1786 metres.

Height gain: 1179 metres.

Average gradient: 6.1%.

Maximum gradient: 12%.

WHAT TO EXPECT

➤ **Two characters.** The first part of Superbagnères uses a valley to gain height, the last part climbs a steep mountain slope to the top in a series of lacets. The valley part of the climb is easier, so save something for the top.

➤ **Changing gradients.** This is a real Pyrenean climb, and there is barely one kilometre where the gradient is constant.

➤ **Chilly on top.** In early and late summer there can be a lot of ice on the high mountains just south of Superbagnères . If the wind blows from that direction it can make the summit cool.

➤ **Point of view.** At the 16-kilometre point there is a viewing point, where you can stop and look at the southern mountains. The highest is the Pic Perdiguère (3222 metres)

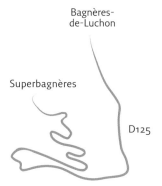

Superbagnères is a ski station that stands on the shoulder of the 3000-metre peaks marking the French and Spanish border south of Bagnères-de-Luchon. You can see the biggest building of the ski station, the Grand Hotel, from Luchon, but the way straight to it is too steep for vehicles and only a cable car and various walking tracks go directly up.

The road to Superbagnères uses the Pique valley for the first six kilometres of its ascent. Here the gradients are variable but none too steep. At the Pont de Ravi the road switches right to climb up the Lys valley, still at relatively modest gradients, but all that changes at some lacets just before the ten-kilometre mark.

Now the climb becomes a much tougher proposition, as the gradient increases to an average of nine percent with one passage of twelve. You also begin to emerge from the trees that have provided shelter so far, but the compensation is some great views of the Spanish border mountains.

Now the bulk of the huge Grand Hotel hoves into view again. This was built in 1922 and is the centre of the ski resort of Superbagnères. It's quite an amazing structure that looks just like someone has taken one of the big hotels of Paris and dumped it onto this rocky outcrop. You would have to travel a long way to improve on the views from its 100 rooms.

The descent is down the same road that you climbed, although there are plenty of opportunities on the way down to turn off and do some exploring. The road to the head of the Lys valley is interesting, and so is the one that continues up the Pique valley. This takes you to the Hospice de France, a shelter built to help pilgrims in the 14th century by the ancient lay fraternity of the Hospitalliers de St John of Jerusalem.

WHICH WAY?

Bagnères-de-Luchon is on the D125, 39 kilometres south of junction 17 of the A64 Autoroute. Follow the D125 through until the Pont de Ravi, where you take the D46 to the top of Superbagnères.

Above: Superbagnères from the Portillon descent showing the Grand Hotel

➤ The road you ride to Superbagnères was opened in 1961, and to celebrate the resort invited the Tour de France there for a stage finish. The Italian, Imerio Massignan won.

➤ One year later the Tour ran a time trial from Bagnères-de-Luchon to Superbagnères, a normal day that had been done before, but the man wearing the yellow jersey was anything but normal for the Tour de France. Since its inception in 1903 no one from outside mainland Europe had led the race, but the previous day a young Englishman called Tom Simpson had taken the yellow jersey. He lost it on Superbagnères , but fought back to third overall with two days to go. Unfortunately he crashed, broke his finger and finished sixth, the best overall placing by a British rider until Robert Millar finished fourth in 1984.

Col du Tourmalet 'THE ELDER STATESMAN'

✪✪✪✪✪ **5 STARS**

Length: 17.1 km.
Altitude: 2115 metres.
Height gain: 1275 metres.
Average gradient: 7.5%.
Maximum gradient: 11%.

WHAT TO EXPECT

➤ **A climb of two halves.** Easy start but a hard finish.

➤ **Snow tunnels.** They protect the road from snow and rock falls, and you ride through several on the first part of the climb.

➤ **Summit views.** A real mountain feeling of exposure looking down from the top.

➤ **Sculpture.** The Tourmalet Giant is a huge metal representation of a cyclist on the summit. There is also a memorial to one of the Tour's most famous race directors, Jacques Goddet.

➤ **Packs of Llamas.** Yes really – they wander free on the grassy slopes after La Mongie.

➤ **A stop at the top.** There's a café and a souvenir shop at the summit.

If the Pyrenees can be distilled into one climb, that climb would be the Tourmalet. It is unpredictable, an easy start invites you to a steep and difficult end. The weather will change. After a bright start you can ride into a world of wind and scudding clouds, then at the top it can be bright sunshine again. The gradient changes constantly, so you shift from one gear to the next. Sitting and standing as conditions change. The Tourmalet is never easy.

The climb starts in the Ardour valley, in the village of Saint-Marie-de-Campan, where during the 1913 Tour de France, Frenchman Eugène Christophe repaired the broken forks of his bike in a Blacksmith's shop.

He walked 14 kilometres to the village, then worked for nearly four hours, watched by officials, his only help the Blacksmith's apprentice who operated the bellows in the forge. The forge is still there, close to the village square. There's a plaque commemorating Christophe's adventure on the wall outside.

Unfortunately the boy's help was Christophe's downfall. He did everything else himself, repaired the forks, got back in the race and finished the stage, but that night the officials who had watched him in the forge disqualified him from the Tour. In those days the race was a solo event with no help in any form allowed.

The first slopes of the Tourmalet are easy – a wooded valley with waterfalls that is a very pleasant place to be. In the hamlet of Gripp things change, the slope racks up to eight percent and doesn't dip below it until the summit.

The character of the mountain shifts again at the ski resort of La Mongie. The pine forests fall away and from here the landscape is bleak and the road steep.

Saint-Marie-
de-Campan

D918

Col du Tourmalet

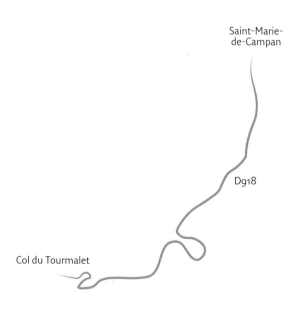

Above: Ski lifts from La Mongie

This bit has to be endured, but the summit view is worth it. It's a real summit too. One minute you're cycling upwards at eight percent, the next plunging into the Gave valley at the same rate.

WHICH WAY.

From Saint-Marie-de-Campan, which is on the D935 south of Bagnères-de-Bigorre, take the D918 following the signs for col du Tourmalet. It's a left turn if you have just descended the Aspin and a right from the Bagnères-de-Bigorre direction.

MOUNTAIN MOMENTS

➤ First climbed by the Tour in 1910, the Tourmalet is one of the longest serving mountains of the Tour de France. First man to the top was Octave Lapize, who became a pilot when the First World War broke out. He died when his plane was shot down over Verdun in 1917.

➤ The Eagle of Toledo, Frederico Bahamontes, a Spaniard who won the Tour in 1959, holds the record for crossing the summit of Tourmalet in first place by doing so four times.

➤ In 1969 Eddy Merckx used the Tourmalet to launch himself into a legendary 120-kilometre breakaway. He was wearing the yellow jersey, so needed to defend, but instead Merckx attacked and won the stage by many minutes. By the close in Paris Merckx had won the Tour by almost 20 minutes. He also won the points and the mountains classification. From that day the press called him 'the Cannibal'.

Left: The summit restaurant   **Above left:** The Tourmalet giant   **Above right:** Tour riders on the Tourmalet

Col de Val Louron ‘INDURAIN’S CONFIRMATION’

⭐⭐ 2 STARS

Length: 7 km.

Altitude: 1420 metres.

Height gain: 560 metres.

Average gradient: 8.2%.

Maximum gradient: 10%.

WHAT TO EXPECT

➤ **Constant climbing.** Val Louron has an eight percent gradient, give or take a few tenths, all the way from the bottom to the top.

➤ **Good finish.** At just eight kilometres, Val Louron is a good way to round off climbing the Péyresourde. Turn left when you see signs for Loudenvielle on the Péyresourde descent. Turn right in Loudenvielle for Génos and do Val Louron. It's five kilometres from the end of the Péyresourde to the start of the Val Louron climb.

➤ **Adventure.** The road to the head of the Louron valley is lonely, beautiful and well worth exploring. From Génos go straight on instead of climbing Val Louron. The metalled road peters out at the Pont du Prat, but the intrepid with suitable bikes can follow a track to the Lassoula shelter right up in among the mountains.

Génos

Val Louron

This climb has only been used once in the Tour, so although that was a quite momentous occasion in the race's history, as it was the point when Miguel Indurain's Tour reign began, I've picked Val Louron as a major climb because it is difficult and because it looks spectacular.

Val Louron is a ski station that sits above the Louron Valley, which stretches from the town of Arreau right up to the high mountains of the Spanish border. The road that was created to take vehicles up to the ski station begins in the village of Génos, and it really is an amazing wriggle of tarmac that,, in a series of lacets, takes you up over 500 metres in just seven kilometres.

That means it is a tough one, with an almost constant gradient of eight percent, and a couple of stretches of ten percent at halfway and just before the finish. The road is unusual for ski resorts in that the top of the climb comes just before a short descent to where the Tour stage finished in 1991, right in the heart of the resort. That is why Indurain is credited with being first over the top of the Val Louron climb, but it was Claudio Chiapucci who won the stage in Val Louron resort that day.

Also unusualy for a ski station, you don't have to descend the same road that you climbed. You can turn right at the top of the Val Louron climb then descend the Col d'Azet, which starts just above the Aure valley. This climb was included in the 1997, 1999 and 2001 Tours. Watch yourself on the descent through

Left: Locals in costume **Above:** Towards Val Louron from Loudenvielle

the village of Azet because the road is very steep here and the buildings either side close in and look extremely solid.

The views from Val Louron are impressive. The high mountains to the south represent the Spanish border, and due west you can see the top of the Col de Péyresourde as a notch between the mountains that separate Haute-Pyrenees from Haute Garonne.

WHICH WAY?

The nearest town to Val Louron is 17 kilometres to the north-west in Arreau, although there is accommodation to be found in several of the places that fill the area of the Louron valley around the bottom of this climb. From Arreau take the D618 south, then turn right on the D25 to Génos and follow the signposts to Val Louron from Génos . The road down the Col d'Azet is the GR10.

MOUNTAIN MOMENTS

➤ The 1991 Tour de France started out as a two-man race between the reigning champion, Greg Lemond and the young pretender Miguel Indurain, but on the stage to Val Louron all that changed. From the first stage Lemond had absorbed everything his Spanish rival could throw at him and there was nothing in it. They were still together all through the first part of this big day in the Pyrenees, but on the Col de Tourmalet, Lemond cracked wide open. Indurain pressed home his advantage, and stormed over the Aspin, then did the same on the climb up to Val Louron. Few could hang on but one who did, Claudio Chiapucci took the stage win. That hardly mattered, Lemond lost over seven minutes and Miguel Indurain all but had his first Tour de France in the bag.

Col d'Azet

Length: 12 km.

Altitude: 1578 metres.

Height gain: 807 metres.

Average gradient: 6.7%.

Maximum gradient: 12%.

A tough Pyrenean climb that has been used three times in the Tour de France. The first time was in 1997 when Marco Pantani tried to break his companions here in an escape close to the stage finish. He went over the Azet in first place but was caught on the descent. A Frenchman, Laurent Brochard won the stage.

The Azet starts in St-Lary-Soulon and is a typical piece of Pyrenean climbing with constant gradient changes and two tough stretches. The first is through the village of Azet, about one-third of the way up. The other is close to the top of the climb. That one is twelve percent – a nasty sting in the tail.

You can make this climb into a nice circuit if you descend to Val Louron then Génos. Then take the D25 and D618 to Arreau. From Arreau there are many lanes running alongside the D929 for a quiet ride back to St-Lary-Soulon.

WHICH WAY? St-Lary-Soulon is 33 kilometres south-west of junction 16 of the A64 Autoroute, and 12 kilometres South-west of Arreau, on the D929. The start of the Col d'Azet is at the southern edge of St-Lary. Look for the D25 left turn going south out of St-Lary. Follow this road to Azet village, where the GR10 take you to the top.

Col de Bagargui

Length: 10 km.

Altitude: 1327 metres.

Height gain: 927 metres.

Average gradient: 7.5%.

Maximum gradient: 12%.

A tough climb that has been used three time by the Tour. It has been climbed from the hamlet of Penin on the east side, and from the west. The east side is the steepest. The climb also has a northern side, making three possible ascents in one session if you like.

The first Tour rider to conquer the Bagargui was Ronan Pensec, a Breton rider who sported a French version of a punk hairstyle when he raced. It was quite tame by British standards, but it got Pensec noticed. He was quite a character anyway and always good for a quote for journalists, who nicknamed him Pin-Pin. Pensec climbed the Bagargui from the west side.

Pensec was sixth overall in the 1986 Tour, but never quite fulfilled the promise he showed that year. He eventually became a trusted team mate of Greg Lemond and lead the 1990 Tour for two days before his team leader took control of the race.

The Col de Bagargui has plenty of twists, turns and changes of gradient. It is only a few kilometres from the Col de Burdincurutcheta, so the two make a good challenge when strung together.

WHICH WAY? Penin is three kilometres north-west of Larrau, which is 40 kilometres south-west of Oloron-Ste-Marie on the D919, D918 and D26. Turn right in Larrau onto the D19 and descend a sharp hill to Penin and the start of the col. Stay on the D19 to the top. The road over the Burdincurutcheta is also the D19

Col de Burdincurutcheta

Length: 19.5 km.
Altitude: 1135 metres.
Height gain: 955 metres.
Average gradient: 4.9%.
Maximum gradient: 12%.

Cauterets

Length: 15 km.
Altitude: 1310 metres.
Height gain: 885 metres.
Average gradient: 5.9%.
Maximum gradient: 8%.

The ultimate climb of two halves. The Burdincurutcheta only climbs up to 300 metres in the first ten kilometres of its length, but then it suddenly rears up and touches ten percent average, with some stretches of eleven and twelve percent, for most of the rest of the way. This makes the climb very hard, as the nine kilometres of steep gradient in the second half are no joke. Make sure you have low-enough gears for this one.

The Tour has climbed the Burdincurutcheta from both sides, but the two-halves side is by far the most interesting, and it's the side that the first Tour rider, Ronan Pensec climbed, in 1986.

This climb was used again by the race in 1987, when Raul Alcala was first to the top. Alcala is Mexican, one of the few riders from that country to make their mark in European pro road racing. He was ninth overall and best young rider in the 1987 Tour, then he won a stage and finished eighth overall in both the 1989 and 1990 Tours.

WHICH WAY? The climb starts at St-Jean-Pied-de-Port, which is 55 kilometres south-east of Biarritz on the D932 and D918. From St-Jean head east on the D933 and turn right at St-Jean-le-Vieux onto the D18 to climb the Burdincurutcheta.

Not a steep climb, but a nice one that starts by scaling the wall of a gorge formed by the river Gave, and gives you some brilliant views. Cauterets is a ski station that has undergone lots of development and extension over the years. The first Tour visit was in 1953, when Jesus Lorono of Spain won, but the finish then was well below the place where Richard Virenque won on Cauterets in 1995. Lorono, a Tour of Spain winner in 1957, was crowned King of the Mountains in the year he won on Cauterets.

The climb starts in Pierrefitte-Nestalas, right at the mouth of the Gorges de Luz. There is a left-hand hairpin to negotiate as you begin the climb, but then it starts ascending the Gave gorge wall and the road twists and turns following the natural lines of the terrain. It isn't very steep, so you get plenty of time to look down at Pierrefitte and the Gave valley, and at the triangular profile of the Pic de Viscos mountain (2142 metres).

In Cauterets follow the right-hand hairpin, ignoring the turn off to the Val de Jeret, and head for Cambasque, which is where the Cauterets climb ends. After you have finished the climb, try descending to the hairpin and the Val de Jeret. Turn off the main road and from there ride to the Pont d'Espagne. This bridge is inside the Pyrenees National Park and is over the river Gave, which at this point is just a series of spectacular and powerful waterfalls.

Cauterets was the first place where Miguel Indurain's potential was revealed to the world when he won his first Tour de France stage there in 1989. He was still a worker for team mate Pedro Delgado in those days and still being developed, but two years later he would win the Tour de France.

WHICH WAY? Pierrefiette-Nestalas is on the D921, six kilometres south of Argelès-Gazost, which is in turn 15 kilometres south-west of Lourdes. The way to Cauterets is clearly signposted in Pierrefiette, follow the D920 to the top.

Col du Pourtalet

Length: 15 km.

Altitude: 1794 metres.

Height gain: 812 metres.

Average gradient: 5.4%.

Maximum gradient: 8%.

This is another border crossing. It has only been climbed once by the Tour, and when they climbed it the riders did so from the Spanish side. Peter De Clerq of Belgium was the first man to the top.

The climb is not very hard, but the road is quite busy. The Col du Pourtalet starts in the village of Escarilla, close to a huge lake in the Valle de Tena. The climb crosses the border at a big semi-circle of mountains called the Cirque d'Anéou, and you get a fantastic view of the Pic Midi d'Ossau (2884 metres) from the summit of the climb.

The French side of the climb starts in the Ossau valley at Larruns, which is on the junction of the D918 and D934 and the climb up is nearly 30 kilometres long. It's a very scenic ride, if a little busy with traffic, especially with French shoppers seeking lower taxed bargains just over the Spanish border.

WHICH WAY? The quickest way to get to Escarrilla to climb the Pourtalet from the Spanish side, as the Tour did, is to go over it from the French side first. Larruns is 30 kilometres from Argeles-Gazost on the D918 over the Col d'Aubisque, or 30 kilometres south of Pau on the D934. From Larruns follow the D934 over the top of the Pourtalet, where the road number changes to the A136, then descend to Escarrilla, where you can turn around and do the climb.

Port de Balès

Length: 19.2 km.

Altitude: 1755 metres.

Height gain: 1179 metres.

Average gradient: 6.2%.

Maximum gradient: 11%.

This was a brand new Tour climb in 2007, when Luxembourg's Kim Kirchen lead over the top. It's a really hard one, very Pyrenean in character, with an easy first seven-and-a-half kilometres, but then it steadily gets harder.

The climb, which starts in Mauléon-Barousse, changes direction and gradient every few hundred metres and the road is narrow with a very heavy surface. Bike tyres roll well on smooth tarmac, but the surface of the Port de Balès is a long way from smooth tarmac.

The descent is as unpredictable as the ride up, so take care on your way down. The road joins the Col de Péyresourde at about one-quarter of the way up that climb. Watch out too for irregularities in the road surface, they can easily throw you off line.

WHICH WAY? Mauléon-Barousse is 16 kilometres south-west of junction 17 of the A64 Autoroute, and 21 kilometres south-west of St Gaudens. Follow the D8 from St Gaudens to the junction with the A645 from junction 17, then take the D33 south and turn right on the N125 and right again on the D925 to Mauléon-Barousse. The D925 is the road over the Port de Balès.

Port de Larrau

Length: 15.3 km.

Altitude: 1573 metres.

Height gain: 1205 metres.

Average gradient: 7.9%.

Maximum gradient: 11.5%.

Another real toughie. The Port de Larrau starts at l'Auberge de Laugibar and isn't much of a climb at all until its fourth kilometre. Then, from there until eleven kilometres the road climbs at a breathtaking ten-percent average. After that it eases a bit as the road crosses the Col d'Erroymendi, but breath deeply and take this part as easy as you can, because the Larreau has a one-kilometre 11.5 percent sting in its tail. It has been climbed twice by the Tour de France, the first time being in 1996 when Richard Virenque was the best.

The Larrau is a very attractive climb that twists and turns its way up to the Spanish border, then descends into Spain in a similar manner. The Spanish side of the climb is a very popular training ground for their cyclists. Miguel Indurain used to make a point of riding this climb to test how his form was progressing at various points during the year. Ironically it was also the last Tour de France climb Indurain ever raced on.

WHICH WAY? Laugibar is on the D26, 42 kilometres south-west of Oloron-St-Marie, using the D919, D918 and D26. The D26 is the road to the top if the climb. The road number changes to the NA2011 as it crosses the Spanish border.

Col du Soudet

Length: 14.7 km.

Altitude: 1540 metres.

Height gain: 1090 metres.

Average gradient: 7.3%.

Maximum gradient: 11.2%.

An attractive climb that has been on the Tour route six times – but only climbed on five of those occasions. In 1995 the riders were scheduled to climb the Soudet, but the stage was cancelled after Fabio Casartelli was killed on the descent of the Portet d'Aspet. The first Tour de France rider to conquer the Soudet was the Frenchman, Robert Forest in 1987.

The climb starts in La Mouline with a brutal bit of fifteen percent, but it immediately eases until nine kilometres. Then the true character of the Soudet is revealed again as the road tilts up at between seven and eleven percent for eight kilometres of twisting and turning road that never stays at one gradient for long.

There are fantastic views as you curl around the edge if the Pic de Guilhers and reach the top of the Col de Labay, which climbs up from your left. That is a beautiful climb too, and well worth trying, even though it has never been used in the Tour.

From the top of the Col de Labay the gradient eases until the Summit of the Soudet. From here it is only three-and-a-half kilometres of descending and climbing to the top of the Col de la Pierre St-Martin, so you could go down that climb, turn around and add the Pierre St-Martin to the Soudet.

WHICH WAY? The Col du Soudet starts in La Mouline, which is 7.5 kilometres south-west of Arette, which in turn is 18 kilometres south-west of Oloron Ste-Marie using the D919 and D918. Turn right in Arette onto the D132 and follow that road to the top of the Soudet. If you want to take in the Pierre St-Martin, continue on the road as it changes to the NA1370 over the Spanish border.

Col du Somport

Length: 28 km.

Altitude: 1640 metres.

Height gain: 1200 metres.

Average gradient: 4.3%.

Maximum gradient: 8%.

This climb is on a main road into Spain. It starts in the small town of Accous and climbs on the N134 up to the Somport tunnel, through which the vast majority of motor vehicles will go. Just before you reach the tunnel there is a left turn onto the old road over the top of the col.

The climb isn't steep until you reach the top part. It traces the Aspet Valley and the course of the Gave d'Aspet until the tunnel starts. At this point two streams join to form the Gave d'Aspet and the road largely follows the path of the left-hand watercourse. This stretch is eight kilometres long and it is where you encounter the steepest gradient. It is a really nice and lonely ride in high country.

It's well worth continuing over the climb into Spain and descending to the tunnel mouth on that side in order to climb back up that part again. The old road from tunnel mouth to tunnel mouth is 17 kilometres long.

WHICH WAY? Accous is on the N134 27 kilometres south of Oloron Ste-Marie, which is 32 kilometres south-west of Pau, again on the N134, The Col du Somport is also on the N134, but to cross the top of it you turn left just before the entrance to the road tunnel.

Col de la Pierre St-Martin

Length: 27 km.

Altitude: 1766 metres.

Height gain: 966 metres.

Average gradient: 3.6%.

Maximum gradient: 7.4%.

Climbed for the first time in 2007 by the King of the Mountains that year, Mauricio Soler of Colombia, the Col de la Pierre St-Martin is another climb that starts in Spain and crosses into France with its summit on the border.

This route is not a major one into France. It begins in and passes through a very sparsely populated but stunningly beautiful corner of Spain. The start village is Isaba in the Navarra region of the Basque country, which borders most of the western Pyrenees and is where bike racing has its greatest popularity in Spain.

Basque bike fans flood out onto the passes of the western Pyrenees to watch the Tour de France every year, and to watch their own Tour of Spain, which also uses many of these climbs. Most of the best racers in Spain are Basques, and the people who live there have made the sport part of their national identity.

The first part of the climb goes straight up the Arroyo de Belagua into the remote Sierra Longa mountains. Once it gets there the road climbs towards the border in a series of lacets, then runs along the edge of the border ridge until it finds the gap that is the Col de la Pierre St-Martin.

From the top the road descends a short distance then climbs for one kilometre to the top of the Col du Soudet, which is firmly in France.

WHICH WAY? The best way to the start of this climb in Isaba is to go over the Col de Soudet from France and descend the Pierre de la St-Martin, then turn around and climb back up it. The start of the Col de Soudet is 26 kilometres south-west of Oloron-Ste-Marie on the D919 to Aramits. Turn left on the D918 to Arette, then right on the D132. Go over the Soudet and Pierre St-Martin on this road and descend into Spain on the NA1370 to Isaba to return and climb the Pierre St-Martin.

Vosges and Jura

The Vosges and Jura almost touch each other, but they are quite different in character. The Vosges are in the north-east of France and are the northernmost mountains that the Tour de France visits. They are largely made from ancient igneous rocks, so the landscape has a well-rounded look. The Jura are limestone mountains that have been affected by several parallel geological faults, turning them into a series of ridges.

They are both very attractive and less well-known parts of France. Top altitudes reached by the Vosges mountains are generally not much over 1000 metres, so although they are quite northerly most are covered in vast forests, making autumn one of the best times to visit.

The Vosges have also seen a lot of action in different wars and national boundaries have swept one way or another over them. As late as the First World War much of the Vosges was part of Germany, so there is a great deal of German influence evident in the local architecture. Strasbourg, Colmar and Belfort are great places from which to explore the Vosges.

The Jura are similarly quite low and accessible. They are generally higher than the Vosges and the parallel ridges lend a regularity to the road network, which tends to run south-west to north-east along the bases of the ridges, and south-east to north-west over them. Great bases for exploring the Jura are Geneva or the smaller towns of Gex, Les Rousses or St-Claude.

Ballon d'Alsace 'THE FIRST MOUNTAIN EVER'

★★ 2 STARS

Length: 9.6 km.

Altitude: 1178 metres.

Height gain: 630 metres.

Average gradient: 6.6%.

Maximum gradient: 8%.

WHAT TO EXPECT

➤ **Good roads.** The road up the Ballon d'Alsace is well-surfaced and well-engineered. The gradient isn't constant, but changes are gradual, which is good for your legs.

➤ **Meeting point.** Four departments and three regions meet at the top of the Ballon d'Alsace.

➤ **Humidity.** The Vosges get their share of rain because there is no higher land to the west to shelter them. Low cloud is also a characteristic of these mountains.

➤ **Technical descent.** It's long and twisting and has some steep bits. It's also within easy reach of Belfort by car, so be careful to stay well over on your side of the road in the corners.

➤ **Memorial.** Just before the summit there is a stone dedicated to the memory of René Pottier. He won the Tour de France in 1906, but the following winter he committed suicide after being rejected by the woman he loved.

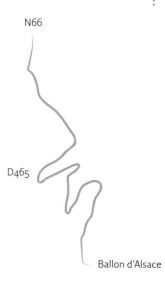

N66

D465

Ballon d'Alsace

The Tour de France grabbed public attention from it's first running in 1903, but when the organisers announced that they were going to run a stage of the race over some real mountains in 1905, everyone thought they had gone too far. A race around the hexagon of France was pushing human endurance to its limits, they thought, making the riders climb mountains was too much.

Some of the organisers thought it might be too much as well. In his newspaper editorial, Henri Desgranges predicted that no rider would be able to scale the Ballon d'Alsace on his bike, and that every one of them would have to get off and walk. But René Pottier didn't walk, he pounded up the wooded slopes, even overtaking and leaving Desgranges behind in his official race car. Man had beaten the mountain – and mountains would be part of the Tour de France for ever.

Compared to some of the climbs in the Alps and Pyrenees, the Ballon d'Alsace isn't at all vicious, but that is just a question of scale. The Vosges climbs are still a challenge, plus they have a charm of their own, and the Ballon d'Alsace captures it all.

The climb starts in Saint-Maurice-sur-Moselle and at first heads toward the Tête

Vogeans sense of humour

Above: Looking towards the summit   **Right:** A war memorial

des Fourneaux, its gradient constantly oscillating between six and seven percent. In the gaps between the trees you will catch some splendid views across the Moselle valley.

A right-hand hairpin signifies the beginning of a series of lacets, and the toughest part of the climb. The road switches back and forth across the mountain side until you reach La Jumenterie, where local historians say that the dukes of Lorraine bred their horses.

Now the gradient eases as you reach a slightly domed plateau. This is the top of the Ballon d'Alsace, and from the summit you can see the tips of the Jura to the south, which is where the pioneer riders were going in 1905 after climbing the first real mountain of the Tour de France.

WHICH WAY?

St-Maurice-sur-Moselle is on the N66, six kilometres east of Le Thillot and 27 kilometres west of Thann, which is 15 kilometres west of the city of Mulhouse and with Belfort the nearest big place for accommodation in this area. The Ballon d'Alsace is clearly signposted in St-Maurice and the road to the top is the D465.

MOUNTAIN MOMENTS

➤ The Tour de France returned many times to the Ballon d'Alsace after its first visit in 1905, including four occasions when the climb hosted the stage finish.

➤ The first of those was in 1967, when you could say that the wrong Frenchman won. It was the 1966 Tour winner Lucien Aimar, but in 1967 the whole French team was working for a Raymond Poulidor victory. His nemesis, Jacques Anquetil wasn't riding and everyone said that Poulidor was now the strongest. Unfortunately the Frenchman managed to blow his chances by crashing on the Ballon d'Alsace stage and it was left to Aimar to salvage French honour that day. France still won the 1967 Tour through Roger Pingeon.

Ballon de Servance 'THE ULTIMATE STING'

⊛⊛⊛ 3 STARS

Length: 10.5 km.
Altitude: 1158 metres.
Height gain: 737 metres.
Average gradient: 7%
Maximum gradient: 12%

WHAT TO EXPECT

➤ **Easy start, tough end.** This climb has the ultimate sting in the tail. It takes a real concerted effort to haul yourself up the final three kilometres.

➤ **Rough road.** The road surface becomes increasingly loose and broken as you approach the summit. Try to avoid the gravel and climb seated wherever possible. However, if you are climbing out of the saddle and your rear wheel spins on the gravel, try moving your body a little further back to put more weight over that wheel.

➤ **Descent caution.** The loose road surface continues over the summit of the climb. Take the corners slowly and brake extra early and smoothly to reduce your speed for the corners and avoid possible wheel lock ups.

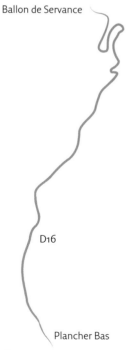

Ballon de Servance

D16

Plancher Bas

The start of this climb hides the truth of its severity. It begins in Plancher-Bas and climbs easily at the start, although it begins to steepen after four kilometres.

After the road joins the Rahin stream, which tumbles down in the opposite direction to the one you are going in, the slope really begins to rack up. Yet it's still not that severe, the shock is yet to come. That happens at a steep left and right hairpin. From there the road becomes incredibly narrow, with hardly room for a car, and it corkscrews giddily upwards at a regular ten and twelve percent for the whole of the last three kilometres of the climb.

The road splits just short of the summit, which is the highest point of the Haute-Saône department. One way plunges down into the Moselle valley at similar gradients to the ones you've just climbed. The other, the right split, carries on to the summit, but don't go that way because it leads to a military establishment with TV cameras and goodness knows what along the way to keep an eye on you.

The descent takes you to the edge of the Plateau of a Thousand Lakes, where the village of Servance is located. This is a very fertile area of land that is studded with lakes and is famous for potato growing.

The Ballon de Servance really is an extraordinary climb. It's extremely quiet, possibly because nobody dares to take their car up the narrow road. Even on the flatter approach to the tough bit all you will see is the occasional van, maybe owned by somebody cutting wood in the vast forest that covers the mountain.

After the Franco-Prussian war of 1870 the Ballon de Servance was of enormous strategic importance to the winners Germany. The whole of Alsace-Lorraine became part of Germany, and a huge fort was built on the Moselle side of the mountain to guard the upper valley from any possible invasion.

WHICH WAY?

Plancher Bas in on the D4, 15 kilometres north-west of Belfort. Use the N19 to go west out of Belfort. After 11.5 kilometres turn right on the D16 and turn right again on the D12. In Plancher-Bas turn left onto the D16 and follow that road to the top of the climb.

Above: Plancher-les-Mines   **Right:** The Rahin mountain stream

MOUNTAIN MOMENTS

➤ The Ballon de Servance has been climbed only once by the Tour de France, in 1988. But it's a fitting tribute to its character that one of the best climbers of his day, Robert Millar was the first man to the top. Millar has become a mystery in cycling. Most ex-Tour riders keep in touch with the race. Many of them work on it, either as full time TV or radio pundits, mechanics, managers or physios, or they spend just the three weeks of the race as a driver or as PR hosts for the sponsoring companies. But Millar has never been back. After he stopped racing in 1995 he was the British national coach for a short time, and he did some product testing for cycling magazines, but slowly he became less and less involved with the sport until he disappeared. No one really knows where he's gone.

Col du Calvaire 'WATCHER OF THE LAKES'

⭐ 1 STAR

Length: 18.8 km.
Altitude: 1134 metres.
Height gain: 804 metres.
Average gradient: 4.3%.
Maximum gradient: 8%.

WHAT TO EXPECT

➤ **Three in one.** You bag three cols in one when you climb the Calvaire.

➤ **Route jig-saw.** There are a lot of roads that wind around the hills of this quiet backwater of France.

➤ **Ironmen, and women.** While you are suffering on the climbs here, spare a thought for the triathletes who until recently used to race the Ironman France on these climbs The event started and finished in Gérardmer, which is 37 kilometres south-west of the Col du Calvaire.

➤ **Super cars.** They manufacture the Bugatti Veyron in a special facility in Molsheim near Strasbourg, on the northern edge of this area. They test the 1000 bhp monsters in the Vosges mountains. And yes, I've seen one on the Calvaire.

This one is a little bit complicated. For a start you get three cols for your money in climbing the Col du Calvaire, because in doing so you also cross the Col du Bonhomme and Col du Louchbach before reaching the Calvaire summit.

The top of the Col du Calvaire stands guard over two lakes, the White Lake and the Black Lake, which both sit in rocky, quarry-like bowls in the Gazon du Faing. Legend has it that there was a castle in this quite menacing area of marshy grass, but the lord living in it angered God and his home was destroyed by a thunderbolt leaving behind the two holes where the lakes are now.

The climb starts in the little village of Hachimont on the main N415 road. The first part is on the main road, a distance of 6.5 kilometres that gradually rises to a peak gradient of 7.4 percent at the halfway point, then relents towards the top of the Col du Bonhomme.

This is the crossroads of the N415 and D148, which if you turn right takes you to Ste-Marie-les-Mines. The name of that town reflects that this area was once a hub of thriving industry based on the mining of metal, including precious ones like gold and silver. A few people got rich, but the mines are gone now. If you are interested in social history, there's a nice little mining museum in Ste-Marie-les-Mines.

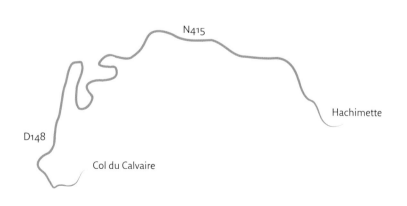

N415

Hachimette

D148

Col du Calvaire

Left: Foret des Deux Lacs from the Calvaire   **Above:** The Tour de France in the Vosges

To continue the climb you turn left on the D148 to climb the four kilometres of just under five percent average to the Col du Louchbach, where the road flattens for a while before the last bit to the Calvaire, which goes up at seven and eight percent and is very tough.

There are a couple of choices at the top if you want to continue riding. And with a good number of interesting roads in this area, there are a number of round trips you can organise that include the Calvaire in them.

WHICH WAY.

Hachimette is on the N415, 15 kilometres north-west of Colmar, which is a big town 19 kilometres west of the river Rhine and the German border. Continue going west on the N415 to the top of the Col du Bonhomme. Turn left at the crossroads with the D148 and follow this road over the Col du Louchbach to the summit of the Calvaire. From the top you can descend the D48II to Orbey which brings you to the N415 and Hachimette again.

MOUNTAIN MOMENTS

➤ First man over the Col du Calvaire was an Italian, Luciano Conati in 1976.

➤ In 2001, on 14 July (which is Bastille day when French Tour riders always try to put on a show), Laurent Jalabert discovered his climbing legs on this route. The stage ran from Strasbourg to Colmar and Jalabert, who started his pro career as a sprinter but developed into an all-round rider, rode away from his breakaway companions with two climbs to go. He was supreme on the Calvaire, pulling away still further to win alone in Colmar. What is more he'd laid the foundations for winning the King of the Mountains title, something he repeated the following year.

Col de la Croix de la Serra

'JEWEL OF THE JURA'

⊛⊛ 2 STARS

Length: 14 km.
Altitude: 1049 metres.
Height gain: 743 metres.
Average gradient: 5.3%.
Maximum gradient: 8%.

WHAT TO EXPECT

➤ **Smooth passage.** The road up the Croix de la Serra is fairly smooth and well made. The gradient is reasonably constant – this, together with the straight road, means you can get a really good climbing rhythm going.

➤ **Straight up, twists down.** The descent runs straight for eight kilometres, but then it twists and turns its way into the Nantua valley.

➤ **Exploring.** There are lots of interesting climbs branching off both the ascent and descent. Ride to the top, then descend back the same way to turn right onto the D25. Go through Les Bouchoux and Les Moussières to finish off an interesting ride that will bring you out almost at the eastern end of the Flumen gorge. It's a great round trip.

➤ **Chamois watch.** There are supposedly quite a few living on the higher ground around here.

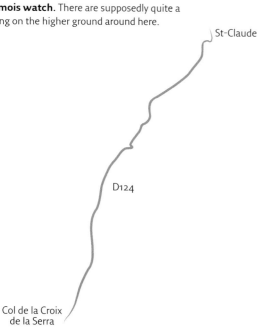

St-Claude

D124

Col de la Croix
de la Serra

This is another Tour de France climb that has only been scaled once by the race, and it didn't even play a big part in that day's racing, but it deserves to be a major climb simply because of the beauty of its setting.

The climb is quite straightforward. It starts in the town of St Claude, which is the capital of the Haute-Jura and is a very pleasant unhurried place to stay while you are visiting the whole area. The road is fairly straight most of the way to the top of the climb and the gradient not too taxing, although there are three short stretches of eight-percent climbing on the way up.

The climb starts with a short descent, which at least gives you a run up at the first eight-percent bit. For the first three kilometres you ride beneath the shadow of the Crêt de Surmontant, which rises up to your right.

Eventually you break clear of this shelter and the climb is much more open as you follow the valley carved out by a stream called the Tacon, which is on your left and has its source at the top of the climb.

The great joy of this climb though, is exploring the Flumen Gorge, which is where the main road east out of St Claude, the D436, goes. It's a spectacular, deep gash in the limestone of the Jura that twists and turns for nine kilometres between St Claude and Septmoncel.

Chapeau
de Gendarme

Above: Just in case you don't think it looks like a policeman's hat

Above left: Start of the climb   **Above right:** The Flumen Gorge   **Below:** The Chapeau de Gendarme

Some amazing features have been carved out by the water that formed the gorge, the best being the Chapeau de Gendarme, which is on your left about halfway along if you are going west to east. The road makers have done their fair share of carving too, and you will pass under several rock arches along the way.

Riding the gorge and the Croix de la Serra really compliment each other and they give you a good taste of this unique and less visited part of France. The Jura is a great place for a holiday, particularly if you are into active pursuits like cycling.

WHICH WAY?

St Claude is 57 kilometres north-east of Bourg-en-Bresse on the D979, D984D, D31 and D436. It is also 53 kilometres west of Geneva on the N5, D936 and D436. From St Claude head east on the D436 for the Flumen gorge, or turn right off the D436 onto the D124 for the Col de la Croix de la Serra. Follow this road to the top.

MOUNTAIN MOMENTS

➤ The first rider over the Col de la Croix de la Serra on the Tour's first and only visit in 1996 was Leo Van Bon from Holland. Van Bon wasn't a climber though, he was a very good sprinter. The Croix de la Serra was the first mountain in the Tour de France that year, and the man who is first to the top of the first climb is always certain of some extra column inches of publicity for himself, and more importantly for his sponsors. It could also be that Van Bon was trying to create a diversion that day by making the others riders chase him, which would have deadened a few legs. If that is what he was doing it worked, because shortly before the finish Van Bon's Dutch team mate, Michael Boogard attacked and hung on to win the stage by a single second.

Col de la Faucille '*GENEVA'S JURA*'

✪✪✪ 3 STARS

Length: 11.8 km.

Altitude: 1323 metres.

Height gain: 703 metres.

Average gradient: 6%.

Maximum gradient: 8.1%.

WHAT TO EXPECT

➤ **Great views.** A stop at the Floriment viewing point is a Faucille must. It is one of the best views in France simply because it takes in so much. From the fleeting aeroplanes taking off and landing at the airport in Geneva, to the permanence of Mont Blanc and the Vanoise glaciers, you can see it all from here.

➤ **Particle acceleration.** Look due south from Floriment and you will see a big complex of futuristic buildings on the edge of Geneva, with a small country's worth of electricity cables going into it. That is C.E.R.N. the European organisation for nuclear research. Basically it's the biggest physics lab in the world where, among others things, boffins accelerate sub-atomic particles in a 27-kilometre circumference tunnel buried 100 metres underground, just to see what happens.

The Jura mountains march like soldiers in battle lines right up to the shores of Lake Léman and Geneva. They act as a natural barrier and are only breached by roads in a few places where the ridge is at its lowest. One of those places is the Col de la Faucille.

This is a beautiful zig-zag climb that starts in the pretty town of Gex, and as you climb you get huge views over Geneva, Lake Léman and its giant fountain, and of the Alps stacking up into the distance beyond that. It's also really something to pause and watch the planes flying below you into and out of Geneva airport.

Gex is 700 years old and was the capital of an ancient principality. It's French-looking and Swiss-clean, reflecting its location close to the Swiss border on the outskirts of Geneva and up the road just east of Divonne-les-Bains.

Col de la Faucile

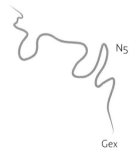

N5

Gex

Left: Mont Rond   **Above left:** Summit of the Faucille   **Above right:** Gex

The climb has a touch of Swiss orderliness about it too. It starts fairly easily, climbing at between four and six percent, up well-made hairpin bends, on a wide and well-surfaced road. Then, seven-and-a-half kilometres into the climb, at the Napoleon's fountain bend, it gets steeper, but it does so with an easy transition from six to seven then eight percent. The last 1500 metres are just four percent.

Apart from the first couple of kilometres, most of this climb is through pine forests. There is a long gap in the trees leading up to a wide viewing point at Florimont, where you can see everything within an arc of 250 degrees.

At the summit there is a restaurant, a hotel and a shop selling local produce. The summit is also a ski station in the winter and there are 140 kilometres of pistes based on Mont-Rond (1614 metres), which you can see on your left as you approach the summit.

Either side of you at the top is a long crest of peaks that is one of the largest protected wildlife preserves in France. The tops of the Jura ridges are home to chamois, many different kinds of deer and lynx – so if you see a pretty kitten up here be careful about approaching it, its mother might be watching and she might be bigger than you expect.

WHICH WAY?

Gex is 17 kilometres north of Geneva on the E21 and N5. The way to the Col de la Faucille is clearly signposted once you enter the town, just follow the N5 to the top. If you descend the Faucille and turn left onto the D936, this becomes the D436 and that will take you to the Flumen gorge and the start of the Col de la Croix de la Serra.

MOUNTAIN MOMENTS

➤ The Tour has climbed the Faucille many times since a Frenchman, Maurice Brocco led the race over it in 1911.

➤ In 1954 the points that Frederico Bahamontes secured by crossing the Faucille in first place won him the first of his six King of the Mountains titles. During that Tour Bahamontes was in first place over the top of ten famous mountains, earning from the press the title that has stuck with him ever since, the Eagle of Toledo.

➤ First on the Faucille in 1975 was a Spanish-born Frenchman, Mariano Martinez, whose son, Miguel was Olympic mountain bike champion in 2000 and whose other son, Yannik looks set to become a pro rider. Mariano was the Tour de France King of the Mountains in 1978.

Le Grand Ballon 'THE ROOF OF THE VOSGES'

✪✪✪ **3 STARS**

Length: 16.2 km.
Altitude: 1343 metres.
Height gain: 975 metres.
Average gradient: 6.1%.
Maximum gradient: 9%.

WHAT TO EXPECT

➤ **Summer heat.** This part of France can get hot and humid in in mid-summer. The region is well into the European land mass, so the cooling effects of the sea are slight. Drink plenty of water when you are climbing in the Vosges, occasionally replacing water with well-diluted electrolyte drinks. If you use energy drinks, make sure they too are diluted in accordance with the manufactures instructions.

➤ **Monument moments.** As well as the Paul Amic memorial, there is a monument on top of the Grand Ballon to the Diables Bleus, a band of soldiers who fought with valour in these mountains during the First World War. There is also a very touching memorial in the trees on the cobbled hairpin just before the top of the Col d'Amic. It is to a local man called Philippe Emporte. It was placed there by his friends because of Phillipe's love for the forests.

The Grand Ballon is the highest of the Vosges mountains. It starts in the village of Willer-sur-Thur, which is just to the north-west of Than on the N66. If you approach this climb by going through Than, look to your right to see the remarkable patchwork of vineyards that cover the south-facing hills.

Turn right onto the D138 in Willer-sur-Thur, a place with lots of German influenced architecture. The climb starts gently enough but the gradient subtly winds up until Goldbach, where it relents a bit before turning up the heat again to peak at nine percent just before the Col d'Amic.

The two hairpins before the Amic are laid with the sort of cobblestones that paved most climbs before the Second World War, and they give you a taste of what racing in the mountains was like 70 or 80 years ago. The col is named after a local war hero, Paul Amic. There is a memorial to him on the hairpin where the D138 meets the D431.

You need to join the D431 by turning left to continue the climb of the Grand Ballon, which gets steadily harder now all the way to the top. In the right season, look out for yellow gentians in the verge – you might not see any but looking helps keep your mind off the pain in your legs.

There is a large hotel-restaurant at the top of the climb, which is nice place to stop for refreshment and to take in the views across the whole of the Vosges, if you get a clear day that is. If you look due north you can pick out the Petit Ballon, and to the east you can see right over the river Rhine and into Germany – beyond, Freiburg and the edges of the Black Forest. Autumn is a lovely time to visit the Vosges: you get good clear days and the forest are a riot of colour.

Grand Ballon

D431

Col Amic

Left: Willer-sur-Tour   **Above:** The Grand Ballon ascent is part of the Route des Crêtes   **Below:** A mountain bike trail sign pointing off into the woods

The Grand Ballon is on the Route des Crêtes, an upland journey that travels up the spine of the Vosges and was engineered during the First World War for strategic reasons. In winter the Route des Crêtes becomes a long distance cross-country ski challenge.

WHICH WAY?

Willer-sur-Thur is on the N66, five kilometres north-west of Than and 15 kilometres north-west of Munster on the same road. The Grand Ballon is clearly signposted on the N66 in Willer. Take the D13BVI north out of the town to the Col d'Amic and turn left there onto the D431 to the top of the Grand Ballon.

MOUNTAIN MOMENTS

➤ The first time the Grand Ballon was climbed by the Tour de France was in 1969, and the man who christened it was arguably the best climber that the Tour de France has ever seen. Lucien Van Impe won the King of the Mountains title six times and won the Tour de France overall in 1976. He had the classic climber's build – short and light but powerful. His greatest weapon was a blistering turn of speed that was impossible to follow. He says that climbing mountains efficiently is a combination of controlling your breathing and always being in the right gear. But Van Impe stresses that is the science of climbing. The extra – what it takes to be one of the best, what Van Impe calls a true climber – depends more on art than science.

Col du Platzerwasel *'CLIMBING THE CRÊTES'*

⭐ 1 STAR

Length: 16.2 km.

Altitude: 1198 metres.

Height gain: 781 metres.

Average gradient: 4.8%.

Maximum gradient: 9%.

WHAT TO EXPECT

➤ **Great views.** The scenery in this part of the Vosges is special. It's like the rest of the mountain range, but somehow scaled down and more intimate.

➤ **Round trips.** There are loads to chose from as the road network is quite dense around the Col du Platzerwasel. The circuit that includes descending the Col de la Schlucht is a good choice because the road is wide and well surfaced with nicely engineered bends.

➤ **Two Ballons.** You could ride to the top of the Petit Ballon on your way to the Col du Platzerwasel, then climb the Grand Ballon.

➤ **Waterfall.** Another nice side trip on the way to the top of the Platzerwasel is to turn right in Merzal and continue up the Fecht to visit the waterfall at the head of the valley

You underestimate this climb at your peril. It's only been in the Tour de France once, but it's worthy of major climb status because of the concerted effort you have to put in to scale the final five kilometres of the climb.

The Col du Platzerwasel starts in the German-named town of Munster. All the place names around this climb speak of this area's German past, and what they don't say the architecture adds quite eloquently.

There are many Munsters in the world. There's a big city called Munster across the Rhine from France in Germany, and one in Ireland. This Munster though gives its name to Munster cheese, a version of which is very popular in America. In France it has its own Appellation Contrôlée, is made from unpasteurised milk and often has caraway seeds added to it.

The climb starts gently on a fairly straight road that winds through a string of villages along the Fecht river valley. At Mezeral the road splits and the route to the Platzerwasel begins to climb out of the valley.

Now the gradient gets serious, and after Sonderbach it gets seriously steep. The road splits again, with the left-hand route heading for the top of the Petit Ballon. You go right and begin the final six kilometres of the climb, which is a succession of hairpin bends and eight- and nine-percent ramps.

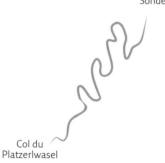

Sonderbach

Col du
Platzerlwasel

Left: German name, German architecture   **Above:** This region is especially pretty in Autumn

The compensation for your effort is the fact that the Col du Platzerwasel is a very pretty climb. From the top you get great 360-degree views of surrounding peaks, and to the west there is a nice view along a good length of the Route des Crêtes.

A short descent takes you to another little pass and then to the junction with the D430 road that traces the Route des Crêtes. From there you could turn left and climb the other side of the Grand Ballon, or right and ride to the crossroads at the top of the Col de la Schlucht. You could then descend the Schlucht and end up back in Munster.

WHICH WAY?

Munster is on the D417, 15 kilometres from Colmar. Turn left from the D417 into Munster town centre and pick up the D10, which goes south-west, then south as it leaves the Fecht valley. At Sonderbach turn right onto the D27 at the first hairpin of the climb. Follow this road to the top of the Col du Platzerwasel.

MOUNTAIN MOMENTS

➤ The only time that the Tour de France has climbed the Col du Platzerwasel was in 1967 when a Spaniard, Jesus Aranzabal was first to the top. The stage he did it on was the one which Lucien Aimar of France won on the top of the Ballon d'Alsace, after the French favourite, Raymond Poulidor had crashed. In 2007 the organisers of the Tour celebrated that stage by running a cyclo-sportif race over the same route and calling it the Etape du Legend. Cyclo-Sportives are the growth industry in cycling at the moment, they give all-comers a chance to ride legendary routes, or they celebrate a big cycling occasion or a famous rider. Many of them are held in the mountains.

Col de la Schlucht

'THE ROAD TO DEVIL'S ROCK'

⭐⭐ 2 STARS

Length: 18 km.
Altitude: 1139 metres.
Height gain: 759 metres.
Average gradient: 4.2%.
Maximum gradient: 5.3%.

WHAT TO EXPECT

➤ **Regular climbing.** The road builders were on song when they made this road and after an easy first three kilometres the whole of the Col de la Schlucht hardly varies from a five-percent gradient.

➤ **Third highest.** The peak you see on your left as you approach the top of the Col de la Schlucht is the Hohneck (1362 metres), the third highest in the Vosges range.

➤ **Glacial lakes.** On the descent you pass three lakes, all formed after the Ice Age by different aspects of glacial activity. Shortly after the top the first, the Retournemer, sits in the bowl in which the glacier was born. The second, the Longemer, fills the hollow that the glacier scooped out as it progressed down the valley while conditions grew colder. The third, in Gerardmer, is water trapped behind the detritus dumped by the glacier when it melted and retreated.

The Col de la Schlucht goes from Munster, crossing the Route de Crêtes at right-angles, before descending through a hole pierced in a formation called the Devil's Rock and arriving at the town of Gerardmer.

It's a main road but not a busy one, and the climb's twists and turns, plus its forgiving gradients, make riding it a very attractive proposition. It affords a nice taste of Tour de France climbing without being too demanding.

From 1871 until 1918 the top of the Col de la Schlucht was the border between France and Germany and an important crossing place. So important that both countries built electric tramways from their respective sides to the top. Today the top is the border between the French departments of the Vosges to the west, and Haut-Rhine the east.

The first three kilometres from Munster are straight, but then the road begins to seek out the easiest lines up the slope in order to maintain an even gradient. There are terrific views across the Fecht valley behind you, and to your right, as you make your way to the top.

About one third of the way up the Schlucht there is an off-shoot road on your right that is worth investigating if you are feeling strong. It's steep and narrow but winds up to a lake just below the Gazon du Faing. A left turn off this road will take you up onto the Route de Crêtes .

Back on the main route the road continues to climb regularly in a series of bends until shortly before the summit, where a buttress of rock that was jutting out into the road builder's path has been pierced through. It's uncannily like the more famous Devil's Rock on the others side.

There's a café at the top of this climb and some good route choices. You could go left or right to explore the Route de Crêtes , or a little further down there's a road that runs parallel with the Crêtes road. Turn right on this to explore the upper Meurthe valley and left for the Vologne hills. Finally you could continue on the descent of the Schlucht to Gerardmer.

WHICH WAY?

Munster is on the D417, 15 kilometres west of Colmar. Continue heading west on the same road to climb the Col de la Schlucht.

D417

Col de la Schlucht

Munster

MOUNTAIN MOMENTS

➤ The Tour de France has visited the Col de la Schlucht many times since the first crossing in 1931, when it was recorded that the whole field reached the top together.

➤ It was a case of local boy makes good in 1967 when Charly Grosskost lead the race over the Col de la Schlucht. Grosskost, who won the prologue time trial of the 1968 Tour de France, was born in Strasbourg where he had a cycle shop for many years after he stopped racing. Sadly he was killed in a road accident while cycling with friends in 2004.

➤ Andreas Klöden of Germany was the best rider on the Col de la Schlucht in 2005. Klöden is one of the most complete riders in the world, but he seems to lack the ambition and necessary steel to win the Tour de France.

Left: Steam at the start of the climb **Above:** Close to the summit

Col d'Amic

Length: 9.6 km.

Altitude: 828 metres.

Height gain: 460 metres.

Average gradient: 4.8%.

Maximum gradient: 7%.

Col du Berthiand

Length: 10 km.

Altitude: 780 metres.

Height gain: 450 metres.

Average gradient: 4.5%.

Maximum gradient: 15%.

This is the first part of the Grand Ballon climb, but there are other ways up the Col d'Amic than the one from Willer-sur-Thur. An eastern route climbs from the town of Soultz-Haut-Rhin, and another starts in Cernay and approaches the col from the south-west. That route picks out a lovely ridge up the climb and is the start of the Route de Crêtes, crossing the Col de Herrenfluh and Col de Siberloch on its way to the Amic.

The ride from Willer-sur-Thur is very pleasant, with just one tough bit coming after you go through Goldbach. From the top of the col there are great views, especially to the south over the Ballons regional park with the top of the Ballon d'Alsace just peeping out above its surrounding forest.

From the Col d'Amic there are a lot of route choices and some great circular rides can be put together, but the ambitious might like to try a crossing of the Route des Crêtes. It starts in Cernay and the Col d'Amic is the first climb. It continues on over the Grand Ballon, Col de la Schlucht and Col du Bonhomme before ending in St-Marie-aux-Mines. The total distance is 93 kilometres.

The first Tour de France rider to cross the Amic was Raphaël Géminiani in 1952. Géminiani was an excellent racer who became a great team manager. One of his charges was Jacques Anquetil and it's said that Géminiani, or the Big Gun as he was known during his racing days, was the only person who could get the headstrong Anquetil to do as he was told. Maybe that was because Géminiani was even more headstrong and stubborn than Anquetil.

WHICH WAY? From Willer-sur-Thur head north on the D13BVI to the top of the Col d'Amic. The road to the top from Cernay is the D431.

Where the Col de la Faucille climbs the first ridge of the Jura mountains counting from the east, the Col du Berthiand climbs the first ridge counting from the west. It's a real gateway climb to the big mountains.

The Berthiand has a shock in store for you too. It starts in Hautecourt-Romanèche and the road quickly climbs a seven-percent stretch before plunging down at the same rate into the Ain gorge. You climb out of that at seven percent, then the road levels out a bit before a left-hand bend. Now comes the shock, facing you is 500 metres of 15 percent. Take a deep breath and go for it.

After that the rest of the climb isn't too bad – although after that last stretch, banging your head against a brick wall wouldn't seem too bad. The road levels off, sweeps right and then left, and finally there is a right-hand hairpin and a seven-percent pull to the top.

The Tour de France has climbed the Berthiand three times, the first time was in 1991 when the feisty Italian, Claudio Chiappucci led the race over the climb. The race has done the climb from both sides. The eastern approach is a short climb and only has 300 metres of height gain.

WHICH WAY? Hautecourt-Romanèche is 18 kilometres east of Bourg-en-Bresse on the D979, and 15 kilometres north-east of junction 9 of the A40 Autoroute on the D984, D42 and D979. In Hautecourt continue east on the D979 to the top of the climb.

Col du Bonhomme

Length: 18.4 km.

Altitude: 949 metres.

Height gain: 589 metres.

Average gradient: 3.2%.

Maximum gradient: 6%.

Col du Champ du Feu

Length: 23.5 km.

Altitude: 1100 metres.

Height gain: 910 metres.

Average gradient: 3.9%.

Maximum gradient: 8.9%.

There are four ways to climb the Bonhomme, the top of which is a crossroads on the Route des Crêtes. One way is on the main N145 road from the east, but I covered that approach when talking about the Col du Calvaire. I think the best is from the north, from Ste-Marie-aux-Mines.

This is part of the Route des Crêtes, the start from the north in fact, but it's a long and leisurely start as the road ambles upwards at under four-percent gradient for all but the final few metres.

The Tour de France first used this climb in 1949, when Fausto Coppi graced it by being the first to the top. Roger Hassenforder, a Frenchman who raced with Coppi has a hotel in this area at Kayserberg, which is on the N415 route up the Col du Bonhomme. The hotel is called the Roger Hassenforder, there is plenty of cycling memorabilia there, and it is still run by his family

WHICH WAY? Ste-Marie-aux-Mines is on the N59, 23 kilometres east of St-Die-des-Vosges and 18 kilometres west of Sélestat, which is on the French side of the river Rhine. Look for the D48 in Ste-Marie and follow that road south-west to the top of the Col du Bonhomme.

This is quite a complicated route through a maze of roads. It begins in Obernai, a town close to the big city of Strasbourg. The first nine kilometres of the climb are very easy, as you skirt the village of Ottrott and ride around a small peak called the Elsberg (673 metres) and head gradually upwards through the Obernai forest.

Towards the end of the forest the tough section of the climb starts, and the next nine kilometres rise at six to nine percent through some really craggy scenery with plenty of waterfalls, unusual rock formations and little off-shoot valleys. This is great walking country as well as cycling country, and the tracks that run off the Champ du Feu road are very popular with walkers, or randonneurs as the French call them.

Another popular way of getting about up here is on *raquettes à neige*, or snow shoes. There are snow shoe races up here in winter, and the equipment the racers use is a long way from the cartoon depiction of strapping tennis rackets to your feet.

From the top of the Col du Champ du Feu you can descend for a couple of kilometres, then if you turn right on the D57 at the crossroads it is just a short distance to the Col du Kreuzweg and the Col de la Charbonnière. The Champ du Messin isn't far from the Col du Champ du Feu either, so a day spent in this area will bag you a lot of Tour de France climbs. Take a map though, because with roads going off in all directions, it is easy to get lost.

The first Tour rider to climb the Champ du Feu was another climbing great, Luis Herrera of Colombia, who achieved the feat in 1985 on his way to becoming the King of the Mountains that year.

WHICH WAY? Take the D426 west out of Obernai. Cross the D35 at Ottrott and skirt this village on the D426. Turn right after four kilometres onto the D214 and continue on this road to the top of the Champ du Feu.

Champ du Messin

Length: 13 km.

Altitude: 1010 metres.

Height gain: 695 metres.

Average gradient: 5.3%.

Maximum gradient: 10%.

Another very pretty climb, but one with a dark past that has nothing to do with the Tour de France. The climb starts in Rothau and follows the Rothaine valley for two kilometres before a left-hand hairpin takes you to the steepest part of the climb.

This ten-percent section doesn't last for long and the road winds this way and that, affording you a great view towards the Serva waterfall before taking you to Struhof, and the location of the Champ du Messin's dark past.

This was where the Struhof concentration camp was located during the Second World War. More than 25,000 people died here, including four officers of the British secret service who had been captured operating inside enemy territory.

Diana Rowden, whose code name was Paulette, and Vera Leigh were two of them. They worked for many months in France relaying messages about troop movements back to their 64 Baker Steet, London headquarters. Rowden's cover was working as a juggler in a circus so she could travel as freely as possible. Rowden was posthumously awarded an MBE by the British and the Croix de Geurre by the French.

Another couple of tough seven-percent stretches after the Struhof camp take you to the summit of the Champ du Messin, which is a wide open grassy place that affords great views of the surrounding mountains. The Donon (1009 metres) can be seen clearly to the north-west, and due south is the Champ du Feu. The top of the Champ du Messin is also a nature reserve.

The first Tour de France rider to climb the Champ du Messin was, fittingly, a rider from the Vosges, called Stéphane Lach. He did it in 1961 while racing for the Paris and North-East France regional team. Lach only rode the Tour twice, but he made a big effort on his home roads and took third place on this 1961 stage. He probably never had to buy a drink for years after it.

Until 1962 the Tour de France was contested by national teams, plus some regional ones from the big cycling countries to make up the numbers, whereas for the rest of the year pro racers competed for their commercially sponsored teams. The race organisers eventually had to bow to sponsor pressure in 1962 and national teams were out. They came back in 1967 and 1968, but since then rider loyalty has been entirely to whoever is paying his wages.

WHICH WAY? Schirmeck is on the N420, 25 kilometres south-west of Strasbourg. From Schirmeck follow the N420 south and turn left onto the D130. Follow this road to the top of the Cham du Feu.

Col de la Charbonnière

Length: 8.66 km.

Altitude: 960 metres.

Height gain: 450 metres.

Average gradient: 6.5%.

Maximum gradient: 8.3%.

This climb starts in Fouday, just down the road from Schirmeck where the Champ du Messin starts. The top of the Champ du Feu is only a couple of kilometres from the Charbonnière summit too. Tour de France climbs come thick and fast in this part of the Vosges.

Fouday is dominated by its Protestant church. There are a lot of these churches in this part of France, because during the 16th century and the time of the Reformation a lot of protestant reformers lived in this area.

At just over eight and a half kilometres The Col de la Charbonnière isn't a long climb, but there are one or two steep bits to test your legs. About halfway up, a road branches off to the left that takes you to the Champ du Feu climb. It goes through La Serva, so you might want to go there to visit the spectacular Serva waterfalls.

Carry straight on for the top of the Charbonnière, which is reached after negotiating some eight-percent climbing and some nicely constructed bends. Up here you get great views over the valley you have just climbed out of. The top of the Charbonnière is a crossroads. Turn left for the summit of the Champ du Feu, and carry straight on to join the road that climbs the Col du Kreuzweg.

The first Tour de France rider over the Charbonnière was Vincent Vitetta, a Frenchman who did it during the 1955 race. The stage was from Metz to Colmar, and Vitetta was part of a four man breakaway group. He was good on the Charbonnière climb, but in the sprint for the stage victory at Colmar he couldn't beat local hero Roger Hassenforder.

In third place that day was a Frenchman called Jean Bobet, whose brother Louison won the 1955 Tour, his third consecutive victory. Bobet was the first man to achieve that feat. Louison died in 1983, but after his cycling career ended, Jean Bobet became a journalist and is now a celebrated and award-winning author in France.

The 1955 Tour de France was also the first in which a British team took part. Of the ten starters only two British riders finished. Brian Robinson was 29th overall and Tony Hoar finished last, the position the race use to call the Lanterne Rouge, or Red Lamp in English. Robinson returned to the Tour six more times and won two stages on his way to becoming the first British cyclist to make a name in European professional road racing.

WHICH WAY? Fouday is on the N420, five kilometres south of Schirmeck. Go into the village and look for the D57 and follow that road to the top of the Col de la Charbonnière. If you also continue after the top to descend on the D57 and cross the D214 you join the D425. Turn left onto the D425 for the top of the Col du Kreuzweg.

Collet du Linge

Length: 10.7 km.
Altitude: 975 metres.
Height gain: 612 metres.
Average gradient: 5.7%.
Maximum gradient: 7.6%.

There are three ways up the Collet du Linge, but the nicest is from Munster. There's even a choice of first parts to the climb on this side. The first starts in the town and climbs a tiny road that I couldn't even find a number for, but it is signposted to Hohrodberg. The second first part, so to speak, starts on the D417 about one kilometre west of Munster. You go out of Munster and turn right onto the D5b, which you follow all the way to the top. The un-named road joins this road just before the village of Hohrodberg.

Both first parts climb upwards in a series of bends, and this theme continues the rest of the way up to the top, where the reason this climb attracts a lot of visitors quickly becomes obvious, and it's nothing to do with the Tour de France.

One day in 1967 a local man, Armand Durlewanger, was walking on the Collet du Linge when he met a veteran of the First World War. The old man had been to the top of the mountain, as was his custom, to remember the 10,000 men who had fallen in defence of it, but he bemoaned the fact that there was no official record of this, and he feared that the fierce battle and brave men of the Collet du Linge were about to be forgotten

His story touched Monsieur Durlewanger, so he decided to do something about it. What he did though was unprecedented. He not only built a memorial but was the driving force in re-creating the whole battlefield of the Collet du Linge. Some say it is the most impressive war memorial in the world – certainly it's one of the most real.

The Tour de France climbed the Collet du Linge for the first time in 1957 when Louis Bergaud was the first man to the top. Bergaud was a good climber who won two stages in his seven Tour appearances. He was a small man who had two nicknames; the Cantal Flea and Lily. I don't know why he was called Lily, but if you are a cyclo-sportive rider and you see an event in the Cantal region of the Massif Central called La Lily Bergaud, it is named after little Louis.

WHICH WAY? Munster is 15 kilometres west of Colmar on the D417. For the first alternative first part of the Collet du Linge you need to go along the main D471 from the Colmar direction, ignoring where part of it splits off to enter Munster town centre, and at the point where the road joins together again, turn right unto an unmarked road that is signposted to Hohrodberg. For the other first part continue on the D417 in a westerly direction and turn right after one kilometre onto the D5B. The two first parts join just before Hohrodberg and you continue on the D5B to the top.

Col du Donon

Length: 9.5 km.

Altitude: 722 metres.

Height gain: 417 metres.

Average gradient: 4.4%.

Maximum gradient: 7.2%.

Another climb that starts in Schirmeck, the Col du Donon climbs the northernmost mountain of the Vosges chain, so it is the northernmost mountain of the Tour de France. You climb from Schirmeck up the opposite side of the valley to the Champ du Messin climb.

The first four kilometres pass by with easy gradients, but the road then steepens for one kilometre of seven percent. After that it relents to three-and-half percent, gets steeper then eases considerably before the summit.

At the top you emerge from the forest that covers the slopes of the Donon, and which until the 18th century was home to many bears. The top is dominated by the Haute Donon, a small peak of 1009 metres that today is topped by a TV transmitter, but in Roman times there were three temples on its slopes – parts of which have now been reconstructed.

The first Tour rider up the Col du Donon was Louis Bergaud in 1961. The man who was unlucky enough to lose the King of the Mountains title by just one point in 1957, found himself in a breakaway group of four soon after the stage start in Metz. He was strongest on the Col du Donon and, eight kilometres before the stage finish in Strasbourg, he attacked leaving his rivals behind to win the stage.

WHICH WAY? From the centre of Schirmeck, which is 25 kilometres west of Strasbourg, find the D392 and head out of town in a westerly direction. Follow the D392 to the top of the climb.

Col du Kreuzweg

Length: 18 km.

Altitude: 768 metres.

Height gain: 589 metres.

Average gradient: 3.3%.

Maximum gradient: 6.5%.

The Col du Kreuzweg starts in St-Pierre-Bois, which is a small village eight kilometres north-west of Sélestat. To get from Selestat to St-Pierre-Bois go west on the N59 and turn right onto the D424 and right again onto the D253. Turn left into St-Pierre village centre and go through the village to turn left onto the D203. At Triembach-au-Val turn right onto the D424 and after St-Martin turn right onto the D425 through Breitenbach to the top of the climb.

The first part is quite easy as you ride north out of St-Pierre-Bois then turn left and head for the villages of Triembach-au-Val, Villé and St Martin, which are all on the flanks of the Kreuzweg.

At St-Martin you turn right and make your way through Breitenbach, where Varta batteries used to have their French factory. Varta sponsored the Colombian cycling team when they began competing in the Tour de France. The climb gets tougher after the village, as the road begins to snake backwards and forwards to vault the final part of the mountain.

The toughness doesn't last long and you are soon on the top of the Kreuzweg, where there are great views to the east over the river Rhine and to the west you can see the tower atop the Champ du Feu.

WHICH WAY? St-Pierre-Bois is eight kilometres north-west of Sélestat, which itself is 17 kilometres north of Colmar. To get from Selestat to St-Marie go west on the N59 and turn right onto the D424 and right again onto the D253. Turn left into St-Pierre village centre and go through the village to turn left onto the D203. At Triembach-au-Val turn right onto the D424 and after St-Martin turn right onto the D425 through Breitenbach to the top of the climb.

Col du Mollendruz

Length: 7 km.

Altitude: 1180 metres.

Height gain: 428 metres.

Average gradient: 6.1%.

Maximum gradient: 14%.

This climb is in the Swiss part of the Jura, in the Vaud Canton and it is in between Lake Léman and Lake Neuchatel. It starts in the large village of Montricher, which was almost totally destroyed by a fire in 1770. Most people had left home to work in the fields when a chimney fire got out of control, and fanned by strong winds it burned down 54 of the village's 57 houses. Remarkably only two people were killed.

The climb has a very tough start, so it's a good idea to be well warmed up before you try it. You ride north out of Montricher and after two wide bends you hit a fourteen-percent wall. This is about 200 metres long, but after it the gradient eases considerably. Two hairpin bends then take you to a long straight stretch of climbing that has 100 metres of ten percent in the middle of it.

The first Tour de France rider over the Mollendruz was a Frenchman Raoul Rémy, who did it in 1952. Remy was a good rider who won two Tour de France stages during his career. One of them was in the 1952 race. It wasn't the day that he lead over the Mollendruz, but some days later in the south of France on the stage from Monaco to Aix-en-Provence. Rémy was from nearby Marseille – so that must have pleased his local supporters.

WHICH WAY? Montricher is 61 kilometres north-east of Geneva. Take the A1-E42 Autoroute east and leave it at the Morges Exit. Go north to Vufflens-le-Château, a name F1 motor racing fans might recognise because Michael Schumacher used to live there. In Apples you will pick up signposts for Montricher. Head east out of the village on an unmarked road and follow this road to the top of the col.

Côte des Rousses

Length: 8 km.
Altitude: 1105 metres.
Height gain: 435 metres.
Average gradient: 5.4%.
Maximum gradient: 5.9%.

This is one of the most regular climbs you will ever ride, with an average and maximum gradient that are only half-a-percent apart. The surveyors really had their theodolites and calculators out for this one. The climb is in the Jura range and starts in Morez. It's quite a busy route as it runs along the main N5 road, but it has had eight visits from the Tour de France, the first being in 1967. A Spaniard called Mariano Diaz was the first man to the top, and he must have liked the climb as he was first over it the following year too.

The road climbs at about three percent coming out of Morez, then there is short descent before the pull up to the town of Les Rousses. It's five-and-a-half percent, give or take a few tenths, all the way to the top. The road is well made and uses nice regular bends to keep itself on such an even keel.

From the top you can follow the N5 and climb the other side of the Col de la Faucile, or descend to Nyon, which is on the north shore of Lake Léman and take in the impressive set of regular lacets that is the Côte de Nyon.

WHICH WAY? Morez is 55 kilometres north of Geneva on the N5. To get there from that direction you have to go through Les Rousses town and descend the Rousses climb. In Morez turn around and follow the N5 south to Les Rousses.

Vue des Alpes

Length: 15.25 km.
Altitude: 1283 metres.
Height gain: 849 metres.
Average gradient: 5.6%.
Maximum gradient: 9.2%.

This climb is entirely in the Swiss Jura, it runs between Neuchâtel and La Chaux-de-Fonds, which are both big places, and the route is an important one into France. It's where the Jura almost touch the Vosges, so Vue des Alpes is the most northerly Tour de France climb in the Jura. The climb gets its name from the magnificent view of the Swiss Bernese Alps including the Jungfrau you get from the top.

The road to the top of this climb is wide and well-surfaced because it used to take all traffic over the Vue des Alpes climb, but now a lot of that travels via an Autoroute that runs quite close to the old route and uses tunnels for part of its journey.

It's an odd climb because there are lots of changes of gradient but the road you ride on is so wide that you can't see them. Your legs will let you know though. The top of the climb is a wide open space, where a lot of people stop to enjoy the Alpine view. The descent into La Chaux de Fonds is quite short.

The Tour de France has only used this climb twice. The first time was in 1948 when Gino Bartali was first to the top on a stage from Lausanne to Mulhouse. Bartali won the Tour in 1948.

WHICH WAY? Neuchâtel is on the auto route that runs along the north shore of Lake Neuchâtel

La Chaud de Fonds is clearly sign posted in Neuchâtel . The Vue des Alpes climb starts outside the main Neuchâtel railway station. Follow the Rue du Rocher north away from the station and continue climbing the main road out of town

Massif Central

The Massif-Central is an area of upland in south-central France that comprises the Auvergne mountains in the north and Cevennes in the south – plus a number of small massifs clustered around the south and west of the Cevennes.

The big geological difference between the Auvergne and Cevennes is that most of the Auvergne is the result of volcanic activity which only ceased some 10,000 years ago. While some of the Cevennes are formed from igneous rocks, the majority of the range are limestone, which lends it its characteristic blocky appearance.

The higher peaks are found in the Auvergne, but both regions are lower than the Alps and the Pyrenees. In character, the Auvergne passes tend to wander between volcanic features like ash cones and lava domes as they link valley to valley, whereas the passes of the Cevennes tend to link rivers in gorges by climbing across huge blocks of limestone.

Aurillac, Clermont-Ferrand and St-Etienne are great bases from which to discover the Auvergne, and there are a lot of smaller towns in the area that are ideal too. Population centres are much more sparse in the Cevennes – Mende and Millau are two of the biggest.

Col de la République 'THE FIRST PASS.'

Length: 18 km.

Altitude: 1161 metres.

Height gain: 674 metres.

Average gradient: 3.8%.

Maximum gradient: 6.3%.

WHAT TO EXPECT

➤ **Father of cycle touring.** There is a memorial stone on top of this climb to Paul de Vivie, a Frenchman from this area who lived from 1853 until 1930 and is credited with inventing cycle touring through his magazine, *Le Cycliste*. He always signed his work 'Velocio' and was also one of the first cyclists to use multiple gearing, including one system where the rider pedalled forward for top gear and backwards for bottom. De Vivie penned ten commandments that all cyclists should abide by. The fifth is "Do not drink wine, at any rate whilst in the saddle", and the seventh is "Never pedal out of vanity". Every June hundreds of cyclists flock to the Col de la République to ride the Journée Velocio, a time trial up the climb from the St Étienne side.

The first real mountain climb iin the Tour de France was the Ballon d'Alsace in 1905, but the first pass to be stormed was the Col de la République, which the riders climbed two years earlier in the first ever Tour.

The col was included in the 1903 route because it has always been seen as a symbol of passing from the north to the south of France. It's said that the *cigales*, a type of cricket that are particularly numerous in Provence, start to sing on the south side of the Col de la République. They could be right too, as the climb is part of the Mont Pilat chain, so part of the ecotone boundary between the continental and Mediteranean climate zones of France.

It isn't difficult, which is why it has never been considered the Tour's first climb, and the first few kilometres out of St Étienne are very gentle. The road is the main N82, but it is wide and Autoroutes have taken the heaviwar traffic away. The middle seven kilometres flit between five and six percent, but the top part is easy too.

The road is fairly straight, and despite it being a main route the dense pine forests on either side towards the top make climbing it an enjoyable experience. One that many Stéphanois cyclists still enjoy today, especially on summer weekends. Stéphanois is the name given to inhabitants of St Étienne , because Étienne is the French equivalent of Stephen.

As well as the Tour de France, the Col de la République features in another famous French professional bike race, the Paris-Nice. This is run every March and

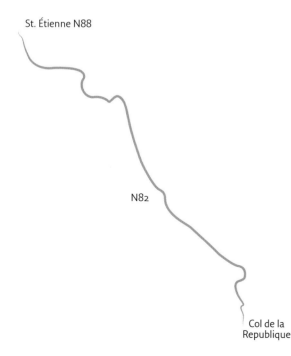

St. Étienne N88

N82

Col de la
Republique

➤ As you might expect with such a long connection the Tour de France has climbed the Col de la République many times since Hippolyte Aucouturier was first to the top in 1903. The race has visited 11 times since 1950, although it seems to have fallen out with the République in recent years.

➤ A Belgian, Stan Ockers was first to the top in 1956. He was world road race champion in 1955 and a great rider, a real winner, but he was killed in a crash on the Antwerp track in October 1956.

➤ In 1971 a young French rider called Cyrille Guimard crossed the col in the lead. He was another really promising rider who was cut off as he approached his prime. Knee trouble curtailed Guimard's career, but he became a very successful team manger who masterminded six Tour de France victories.

is called the 'race to the sun' because it starts in the wintry north of France and ends on the sunny Côte d'Azur. The Col de la République is a different proposition in March to the climb you will find in high summer. Its slopes are often covered in snow and the riders have to struggle along a ribbon of black tarmac set against an all-white background.

The descent to Bourg-Argental has some really nice wide sweeping bends and the road surface is excellent, so it's a nice place to enjoy the thrill of descending a climb on two wheels. Watch out for the seven-percent down slope just before the hamlet of Argental.

WHICH WAY?

The climb starts just after junction 24 of the N88 St Étienne south ring road. Continue south-east on the N82 to the top of the climb. The start is only one kilometre from the start of the Croix de Chaubouret, and there are a couple of connecting roads between the two, both of which go through a village called Tarantaise.

Col d'Oeillon 'THE RHÔNE LOOKOUT'

★★★ 3 STARS

Length: 20 km.

Altitude: 1210 metres.

Height gain: 1079 metres.

Average gradient: 5.4%.

Maximum gradient: 8.5%.

WHAT TO EXPECT

➤ **Military presence.** Some of the summit of the Crêt d'Oeillon is fenced off for military purposes.

➤ **Mediteranean air.** You are climbing the Mediteranean climate side of the Mont Pilat chain. Chavanay and the towns south of it have a real south of France feel.

➤ **View point.** There is an orientation table right at the top of the Crêt d'Oeillon, next to the big telecommunications tower. You'll be amazed at what you can see.

➤ **Nuclear power.** Look due east from the Crêt d'Oeillon, and right next to the Rhône you can see the huge St Alban nuclear power station, one of 59 in France that produce getting on for 80 percent of the country's electricity at a carbon cost of one tenth of electricity production in the United Kingdom.

Thrusting upwards out of the flat Rhône valley the Col d'Oeillon is the most easterly high part of the Mont Pilat chain, and its summit offers unrivalled views across the Rhône valley to the Alps and the amazing sight of Mont Blanc towering above everything.

The climb starts right next to the Rhône in Chavanay, and it ascends at a relatively easy five and six percent until Pélussin, a small town that occupies a unique place in French cycling history.

French cycling was undergoing a bit of a recession at the start of the 1980s and there wasn't much money for new professional teams, so an ex-pro racer from the 1960s who lived in the area, Michel Nedelec, decided to register his local amateur cycling club, UC St-Étienne-Pélussin as a pro team, hoping to attract sponsorship along the way. It was a plucky move, but it didn't work. A couple of riders from the club managed to make it as pros though, including Vincent Lavenu, who now manages the AG2R Tour de France team.

The road steepens at Soyère as the route turns off the main road and begins to twist and turn to find the easiest route up the steepest part of the climb. A stretch of eight percent takes you into the Pélussin forest and up to the Collet de Doizieu, where the gradient relents to five percent.

Use this stretch to recover as there is more steep stuff to come, including a bit that is over eight percent at the Chapelle de la Magdelaine. This relents at a weird-looking rock formation that stands on your left – and the last kilometre is very easy.

At the top of the col you can climb to the telecommunications tower up at the top of the mountain, which is called the Crête de l'Oellion. This is the place for some of the most amazing and far-reaching views in the whole of France. As well as Mont Blanc to the east, on clear days you can see as far south as Mont Ventoux in Provence. Then to the north and east are the Puys of the Auvergne. Enjoy!

D63 D7 Chavanay N86

Col d'Oiellon

Above: Looking from the Crête de l'Oeillon towards Mont Ventoux

WHICH WAY?

Chavanay is on the N86, which is one of the main routes along the Rhône Valley. It is also close to the A7 Autoroute. Take junction 12 and go north on the N86 to Chavanay. Once there take the D7 west and turn left just after Pélussin onto the D63 and follow that road to the top of the climb.

MOUNTAIN MOMENTS

➤ The Col d'Oeillon was first climbed in the Tour de France by mountains legend Frederico Bahamontes in the 1956 race.

➤ It has been climbed three time since in the race, and each time either a Spaniard or a Colombian was first to the top, underlining the contribution those two countries have made to the great mountain moments of the Tour de France.

➤ Top man in 1985 was Colombian King of the Mountains, Lucho Herrera. Clad in the polka dot jersey of the mountains leader he romped up the climb, dropping the five times Tour winner Bernard Hinault in the process. Over the other side Herrera hurtled down into St Étienne to win the stage. A mountain great, Herrera was King of the mountains in the Tours of France, Italy and Spain during his career.

Col de la Croix de Chaubouret

'PRINCE OF THE PILAT'

⭐ 1 STAR

Length: 16 km.

Altitude: 1201 metres.

Height gain: 611 metres.

Average gradient: 3.8%.

Maximum gradient: 7.2%.

WHAT TO EXPECT

➤ **Company.** Being so close to a major conurbation you can expect a few cyclists to be climbing this one.

➤ **Welcoming.** There's nothing too demanding about the Croix de la Chaubouret, so it's perfect for beginners and for easing yourself back into climbing mountains.

➤ **Alpine view.** You can see the Alps from the crossroads summit.

➤ **Super descent.** Continuing over the top of the climb and descending on the D8 to St-Julien-Molin-Molette is great fun because the road is a twisting test of your descending skills. Take it easy and line up for the corners so that you come out of them well-over on your own side of the road.

This popular climb starts almost in the city of St-Étienne, which at one time was the capital of the French cycle industry and still retains strong bonds with the bike. The route climbs into the Pilat regional park that lies to the south of the city, and the road up it runs parallel to the main road crossing of the Pilat, the Col de la République. The Croix de Chaubouret is also a nice warm-up before the nearby Col d'Oeillon.

The Pilat chain of mountains are most easterly of this region. They run diagonally from south-west to north-east and border onto the Rhône valley in the east. The spine of the mountains form a climate border – the northern side has a continental climate and the southern a Mediteranean climate.

The climb starts just south of the busy N88, which forms part of the ring road around St Etienne. The first three kilometres are an easy three- to four-percent climb, but then gradients increase as you pass through the pretty village of Rochetaillée, where you will see signposts to the Gouffre d'Enfer (the Abyss of Hell) which has an exciting Via Ferrata, which you can explore if you are carrying suitable footwear – or come back later.

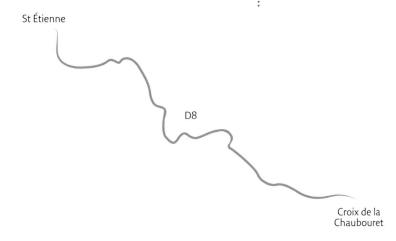

Left: Le Bossat **Above:** The Croix de la Chaubouret is part of the Mont Pilat range

The gradient increases after Rochetaillée to just over seven percent and the maximum for the climb. After that it eases to around five percent, then just over three to the top. This is a crossroads, with the main road carrying on towards the south of France and side roads on your left entering the Pilat mountain range. The third left, the D63 is the way to the Tour de France climb of the Col d'Oeillon.

The first left takes you back towards St Étienne's eastern suburbs. If you turn left after this descent onto the D36 you can avoid busier roads in the city to make a nice triangular round trip of 46 kilometres. There is also a connecting road to the Col de la République between Le Bessat and Rochetaillée for another round trip or an assault on the République after you've climbed the Croix de Chaubouret.

WHICH WAY?

From Junction 21 of the N88 in St Étienne take the D8 south out of the city and continue to the top of the Croix de la Chaubouret.

 **MOUNTAIN MOMENTS**

➤ First Tour rider over the Croix de la Chaubouret was Switzerland's Ferdi Kübler in 1950. The climb has been used seven times since by the Tour. In 1997 the Croix de la Chaubouret was part of a 55-kilometre time trial that started and finished in St Étienne. The winner was Jan Ullrich, who went on to win the Tour.

➤ First to the top in 1999 was a Belgian, Ludo Diercksens, who was on his way to winning a stage in St Étienne. Diercksens was a late arrival into the world of pro cycling who worked for years in the Daf trucks factory painting lorries and racing as a semi-pro at weekends. Eventually his persistence paid off and he found a place in a full-time pro team at the age of 30.

Col de la Croix-de-l'Homme Mort

'DEAD MAN'S CROSS'

⭐⭐ 2 STARS

Length: 15 km.

Altitude: 1163 metres.

Height gain: 742 metres.

Average gradient: 5%.

Maximum gradient: 6%.

WHAT TO EXPECT

➤ **Relaxed atmosphere.** This is a really quiet part of France. The climb is on a main road, but relatively little traffic uses it. It's also a very benevolent climb, so perfect for beginners.

➤ **Round trips.** There is a maze of roads branching off the Croix-de-l'Homme Mort, both to the north and the south of the main road. They are perfect for creating your own rides to discover the Forez.

➤ **Competitions.** Two cyclo sportive events are held in the Forez each year, Les Copians and the Monts du Forez. Visit www.velo101.com for more information.

➤ **Upper Loire.** Montbrison and St Étienne are great bases for discovering the upper Loire valley, which has its source in the Massif Central. Here the longest river in France has a very different character to the languid giant you find flowing through Saumur and Nantes

Dead man's cross. That is what Croix-de-l'Homme Mort means in English. It sounds terrible, but there isn't to much for cyclists to worry about with this climb. It's long and the height gain is quite impressive, but six percent is the steepest gradient you will encounter on this attractive amble out of the Loire Valley and into the eastern entrance of the Massif-Central.

There are well over 1000 place names with the word cross in them in the Massif-Central, and their reason for being seems to be nothing more sinister than the fact that crosses were used in the Middle Ages to mark mountain summits or crossroads.

The Croix de l'Homme Mort takes you from Montbrison, a large, walled town that used to be the prefecture of the upper Loire, but is now a sub-prefecture. It's still an important bustling place though, and an ideal base for exploring the climbs of the Forez, which is what this area of the Massif-Central is called.

It's an area of lush forest, few main roads and an absence of noise. There is a remote feel to this part of France that makes it very bike friendly. But you need to enjoy climbing as the roads here tend to run between river valleys, rather than along them.

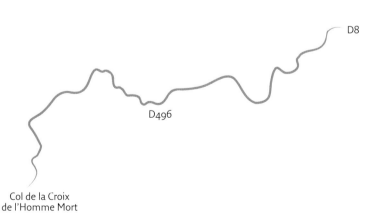

D8

D496

Col de la Croix
de l'Homme Mort

Left: View of the Puys to the west   **Above:** View of the Puys to the west

The climb from Montbrison twists and turns gently to the summit, where you get a great view back over the Loire and across the valley to the vast sprawl of Lyon in the distance. The descent to St Anthème is quite demanding of your cornering skills.

If you continue west after St Anthème you have to negotiate another Tour de France climb, the Col des Pradeaux before descending to the town of Ambert, which has a perfectly circular town hall.

You are now in Livardois-Forez, which in 2007 celebrated 40 years as a regional park. This area is famous for the production of cutlery and paper and its scenery is a halfway house between the rolling wooded hills of the Forez to the east and the volcanic scenery of the Puys to the west.

WHICH WAY?

Montbrison is about 50 kilometres west of Lyon as the crow flies, although the connecting roads are anything but straight. It is also 20 kilometres north-west of St-Étienne. Pick up the D8 in St Étienne and go north-west to Montbrison. Turn left at the south-eastern edge of town onto the D496 and follow this to the top of the climb.

MOUNTAIN MOMENTS

➤ First Tour rider to the top of the Croix-de-l'Homme Mort was Jean Forestier in 1956. Forestier came from nearby Lyon and was a great rider for the northern single day races. He won Paris-Roubaix in 1955 and the Tour of Flanders in 1956. He also won four stages in the Tour de France and wore the Yellow Jersey once. He won the Tour de France points classification, the green jersey, in 1957.
➤ First over the climb in 1971 was another Frenchman, Jean-Pierre Danguillaume. He was a good rider from a cycling family. His uncle, Camille had been a Tour rider before him. After he retired from racing Danguillaume worked on the Tour for one of the race's first sponsors from outside Europe, Coca Cola, who were attracted to the race by the American Greg Lemond's success.

Col de la Croix Morand

'STEPHEN'S LAST STAND'

⊛⊛⊛ **3 STARS**

Length: 10.5 km.

Altitude: 1401 metres.

Height gain: 511 metres.

Average gradient: 4.9%.

Maximum gradient: 8.2%.

WHAT TO EXPECT

➤ **Heavy roads.** Roads in this part of France are usually granite chipped, making them what cyclists call heavy roads. Tyres don't roll well on granite, compared to asphalt or tarmac. It almost feels like the roads suck at your tyres, dragging you back. It's not an overwhelming feeling, but it mounts up on a long ride.

➤ **Heavy weather.** The Auvergne has hot summers and cold winters. Spring and autumn are perhaps the best seasons for cycling here. You don't have to worry too much about snow blocking the climbs, especially in Autumn, as altitudes aren't as high as in the Alps or Pyrenees. Of course in winter there is snow on most of the hills, and that sometimes lingers into spring.

➤ **Restaurant.** There's one on the top of the climb called the Buron du Col that as well as food sells whole animal skins.

A beautiful mountain climb close to the city of Clermont-Ferrand, the Col de la Croix Morand, which is also called the Col de Dyane, was the inspiration for a song written by the celebrated French singer and guitarist, Jean-Louis Murat. He was born in nearby La Bourboule and has lived all his life in this area. Much of Murat's work has been inspired by nature and the landscape of the Auvergne.

The Croix Morand is in the Puys d'Auvergne regional park. Puy is a name you will see time and again in this part of France. Basically it's a French word that describes the peaks here, which are mostly ancient volcanic ash cones or lava domes.

The region isn't volcanically active now, the last eruptions occurred in 7500 BC, give or take about 300 years, and the most recent volcano is the Puy de la Vache, which is about 20 kilometres north-east of the Croix Morand.

The climb of the Col de la Croix Morand starts in Chambon sur Lac and begins with a leisurely two kilometres of 1.7-percent climbing, but then the road immediately kicks up to just over eight percent, the steepest part of the climb.

The steepest bit is less than one kilometre long and once it's behind you the Croix Morand presents a benevolent face as it twists and turns gently upwards past a small peak called the Saut de la Pucelle.

After that the road straightens and the gradient increases to eight percent again for a short stretch before flattening to the summit. Its worth stopping here take in the views. You can see the classic volcano cone shapes of some of the surrounding mountains, and you can see the highest of the Auvergne peaks, the Puy de Dôme almost due north from the top of the Croix Morand.

Col de la Croix
Morand

Murol

D996

Above: Top of the Croix Morand with volcanic features in the distance

➤ The first Tour de France rider over the Croix de la Morand was Bernardo Ruiz from Spain in 1951. In 1992 this climb saw the last exploit of Irishman Stephen Roche, who crossed the Croix de la Morand alone to win his last stage in the Tour de France at La Bourboule, setting the seal on his fight back to fitness after a fallow period. Victory to near obscurity was the see-saw of Roche's cycling career. His body seemed unable to support his class, as brilliance would be followed by long periods of injury and rehabilitation. The one year Roche got it all together, 1987, saw him win the Tours of Italy and France, and the world championships. Eddy Merckx is the only other rider to have matched this in one year.

Left page: The Puy de la Tache above the Croix Morand **Above:** The summit restaurant is a civilised idea

WHICH WAY?

The nearest town to the Col de la Croix Morand is Murol on the D996, which is 40 kilometres south-west of Clermont-Ferrand on the N89 and D5. Turn right onto the D996 for Murol and continue on that road to the top of the climb.

Plomb du Cantal 'TOP OF THE AUVERGNE'

⊙⊙ 2 STARS

Length: 10 km.

Altitude: 1383 metres.

Height gain: 583 metres.

Average gradient: 5.8%.

Maximum gradient: 8%.

WHAT TO EXPECT

➤ **Lonely road.** Not many people use this pass, and the Cantal is fairly quiet anyway. The top of the climb is quite wild looking too.

➤ **Outdoor pursuits.** The Cantal is a haven for them. Mountain biking, Kayaking and hill walking are all catered for. Cross-country skiing is big in winter, and if you look to the top of the Plomb du Cantal you can just see the buildings that mark the top of the Super Lioran ski runs, which sweep down the north-western side of the mountain.

➤ **Misty mornings.** As well as having cold winters, another feature of this region are warm days and cold nights, even in summer. This sometimes causes mists in the early mornings, but they soon lift because Cantal is well up there in the French total annual sunshine stakes.

At 1855 metres the Plomb du Cantal is the highest mountain in the Auvergne, but the pass you climb doesn't go right over the top of the mountain. In fact even though the Tour de France calls this climb the Plomb du Cantal, locally the pass is called the Col de la Tombe du Père and it sits just below the Plomb du Cantal peak.

The Plomb du Cantal and surrounding peaks, like the Puy du Rocher (1813 metres) are all that is left of a huge volcano that dominated this area, and was 60 kilometres in diameter and over 3000 metres high.

This climb starts just to the south-west of the town of Murat at the junction of the N122 and the D39, right next to a small industrial estate. The road is straight for virtually the whole of the climb, and it ascends at a fairly constant gradient. The steepest bit comes just after a right and left bend through the village of Albepierre-Bredons.

The road then continues to follow the course of the Lagnon stream upwards through an increasingly sparse forest until it breaks out into the open at the summit at a cluster of wooden buildings called Prat-de-Bouc.

During the winter the Plomb du Cantal is one of the coldest places in France. The department of Cantal is one of the most central in the country, so has a typical

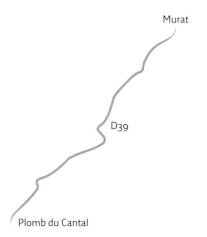

Above: Highest peak in the Auvergne

Above left: Prat du Bouc   **Above right:** There's plenty to do up here

hot summer/cold winter continental climate. Temperatures of minus 15 degrees centigrade and less are quite common on many of these central mountains and being the highest, Plumb du Cantal is the coldest: minus 28 degrees centigrade has been recorded there.

Evidence of volcanic activity is all over this region. For example, in the town of Murat at the base of this climb you will find the Rocher de Bonnevie. It's a huge rock made from columnar basalt, a formation that occurs when the rock solidifies from a molten state and forms columns as it does so because of the rate at which it cools. This is similar to what happened at the Giants Causeway in Antrim, Northern Ireland. You can't miss the Rocher de Bonnevie, because there is a huge white statue of the Virgin Mary on top of it.

WHICH WAY?

Murat is 25 kilometres north-west of St Flour, which you can access by using junctions 28 or 29 of the A75 Autoroute. Take the D926 from St Flour. Turn left in Murat onto the N122. Turn left after one kilometre onto the D39 and continue to the top of the climb.

MOUNTAIN MOMENTS

➤ First Tour de France rider to the top of the Plomb du Cantal was Eddy Merckx in 1975. The stage that day ended a few kilometres later in Super Lioran, and Merckx finished second. He led overall by one-and-a-half minutes from Frenchman, Bernard Thévenet and looked good for his sixth Tour de France victory. However, the following day on the Puy de Dôme, still in the Auvergne, Merckx was attacked by a spectator who punched him in the kidneys. The Belgian champion suffered agonies to finish the stage in third place. He still led the race, but was administered blood thinning drugs by the race doctor to help his injury heal. A few days later Merckx suffered a spectacular slowing down on the climb to Pra Loup and Thévenet took over the race lead, defeating Merckx again the next day. A proud Merckx still believes that the blood thinners cost him the 1975 Tour de France.

Puy de Dôme 'VOLCANIC ACTION'

✪✪✪✪✪ 5 STARS

Length: 4.4 km.

Altitude: 1415 metres.

Height gain: 488 metres.

Average gradient: 11%.

Maximum gradient: 13%.

WHAT TO EXPECT

➤ **One road up and down.** The road is narrow, keep well over on your own side going up and down to avoid problems with people coming the other way.

➤ **Timed ascent.** The first recorded ascent on a bike was in 1871, and it took the un-named rider 28 minutes to do the final four kilometres of the climb.

➤ **Kilometre stones.** There are special stones by the side of the road with information on them, so you can tick off your upward progress.

➤ **Competition.** On cyclists-only Sunday mornings a bit of an unofficial race can develop on this climb. Don't get sucked in to it, unless you want to of course.

➤ **Runners.** The Puy de Dôme is a challenge for them too. Only they use the footpaths, one of which crosses the road at the end of the first steep section. They should stop and look before they cross, but some don't.

A Tour de France classic. One of the steepest and most feared climbs in the race, the Puy de Dôme isn't long but if a rider isn't at his best when climbing it he can lose a hatful of time. Only the best climbers in the race's history have succeeded on this huge lump of rock that sticks up like a giant thumb pointing skywards on the west side of Clermont-Ferrand.

Technically the climb starts in the city of Clermont-Ferrand, and if you decide to start there the climb is 11 kilometres long with a height gain of 965 metres and an average gradient of nearly nine percent. But there are good reasons for not starting there, the principal one being that you don't get much of a time window in which to ride to the top and back.

The last four kilometres of road are privately owned, and motor vehicles are charged for going to the top. It was decided a few years ago that cars, buses and bikes don't mix on the narrow roads, so now cycling is only allowed from 7.00 a.m. every Sunday, and you have to be back down by 9.00 a.m.

Above: Craters below Puy de Dome

➤ The first Tour rider to the top of the Puy de Dôme was Fausto Coppi in 1952.

➤ The biggest Puy de Dôme moment was the battle between Jacques Anquetil and Raymond Poulidor in 1964. Poulidor was strong that year. Anquetil had won a tough Tour of Italy, he led the Tour but he was slowly coming unglued. Poulidor should have attacked lower down the climb, but he let Anquetil bluff him. Instead of riding behind as the two fought their way to the top, Anquetil rode alongside his rival making him think that he was stronger than he was. Afraid of losing what he had for what he might gain, Poulidor left his attack too late. He put time into Anquetil, but not enough time.

➤ In 1978 Dutchman Joop Zoetemelk won a 59-km time-trial stage that ended with the Puy de Dôme climb.

Above: Only 807 metres to go   **Below:** Ash cones from Puy de Dome

The best way to do the Puy de Dôme is to start at the toll gate, where there is a huge car park. You aren't cheating by starting here because while the Tour has approached this climb from many directions, this bit is always the same.

The gradient is brutal from the off. The first kilometre is the steepest of the whole climb. It's thirteen percent and you need your lowest gear. You must also save something because the rest of the climb is pretty steep too.

It's hard and it doesn't help that the road is straight. Try not to look too far ahead. Eventually the road curves round to the right as it begins to spiral around the cone-shaped top of the climb which is an unusual lava dome. On your left you get great views down into the craters of surrounding ash cone volcanoes. Eventually you curl around the climb to the top but don't spend too long there, remember you have to be back down again by nine.

WHICH WAY?

Clermont-Ferrand is right next to the A75 motorway. Take the D68 west from the centre of the city and cross the D914. The climb and the toll booth are well signposted. From any direction though it is difficult to miss the Puy de Dôme, it is much higher than surrounding peaks and has a tall mast at its summit.

Puy-Mary 'HIGHEST MASSIF ROAD'

★★★ 3 STARS

Length: 13.3 km.
Altitude: 1589 metres.
Height gain: 647 metres.
Average gradient: 4.9%.
Maximum gradient: 7%.

WHAT TO EXPECT

➤ **Busy in summer.** The Puy Mary is a favoured countryside destination for people who live in Aurillac. It can get busy up here on summer weekends.

➤ **Ambitious plans.** There are plans to build an interpretation centre on the Puy Mary to help explain how it, and the other volcanoes of the Auvergne were formed. At least they will have a large car park, which will end the problems of people parking on the narrow roads on busy days.

➤ **Tipsy flowers.** Yellow gentians grow on the Puy Mary. Locals make a fierce aperitif from this flower called Avèze.

➤ **Gastronomie.** Cantal produces many delicacies, including Cantal and three other appellation contrôlée cheeses. One of those, Salers, comes from the cows of the Puy-Mary. They also do a kind of Haggis, using sheep's stomach.

There are three ways up the Puy Mary, but the one that the Tour has used most in its seven visits, is the route from the Cantal city of Aurillac, which starts at St-Julien-de-Jordanne. Like the Plomb du Cantal, this climb has another name – is also known as the Pas de Peyrol after the Puy Peyrol (1809 metres), which stands just behind the Puy Mary peak (1787 metres).

The Jordanne flows through Aurillac, and the ride from the city up its valley to St Julien is a treat worth trying. All the way up it you can see the peak of Puy-Mary towering in front of you. While you are riding this section note the elegant and quite tiny semi-circular grey tiles that cover the roofs of the oldest houses in this area.

The Jordanne route climbs imperceptibly, but at St Julien the gradient bites. The Jordanne gets playful as you climb, and you pass a waterfall while negotiating

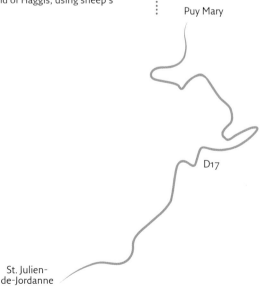

Puy Mary

D17

St. Julien-
de-Jordanne

Left: Puy Mary is surrounded by other peaks, remnants of a giant volcano   **Above:** The road cuts through old lava flows

two wide hairpins. Then at a tight 180-degree bend you leave the babbling Jordanne behind as the route heads for the pass.

The gradient is fairly steady at five to six percent all the way up this climb. It's only in the last stage that you encounter a few short stretches of seven percent. You get plenty of time to take in the beautiful views – unlike the last part of the climb up the western flank of the Puy-Mary from Salers, where the last two-and-a-half kilometres go upwards an average of twelve percent.

As you near the top, not only are you on the highest road in the Massif-Central, but you are getting close to the heart of the huge volcano that the Plomb du Cantal was also part of. Looking down and around you from the top you are looking down on a mini version of the colossus that once was. The rocky peaks you see are ash cones, lava domes and the remnants of ancient lava flows.

WHICH WAY?

Take the D17 north out of Aurillac and follow this route all the way to the summit. Aurillac has good road and rail links with the rest of France, and it has its own small airport.

 **MOUNTAIN MOMENTS**

➤ The first Tour de France rider to conquer the Puy-Mary was Louis Bergaud in 1959. Bergaud was a local rider who was nicknamed the Cantal Flea. He must have found his local knowledge invaluable, as he attacked right after the stage start in Aurillac to ensure that he christened the Puy-Mary in local style.
➤ First to the top of the Puy-Mary in 1985, only coming the other way to the one I recommend you climb, was the Spaniard Eduardo Chozas. He crossed the climb alone and descended to win the stage in Aurillac by nearly 10 minutes, something that very rarely happens nowadays. Chozas is still active in cycling, running training camps in Spain.

Mont Aigoual

Length: 37 km.
Altitude: 1562 metres.
Height gain: 1336 metres.
Average gradient: 3.6%.
Maximum gradient: 6.4%.

You could spend a week exploring this mountain on your bike. The Tour de France has climbed to the top once, in 1987 when an Italian rider, Silvano Contini was first to get there, but there are four other main routes up the mountain and the Tour has used them all on a number of occasions. Plus there are a lot of smaller roads that the race hasn't used yet.

This route is quite formidable, it's 37 kilometres from the town of Le Vigan to the top, although not all of those kilometres are uphill, but each one of them is something you will enjoy and remember forever.

Mont Aigoual is the highest point of the Gard, and part of the Cévennes mountains that form the southern part of the Massif-Central. All the roads up this climb meander beautifully to the top through the lush green countryside that is the product of Mont Aigoual's unique climate.

Aigoual was originally Aiqualis, which means watery one. The mountain gets a lot of rain because it is where cold Atlantic air meets warm air from the Mediteranean. Mont Aigoual is a major watershed for rivers running to both ocean and sea.

After an easy start from Le Vigan the road rises at four to six percent for 20 kilometres until the Col du Minier, after which the road descends for six kilometres, but only at a little under two percent. Then you begin climbing again at L'Espérou for the last few kilometres to the summit.

The Col du Minier was used in the 1955 Tour de France, but the riders descended at l'Esperou after crossing it and didn't climb to the top of Mont Aigoual. The first rider to the summit of the Minier was Louis Caput. Caput wasn't one of the best bike racers of his era, but he later became one of the best team managers.

The other major routes up Mont Aigoual start at Rousses, which is the steepest ascent, Meyruis and Valleraugue. It's also possible to ride a 5-kilometre circuit of the mountain summit, around an observatory that looks like a castle.

WHICH WAY? Le Vigan is on the D999, 52 kilometres north-west of Montpellier on the D986 and D999. Turn right just after Le Vigan onto the D48. Turn left onto the D986 at L'Espérou and then right onto the D269 for the top of the climb. This road circles the summit, starting and ending at Prat Peyrot.

Causse Noir

Length: 13 km.
Altitude: 820 metres.
Height gain: 460 metres.
Average gradient: 3.5%.
Maximum gradient: 7%.

The Causses is an area of limestone plateaux just to the west of the Cevennes, but still part of the Massif-Central. The plateaux are deeply dissected by rivers that cut through the porous limestone until they strike impermeable rocks beneath. Causse Noir, for example, is cut through by the river Tarn. Together the Causses make up the Grand Causses regional park.

The Causse Noir climb has only been used once by the Tour de France, as a stage finish in 1990. The winner was Marino Lejarreta of Spain, who was a good stage race rider and climber who raced in the Tours of Italy, France and Spain in the same year four times during his career. A man of classic climber's build, Lejarreta was known to his fans as the Reed of Berriz.

The climb starts in Millau, where you should pause to take in the splendour of the newly constructed Millau viaduct that carries the A75 Paris-Béziers Autoroute over the Tarn. It is the tallest vehicular bridge in the world, and one of its elegant

Causse de Sauvaterre

Length: 9 km.

Altitude: 1020 metres.

Height gain: 620 metres.

Average gradient: 6.8%.

Maximum gradient: 7%.

towers is 343-metres high, taller than the Eifel Tower and only just shorter than the Empire State Building.

The climb of Causse Noir isn't too demanding, the steepest bit comes in the first three kilometres and after that the gradients are milf. As you near the summit, it's hard to decide where the exact top is, as the bare plateau undulates slightly. You could spend hours exploring the numerous roads on it, and there are several other ways up and down. If you've time, try the Corniche de Causse Noir on the north side of the plateau, which is the D29 from Le Rosier. The Tour hasn't climbed this way yet, but it is a very beautiful road.

WHICH WAY? Millau is at the junction of the N 9, D992 and D911. Junctions 45, 46 and 47 of the A75 also give access to the town. Follow the D991 east out of Millau over the Tarn, and turn left onto the D110. The climb finishes along this road at Longuiers.

This pass links the Tarn and the Lot valleys, climbing another block of limestone upland that is somehow reminiscent of Britain's Yorkshire Dales, only a lot warmer. The climb starts in St Enimie and eventually links with the town of Mende.

This is a remote part of France. In fact there's a French saying that you have to be going to Mende, because it's not on the road to anywhere. But if you like peaceful cycling that is good news. The countryside here isn't as dramatically beautiful as the Alps or Pyrenees, or even the rest of the Massif-Central perhaps, but it has its own quiet charm.

The Tour de France has climbed this road only once, in 1954 when a Frenchman Robert Varnajo was first to the top. Varnajo won the last stage of the Tour in 1954, his only stage victory. Later in his career he specialized in a form of racing that is almost extinct now, motor-paced cycling on Velodromes, where the riders raced behind huge motor bikes and got up to speeds of 80 to 100 kilometres an hour.

WHICH WAY? As you might expect, St Enimie isn't really near to anywhere big. You could stay in Mende and ride the other side of the climb, then turn around and come back, or stay in Florac, which is on the N100. Go north on that road then turn left onto D31 then D907b to St-Enimie. Just after the village turn right onto the D986 and follow that road to the top. Continue on the descent and turn right onto the N88 for Mende.

Col de Ceyssat

Length: 12 km.

Altitude: 1076 metres.

Height gain: 494 metres.

Average gradient: 4.9%.

Maximum gradient: 6%.

This is another climb to do in the Puy de Dôme area when the Puy itself is closed to cyclists, which is every day apart from two hours early on a Sunday morning. The climb starts in the Clermont-Ferrand suburb of Chamalières and runs almost alongside the Puy, just missing out the ancient lava dome that forms the top of the Massif-Central's most iconic climb.

The way up the Ceysset involves crossing the busy D941A, so be careful there. The gradients aren't hard, although there is a steep section just before you turn off the road to the Puy de Dôme, near to a Zoo.

The first Tour de France rider to climb this col was Raphaël Géminiani in 1951. The Tour hasn't used the whole of this climb since, but has used parts of it when heading for the Puy de Dôme.

WHICH WAY? Chamalières is on the west side of Clermont-Ferrand. From Chamalières take the D68 west, cross the D941A and at the Zoo turn left on the D52 for the top of the climb.

Col des Fourches

Length: 11 km.

Altitude: 970 metres.

Height gain: 470 metres.

Average gradient: 4.7%.

Maximum gradient: 7%.

Starting in the town of Ambert, in Livradois-Forez, just to the west of the Col de la Croix de l'Homme Mort, the Col des Fourches has been climbed in both directions once each by the Tour de France. The first time was when Jean-Pierre Danguillaume led over the climb in 1971 going west to east, and on the second occasion Bernard Hinault took the mountain points going east to west.

The east side is the hardest of this climb. It begins once you cross the river Dore, and just after a sweeping left hand bend at St Pardoux the gradient hits seven percent for a few hundred metres. It relents as the road straightens, but there are another three short stretches of seven percent before the top.

The D37 joins the road from the left at the top of the climb, but just before it does it splits in two. From above, this arrangement of roads looks like a pitchfork, and *fourches* is the French word for pitchfork, as well as the forks on a bike.

WHICH WAY? Ambert is 46 kilometres west of Montbrison on the D496 and D996. Once in Ambert follow the D996 west to the top of the climb.

Col de Lachamp

Length: 17 km.

Altitude: 1320 metres.

Height gain: 670 metres.

Average gradient: 3.5%.

Maximum gradient: 7%.

This is a nice climb situated in the northern Ardèche that ambles gently up to the source of France's longest river. None of the climbs in this area are particularly brutal, but there are very few roads, so be prepared if you go for a long ride around here because there are very few short cuts. All in all though, the Ardèche is great cycling country.

The Col de Lachamp starts in the village of Dornas, and the road heads south finding the natural lines and easiest ways to climb. At Mézilhac the route switches right to run west up to Lachamp-Raphael and the top of the climb.

If you continue down the other side for about four kilometres to the Roche des Baux, a lump of rock that will be on your left, a spring in the field to your right is the source of the river Loire, from where it starts its 1020-kilometre journey to the Atlantic at Nantes.

The Tour de France has climbed the Col de Lachamp once, in 1996. First to the top was an Italian, Mirko Gualdi, who was part of a four-man breakaway group that contested the stage finish that day in Le Puy. Gualdi, who was the world amateur road race champion in 1990, but never quite made it as a pro. He was third on the stage.

WHICH WAY? Dornas is a pretty long way from everywhere. The nearest big place is Valence on the A7 Autourote, and that is 60 kilometres south-west of Grenoble. Head west from Valance on the D533, then turn left onto the D578 through Le Cheylard for Dornas. For the Col de Lachamp stay on the D578 but turn right onto the D122 at Mezillac for the top of the climb.

Col de Lalouvesc

Length: 11 km.

Altitude: 1120 metres.

Height gain: 657 metres.

Average gradient: 5%.

Maximum gradient: 7%.

A climb on the eastern edge of the Massif-Central, this one goes up to the town of Lalouvesc and has been used once by the Tour de France. It is also well known in French running circles, as it has been used several times for their national hill running championships.

The first Tour bike racer up to Lalouvesc was Joachim Agostinho, a Portuguese rider who won a number of stages in the Tour de France. Agostinho started his working life as a soldier and fought in the Angolan conflict before deciding that bike racing was easier than being shot at. He loved the sport so much that he was still racing in 1984 at the age of 42 when a dog ran in front of him during a stage in the Tour of Portugal. He crashed and died later from head injuries.

Lalouvesc starts in Satillieu and climbs at a fairly even gradient. You have to turn right in the village for the top of the Tour de France climb, which ends just where there is a left turn onto an unmarked road that has a direction sign to La Bruyère.

WHICH WAY? Lalouvesc is 25 kilometres south-west of Annonay, which is 40 kilometres south-east of St-Étienne on the N82 and D206. Take the D578 and D578A south-west out of Annonay. Continue through Satillieu on the D578A to Lalouvesc. Turn right at the crossroads in the village centre onto the D532 for the top of the climb.

Côte de Lestival

Length: 7.5 km.

Altitude: 963 metres.

Height gain: 470 metres.

Average gradient: 6.2%.

Maximum gradient: 7%.

This is a climb in the west of the Massif Central that starts in the town of Langeac on the Allier river and climbs quite steeply to the village of Lestival. The gradient is a fairly even six percent with a couple of stretches of seven. It's only been used in one Tour de France, and Steve De Wolf of Belgium was first to the top.

WHICH WAY? Langeac is 29 kilometres west of Le-Puy-en-Velay, using the D590 road. Cross the Allier river into town and continue left on the D590 to the top of the climb.

Col de Montjaux

Length: 11 km.
Altitude: 1030 metres.
Height gain: 720 metres.
Average gradient: 6.4%.
Maximum gradient: 10%.

A tough climb up onto the Plateau du Lévézou, which is just to the west of Millau, the Col de Montjaux has been climbed twice by the Tour de France, but just to underline its credentials, on both occasions the first rider to the top was someone special. In 1965 Frederico Bahamontès was first to the top, and in 1983 it was Robert Millar. Kings of the Mountains both of them.

The Col de Montjaux starts right next to the river Tarn, just over the bridge from St-Rome-de-Tarn. The road up is hard from the off, as it snakes around natural contours to find its way up the steepest part of the climb. All of the climbs up onto the plateaux in this area have a hard start, so getting a warm-up before you begin is essential.

After four kilometres the tough stuff ends with a few hundred metres of ten-percent climbing, after which the road meanders gently up to Montjaux, where you turn left for the top of the climb and some great views south over the river Tarn.

WHICH WAY? Millau is on the A75 Paris to Béziers Autoroute. Find the D992 which runs along the south side of town and head west. Turn right at St-Rome-de-Cernon onto the D31 and right again onto the D993 to St-Rome-de-Tarn and follow that road to Montjaux. In the village turn left onto the D169 and follow that to the top of the climb.

Côte de Montsalvy

Length: 11 km.
Altitude: 733 metres.
Height gain: 513 metres.
Average gradient: 4.2%.
Maximum gradient: 7%.

This is a main road climb in the Aveyron department that has been used three times by the Tour de France. Valentin Huot in 1959 was the first Tour rider to cross the Montsalvy. The most recent was another Frenchman, and a local, David Moncoutie, who led here on his way to winning the day's stage in Figeac.

The climb starts in Entraygues-sur-Truyère, a town that sits on the confluence of the Lot and Truyère rivers. It has three short sections of seven-percent climbing, the first of which comes on the first straight of the climb. A sharp right-hand hairpin give you some great views over the town on the second straight, after which the road wriggles out of sight. The last seven-percent stretch comes where the road begins to straighten, just before the top.

WHICH WAY? Entraygues is 57 kilometres north of Rodez on the D988 and D920. Carry on the D920 for the top of the climb.

Col de la Moreno

Length: 16 km.
Altitude: 1065 metres.
Height gain: 675 metres.
Average gradient: 4.2%.
Maximum gradient: 7%.

A bit of an up-and-down complicated climb, the Col de la Moreno starts in the Clermont-Ferrand suburb of Beaumont and jumps from road to road, past the motor racing circuit of Charade before passing through the villages of Manson and Laschamps to reach the top.

The climb has been used once by the Tour de France, in 1951 when local hero Raphaël Géminiani romped up its slopes before turning right at the top and descending back into Clermont-Ferrand to take the stage victory.

WHICH WAY? Find the D941C in Beaumont on the south-western side of Clermont-Ferrand. Follow this road until the left turn onto the D5. Follow the D5 to the Charade motor circuit and turn left onto the D761. Turn right onto the D52 at Laschamps for the top of the climb.

Col des Pradeaux

Length: 11.3 km.

Altitude: 1196 metres.

Height gain: 643 metres.

Average gradient: 5.7%.

Maximum gradient: 7%.

Côte de Saint-Anastaise

Length: 5.5 km.

Altitude: 1160 metres.

Height gain: 490 metres.

Average gradient: 8.9%.

Maximum gradient: 12%.

Another climb that starts in Ambert, this one heads east into Forez. It was first used by the Tour de France in 1959 when Valentin Huot was first to the top. It has been used twice since, and has been climbed in both directions. The last time it was climbed was in 2005, and it was this, the longer side, that the race used.

First over the climb that day was a Spaniard, Óscar Pereiro, the man destined to be crowned winner of the 2006 Tour de France over a year after it finished, due to the disqualification of Floyd Landis once the doping case against him had been proved.

WHICH WAY? Ambert is 60 kilometres north east of Issoire on the D996, which in turn is 23 kilometres south of Clermont-Ferrand on the A75 Autoroute. Continue east through Ambert on the D996 for the top of the Col des Pradeaux.

A short sharp shock of a climb on the south side of the Monts Dore, between the volcanoes centred on Puy Mary and those around the Puy de Dôme, the Côte de Saint-Anastaise has been climbed twice by the Tour de France. The first success fell to a Spanish rider Bernardo Ruiz in 1951, who was on his way to a stage win that day.

The climb starts in Valbeleix, and it is a really hard slog with a section of twelve percent coming after the first kilometre. The gradient relents for a bit to around seven percent, but you are not out of the woods yet because there is another twelve-percent ramp just before the village of Saint-Anastaise. The gradient eases during the final run to the top, where you get some great views of the Monts Dore range.

WHICH WAY? Valbeleix is not very accessible. Issoire is about 50 kilometres to the north-east. Take the D996 west, then turn left onto the D26 and left again at Saurier onto the D26, which runs along the Courgoul Gorge to Valbeix. Turn right in the village onto the D127 to start the climb, then left where the D127 meets the D619. Continue on the D127 through Saint-Anastaise to the junction with the D624 where the climb ends.

Côte de Saraille

Length: 9 km.

Altitude: 810 metres.

Height gain: 580 metres.

Average gradient: 6.4%.

Maximum gradient: 8%.

A new addition to the Tour de France in 2007 when David de la Fuente of Spain was first to the top, the Côte de Saraille is right on the southern tip of the Massif Central in a range of hills called the Black Mountains. From the top of them you can see the Mediteranean to the south-east and the Pyrenees to the south-west.

The mountains are part of the Haute Languedoc regional park and the nearest sizable town to the climb is Mazamet, the birthplace of former Tour de France King of the Mountains, Laurent Jalabert. The name Languedoc comes from a time when people in this area said "Oc" instead of "Oui" for yes.

WHICH WAY? Mazamet is 17 kilometres south-east of Castres on the D612. Continue through town following directions to Carcassonne and you will pick up the D118. Continue on this road to the top of the climb.

Col de la Sereyrede

Length: 20 km.

Altitude: 1190 metres.

Height gain: 860 metres.

Average gradient: 4.3%.

Maximum gradient: 7%.

Another way to climb the beautiful Mont Aigoual, the Col de la Sereyrede was first climbed in 1955 by the Tour rider Louis Caput, although he did only the top part after climbing the Col du Minier.

It starts in Valleraugue, which sits beside the infant Hérault river. The first part of the climb is quite easy, but once the road bends right to cope with the slopes of Mont Aigoual you will find you have to make a greater effort. The gradients increase to five and six percent, with one short stretch of seven to negotiate.

If you turn right at the summit you can add Mont Aigoual to your collection of Tour de France climbs. In fact there are all sorts of opportunities to explore this fascinating climb, as all the main ways up have tiny roads running off them.

WHICH WAY? Valleraugue is 23 kilometres north of Le Vigan. Head east on the D999 and turn left at Pont Hérault onto the D986. Follow that road through Valleraugue for the Col de la Sereyrede.

Col de Sié

Length: 10 km.

Altitude: 1020 metres.

Height gain: 530 metres.

Average gradient: 5.3%.

Maximum gradient: 6%.

The Col de Sié is on the southern tip of the Causses, just before they become the Monts de Lacaune, which are the south-western edge of the Cévennes. It's been climbed twice in Tour de France history, once in 1990 when Thierry Claveyrolat was first to the top and the second time in 1995 when an Italian, Bruno Cenghialta triumphed.

The climb starts in Belmont-sur-Rance and it isn't particularly tough. Shortly before the summit you cross the border between the Tarn and Hérault departments. The top of the col is the meeting point of three roads, and the descent to Lacaune is short but quite steep.

From Lacaune south you start to see evidence of Occitan, the Catalan-influenced language that used to be spoken in the Eastern Pyrenees and as far south as Barcelona in Spain.

WHICH WAY? The nearest largish town north of Belmont-sur-Rance is St-Affrique, which is 30 kilometres south-west of Millau on the D992 and D999. From St-Affrique follow the D999 south-west for 18 kilometres to Petit St-Jean and turn left there onto the D32. Follow the D32 to the top of the climb. For the very top of the col you need to turn right and ride another 400 metres on the D607.

Super Besse

Length: 23 km.

Altitude: 1350 metres.

Height gain: 829 metres.

Average gradient: 3.6%.

Maximum gradient: 10%.

Super Besse is a ski station on the Monts Dore massif, with runs coming down off the Puy Ferrand (1816 metres). The Tour de France has visited here twice. The first when Super-Besse was a stage finish in 1978 and a Belgian, Paul Wellens won.

The climb is a long one but quite gentle. It starts at the junction of the D996 and D 978 and wanders upwards through St Diéry and Besse-Et-St-Anastaise, with just three short stretches of seven percent to cause you trouble. After Besse-Et-St-Anastaise you turn right off the main road and proceed to Super-Besse.

Now the climb has a shock for you, as you have to negotiate 100 metres of ten percent, which relents to seven before letting you go for the summit. If you continue through Super-Besse you will eventually get to the top of the Col de la Geneste, which hasn't been used in the Tour so far, but it's there – so you may as well go for it.

WHICH WAY? The climb starts 19 kilometres west of Issoire on the D996. Turn left onto the D978 when you see the signs to Besse-et-St-Anastaise. Turn right onto the D49 when you see the sign to Super Besse.

Super Lioran

Length: 21 km.

Altitude: 1326 metres.

Height gain: 654 metres.

Average gradient: 3.2%.

Maximum gradient: 8%.

This is a largely main road climb along and up the north-west face of the Plomb du Cantal. It starts in Vic-sur-Cère and climbs steadily on the fairly straight but not too busy N122. Just after Thiézac two short sections of eight percent come in quick succession.

The climb gets really interesting where you turn off the main road shortly before it goes through the Lioran tunnel. The road snakes around some of the Puys of the Puy Mary group to find the easiest way up to the resort.

Super Lioran is one of the oldest ski resorts in France, having been created in 1878. It main ski lift up to the top of the Plomb du Cantal was opened in 1967 by George Pompidou, who was then president of France. Pompidou came from the Cantal region.

Super Lioran's first and only Tour de France visit was in 1975 when a Belgian, Michele Pollentier won a stage there. Pollentier was a good climber who could time trial well, in spite of the fact that he had a most ungainly style.

WHICH WAY? Vic-sur-Cère is 19 kilometres north-east of Aurillac on the N122. Continue on the N122 until you see signs directing you to a left turn for the resort of Super-Besse. Turn right when you see the ski lifts into the resort. The climb finishes in the middle of the built up area.

Côte des Vignes

Length: 9 km.

Altitude: 920 metres.

Height gain: 520 metres.

Average gradient: 5.7%.

Maximum gradient: 10%.

A beautiful little climb out of the Tarn gorge that has only been used once by the Tour de France. That was in 1984 when a Spaniard, Celestino Prieto was first to the top. It is nonetheless worth a visit if you are doing any of the climbs of the Causses around Millau.

The climb starts in Vignes, a village right in the Tarn gorge that at this point separates the Causses Méjean and Sauveterre. The climb tackles the Causses Sauveterre, and like all the plateaux climbs in this area the first part is the hardest part.

A series of lacets take you to the hamlet of St-Rome-de-Dolan, and a couple of the straights between the hairpin bends have stretches of eight- and ten-percent climbing on them.

Once you've got over that bit, the rest is easy, and if you continue over the top to Le Massegros you can turn right onto the D32, then turn right again 18 kilometres later onto the D998, which will take you to Ste-Enimie and the start of the Causse de Sauveterre climb.

WHICH WAY? Les Vignes is 32 kilometres north-east of Millau on the N9, D907 and D907B. In Vignes turn left onto the D995 for the top of the climb.

Northern Alps

The Northern Alps run south from Lake Léman near Geneva, to include the Vanoise massif and northern Maurienne climbs – and are dominated by the huge bulk of Mont Blanc in the east. For cyclists they are quieter and less-well explored than the Central Alps.

This is where the biggest ski resorts in France are located, and the whole place is an outdoor enthusiast's playground. Climbing, Kayaking, paragliding and mountain biking are big sports in the northern Alps, and are all well catered for.

The climbs are of a similar character to those you find in the central Alps. The ski resort climbs tend to be versions of Alpe d'Huez, but the Cormet de Roselend is one example of a northern alpine climb with a character all of its own. My favourites are the Col de la Joux-Plane for its sheer uncompromising toughness, and the lonely untamed Iseran for its high-altitude wildness.

The northern Alps don't have a uniform climate, Mont Blanc's icy summit affects the weather in the whole region, but in different ways. The nearest thing to predictable weather is found in the far north around Morzine, where plenty of summer sunshine is a fairly good bet.

Good places to stay when exploring this area are Cluses or Morzine for the far north, Annecy for the western climbs such as the Col des Aravis, and Bourg St Maurice for the Isère valley climbs such as the three valleys ski resorts or the Col d'Iseran.

Col des Aravis

'FAVOURITE OF THE BRITISH MOUNTAIN KING'

⭐⭐ 2 STARS

Length: 18.9 km.
Altitude: 1486 metres.
Height gain: 630 metres.
Average gradient: 4.5%.
Maximum gradient: 8%.

WHAT TO EXPECT

➤ **Straying cattle.** Especially near the top on both sides of the climb.

➤ **High spirits.** Liquer des Aravis is a highly potent drink distilled from a mix of Alpine herbs and plants.

➤ **Summit Chapel.** This was built in the 17th century as a shelter for unfortunate travellers who got trapped by bad weather at the top.

➤ **Twin peaks.** The Aravis makes a nice pair of mountains to climb with the Col de la Colombière. Take the D4 out of St Jean-de-Sixt for the Colombière

➤ **Diversion.** You can miss out the gentle bit and give yourself an extra challenge by taking the D12 south out of Thônes then climbing the Croix Fry, and descending to the road up the Aravis just as it gets interesting south of La Clusaz.

This climb goes over a pass that sits right in the middle of a high ridge called the Aravis chain, a natural dividing line between the Savoie and Haute Savoie. It's slopes are also home to the cows that provide milk for Reblochon cheese.

The word Reblocher literally means to pinch a cow's udder, and it comes from the 14th century when most farmers in France were tenants. The milk from their cows went to the landowners as part of their rent, however, the crafty farmers of this area didn't fully milk their cows until after the landowners had collected their milk. The milk left inside the cow grew richer, so when the landowners left the farmers finished milking their cows and used this milk to make the Reblochon cheese.

D909

Thônes

Col des Aravis

Above: Part of the Chaine des Aravis

The town where this climb starts, Thônes is still the capital of Reblochon cheese making today. The first part of the climb is quite steady, so you get plenty of time to admire the verdant meadows that lie on either side of the road.

The real climbing starts at La Clusaz, a ski resort with 200 kilometres of pistes. There is steep bit straight after the resort, and on your right you will see the road to the Col de la Croix Fry, another Tour climb but one without the history of the Aravis.

After 15 kilometres the road, which has been quite straight so far, begins to writhe around as the route gets steeper, with several sections of eight percent to be overcome before you reach the top.

There's a bar and restaurant at the top, plus a chapel if you need sustenance of a more spiritual nature. The first part of the descent is very twisty, but it straightens as you enter the Gorge de L'Arondine. You can see Mont Blanc from the summit of the Aravis, but it's well worth turning left at the bottom of the climb onto the N212 and riding through Megève for a really good look at just how big it is.

WHICH WAY?

Thônes is just off the D909 about 20 kilometres from Annecy, a city with lots of accommodation that makes a good base for the north-west section of the northern Alps.

From Thônes, continue along the D909 in an easterly direction. At St Jean-de-Sixt the road bends sharply right, then through La Clusaz follow the D909 right to the top.

Above left: Looking down the ascent towards Le Clusaz   **Below left:** No danger of not knowing where you are

MOUNTAIN MOMENTS

➤ First Tour riders over the Aravis were George Duboc and Emile Georget in a dead heat in 1911. The Tour has climbed the Aravis on 32 occasions since. British riders have been first over the top only twice. Barry Hoban managed it on the way to winning a stage in 1968, and Robert Millar did it in 1984 on his way to winning the King of the Mountains title. Millar says that the Aravis was his favourite Tour de France climb.

➤ Gino Bartali had cause to curse the Second World War for a different reason than most. He won the Tour in 1938 as a 24-year-old. Then it was impossible for him to compete again until 1948, when he won again. When he did so he delivered the coup de grâce to his rival Lousion Bobet on the Col des Aravis.

Les Arcs 'RACING THE TRAIN'

★★ 2 STARS

Length: 21 km.

Altitude: 2120 metres.

Height gain: 1305 metres.

Average gradient: 6.2%.

Maximum gradient: 10%.

WHAT TO EXPECT

➤ **Wide, well engineered roads.** There is a fair bit of traffic going up and down the mountain, but there's plenty of room for everyone.

➤ **Mountain biking.** Like many ski resorts Les Arcs is becoming a Mecca for two-wheeled downhillers. Mind you, the resort has always been innovative – it was one of the places where snowboarding was developed.

➤ **Linking up.** The route I've given you is to Arc 2000, the highest of the stations, but if you turn right on the D120 at Les Arcs and go to Arc 1800 there is a road that links with the village of Vallandry and the next valley. Climb to Les Arcs, then Arc 2000, then descend and turn left to Arc 1800 and the next valley for a round trip.

You have no chance of beating the train up to Les Arcs. It isn't one of those scary old cog railways that you find grinding up the slopes of some Alpine resorts, but a high-speed funicular that whisks passengers up from the station at Bourg St Maurice to Les Arcs in seven minutes flat. You see the train from time to time though, as the road wriggles under its tracks a couple of times on the way up to the top.

Like those going to most ski resorts, the road is well made and the gradient fairly even. There is a section of ten-percent climbing after eight kilometres, then a flat and sometimes down-hill bit between 14 and 16 kilometres. After that it's a more or less constant seven percent to the top. There are trees most of the way up that will protect you from the worst of the sun and wind.

Les Arcs is one of several resorts on the Vannoise Massif, and the local area is called the Tarantaise. There are a mass of mountains to look at when you get to the top of Les Arcs. One, Mount Pourri, thrusts up towards 4000 metres.

The town at the foot of the climb, Bourg-St Maurice was famous long before

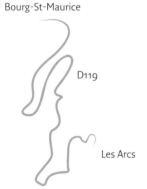

Bourg-St-Maurice

D119

Les Arcs

Left: Towards Les Arcs from the opposite side of the Isere valley   **Above:** Tour de France riders in the Alps

skiing became a popular pastime. It sits at the bottom of the Petit St Bernard pass, a famous route into Italy, so it has been an important stopping-off point since Roman times. Skiing and cycling aren't the only big sports that Bourg hosts. The world canoeing championships have been held on the white water that tumbles down between its closely packed streets.

Bourg-St-Maurice is an excellent base for Alpine cycling . At least seven Tour de France climbs are within easy riding distance. The town has hosted two stage finishes and one stage start of the Tour de France.

WHICH WAY?

Bourg-St-Maurice is on the N90, 27 kilometres north-east of Moutiers, which in turn is about the same distance by the N90 south of Albertville. The road to Les Arcs, the D119, starts at a roundabout on the N90, just as you leave Bourg going north-east. Simply follow the D119 to the ski resort. When you descend turn right on the D120 if you want to go to Arc 2000..

MOUNTAIN MOMENTS

➤ Les Arcs has only been visited once by the Tour, when a stage of the 1996 race finished at the ski resort. The winner was an enigmatic Frenchman called Luc Leblanc. Given to incomprehensible Eric Cantona-like utterances, Leblanc never seemed to sit easy in his own skin. He was a prodigiously talented bike rider who wore the Yellow Jersey for a day in the 1991 Tour de France, when he was fifth overall, and was the world champion in 1994. But Leblanc always seemed to be at war with someone, most often with himself. Leblanc was sixth in the 1996 Tour. His best placing was fourth overall in 1994, and in the same year Leblanc won the King of the Mountains title in the Tour of Spain.

Morzine-Avoriaz 'THE ALPINE NORTH END'

⭐⭐⭐ 3 STARS

Length: 14 km.

Altitude: 1800 metres.

Height gain: 840 metres.

Average gradient: 6%

Maximum gradient: 11%

WHAT TO EXPECT

➤ **Sunny weather.** This are is not called the Portes de Soleil for nothing. The weather here is very sunny, but the cooling effect of all the ice still present in summer on the high mountains, to the south keeps temperatures down. It makes for perfect weather for cycling up big hills.

➤ **A double challenge.** After you've climbed Morzine-Avoriaz, descend to Morzine and turn right on the D228 to climb the Joux-Verte.

➤ **Needle point.** If you look south from the road just before Avoriaz you can see the Aiguilles Rouge, or red needles, range of mountains pointing up at the sky.

➤ **Posh sunglasses.** Jean Vuarnet comes from Morzine. He won a gold medal for downhill skiing at the winter Olympics in 1960, but is better known for the Vuarnet sunglasses that are favoured by well-healed French skiers.

Morzine-Avoriaz is a ski resort, part of an area of similar resorts in France and Switzerland known as the Portes de Soleil. Morzine is a market town with some ski facilities at the foot of the climb, Avoriaz is the ski resort at the top, and the climb is the road that links the two.

This climb is situated at the northern tip of the northern Alps, very close to the Swiss border and not far from the French side of Lake Léman. There are no big Alpine climbs used by Tour de France north of Morzine-Avoriaz, but it is a tough farewell to the big mountains.

It's a climb that only the best climbers win, a fact mostly due to its tough start and the fact that it is the last climb on any stage that uses it, because there is nowhere to go after Avoriaz.

Morzine — D338 — Avoriaz

Left: A toboggan track near Morzine **Above left:** The Aiguilles Rouge in the distance **Above right:** Spring sculpture

The climbing starts in Morzine and at first the going is quite gentle, but after three kilometres you come to a series of lacets with vicious corners and tough straights. Most of this section climbs at just under ten percent and there is a one kilometre stretch of eleven percent halfway through this section. The road is well made and shaded by trees.

After six kilometres the gradient lessens and you break out of the trees. The road is fairly straight and you can see the space-age tower buildings of Avoriaz a bit above you and to your right. The locals use unusual wood sculptures to house spring-water pipes that pour their contents into troughs in this area, and there are a couple of examples by the side of the road along this stretch.

The gradient starts to increase as you approach a right-hand bend with two one kilometre stretches of seven percent. The bend marks the top of the Col de la Joux Verte, another Tour climb but one that hasn't been used as often as Morzine-Avoriaz. After that the road goes straight on to the top of the climb in Avoriaz, with the gradient relenting all the time.

WHICH WAY?

Morzine is just off the D902 that links Cluses with Thonon-les-Bains. Cluses is 45 kilometres east of Geneva on the A40 Autoroute, and Thonon is 33 kilometres north-east of the Swiss city on the southern shore of Lake Léman. Take the D338 from the D902 to Morzine and follow signposts to Avoriaz. The climb ends where the road flattens out in Avoriaz.

MOUNTAIN MOMENTS

➤ First climbed in the Tour de France by Spanish ace Vincente Lopez-Carril, Morzine-Avoriaz has witnessed some of the best climbing performances ever seen in the Tour. Lucien Van Impe won here in 1977 and 1983. Bernard Hinault won in 1979 and a Colombian, 'Lucho' Herrera won in 1985.

➤ The mid-1980s saw an influx into the Tour de France of great climbers from Colombia. Cycling is big in that country, and with races having the Andes to play with, they weren't short of climbing talent. Herrera and Fabio Parra were seen as potential winners of the Tour, and both made their marks in the mountains, but neither could quite cope with the flat stages and time trials that ensure that a Tour de France winner leans towards being an all-round athlete.

Col de la Colombière

'A CLIMB OF TWO HALVES'

⊛⊛⊛ 3 STARS

Length: 16.3 km.

Altitude: 1613 metres.

Height gain: 1108 metres.

Average gradient: 6.8%

Maximum gradient: 10.8%

WHAT TO EXPECT

➤ **Loneliness.** Not many people live on the climb and the road is not a major link route.

➤ **Straying cattle.** They graze free from about one-third up, but they are a problem on the road during the middle part of the climb. The road slopes gently here but so does the pasture down to it. Nearer the top you are fairly safe as terrain by the side of the road is very rocky.

➤ **Headwinds.** The north side often has a nagging headwind to cope with, in addition to its gradients.

➤ **Round trip.** If you descend the Colombière and turn right onto the D12 just after La Grand Bornand there is an interesting road that ends by going through the Gorge des Eveaux. From the village at the end of it, St Pierre-en-Faucigny, take the D19 back to Cluses.

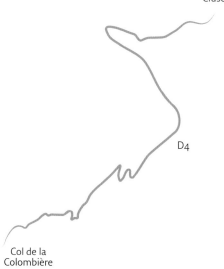

Cluses

D4

Col de la
Colombière

The Col de la Colombière is made up of two six-kilometre stretches of hard work separated by four kilometres of easy climbing in the middle. It also has an indefinable wild feel to it, even though it is quite close to big centres of population and is often the first or last climb in a Tour de France stage.

It starts gently enough in the village of Scizonier, which is just the other side of the A40 Autoroute Blanche from the town of Cluses. After two kilometres though there is a sharp hairpin left-hand bend and the real climbing begins. Now it's seven to eight percent until the easy middle bit. There are some really nicely constructed lacets to negotiate at Le Reposoir too, and some of the hairpins are very steep.

After the first bends the road straightens and the gradient lessens as you climb though pastures and along the side of the lower ground between the Bargy chain of peaks on your right, and the Aravis chain on your left.

Too soon though, there are more lacets and the road steepens again, twisting and turning to the top where the highest peaks of the Bargy and Aravis chains, Pointe Blanche (2437 metres) and Pointe Percée (2752 metres) face each other across the pass.

There are very few people living on the sides of the Colombière, despite it being fairly close to Geneva and the surrounding centres of population. Le Reposoir is the only village on the north side of the climb, and that is no more than a tiny hamlet. It's this isolation that gives the Colombière its wild feel.

If you descend from the summit of the climb to Le Grand Bornand and St Jean-de-Sixt, and turn left to La Clusaz, you are at the beginning of the tough bit of the Col d'Aravis. Take great care descending through the hairpins just after the summit and through La Grand Bornand – they can be quite busy.

WHICH WAY?

Head for Cluses, either on the A40 (junction 2) or N205. There are two roundabouts on the N205 on the south side of the town. Look for the one with signposts to La Grand Bornand/D4. Follow this road to the top of the Colombière.

➤ The Colombière has been used 17 times since 1960 when Spaniard Jesus Manzanque was the first Tour de France rider to climb it.

➤ In keeping with its gateway to Alps position, the Col de la Colombière was the first mountain to be climbed in the 2007 Tour. The young German, Linus Gerdemann was first to the top on his way to winning the stage and taking the yellow jersey for a day. His ride was good enough to convince everyone that he is a big prospect for the future.

➤ First on the Colombière in 1990 and 1991 was the Frenchman, Thierry Claveyrolat. He was another talented climber, along with René Pottier and Luis Ocana, who took his own life. Like Ocana, Claveyrolat succeeded in cycling only to fail in business, and failure was something he couldn't live with. Claveyrolat was King of the Mountains in 1990.

Above: Looking down on the TV helicopter looking down on the riders

Courchevel *'HEAD OF THE FIVE VALLEYS'*

⚫⚫ 2 STARS

Length: 21.7 km.

Altitude: 2000 metres.

Height gain: 1420 metres.

Average gradient: 6.5%.

Maximum gradient: 10%.

WHAT TO EXPECT

➤ **Traffic.** Courchevel is quite a large place and the road to it is quite busy, but it is wide and well engineered, so other road users aren't really a problem. It just means that this climb isn't one where you will find notable peace and quiet.

➤ **Plenty to see.** There are a number of villages on the way up to Courchevel, many linked by a quiet but narrow road, the D89, which makes a nice alternative to the main one. It's not the way the Tour goes, but you get on it at Salins-les-Thermes, just south of Moutiers, and it joins the D915 at Bozal. You then need to turn right and pick up the D91 by turning left at the junction. Now you are back on the Tour route again.

➤ **Triple header.** The climbs of Val Thorens, Méribel and Courchevel all start within five kilometres of each other. It's a very worthy achievement to climb them all in one day.

A busy road up to a busy ski resort – the climbs up to neighbouring Méribel or Val Thorens are more enjoyable – but Courchevel is part of Tour de France history, so it has to be ticked off if you are bagging all the Tour peaks.

The climb starts in Brides-les-Bains, where the climb to Méribel begins as well. The gradient fluctuates between four and eight percent most of the way to the top, but it is never at either for very long so you don't get much rest. This fluctuation means that it's hard to find a rhythm on Courchevel, although the best way to deal with that is to remember that in the Tour the good climbers relish such conditions. Climbs that break up the rhythm sap the strength of all but the most talented up-hillers. Courchevel is a good test.

There are steep bits of ten percent early on, when the road is fairly straight. The second half of the climb twists and turns in big arcs across the mountain side. There is a road at the apex of the second arc that connects with Méribel village.

The top of the climb comes just after the highest part of the resort's built-up area, on the way to an infamous air strip that is only 525 metres long and angles up at 18.5 percent to help slow down landing aircraft.

Courchevel is actually a collection of resorts, each at different altitudes and with their altitudes incorporated into their names. The place was planned

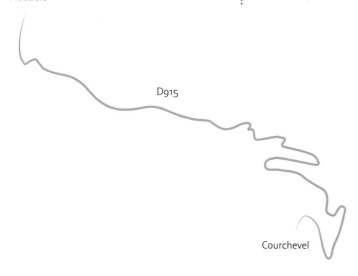

Moûtiers

D915

Courchevel

Left: Brides-les-Bains **Above:** Part of the Vanoise Mountains behind Courchevel

by the Vichy government during the Second World War. In fact Courchevel 1850 (as in 1850 metres) was the first purpose-built ski resort in France. It should be noted that the highest point in Courchevel is only 1747 metres, but the planners didn't want their arch rivals, Val d'Isere to know that.

Like all of the nearby resorts the top of the climb is ringed by the big peaks of the Vanoise range, and there are hundreds of kilometres of ski pistes connected to the resort, many of which are also used by mountain bikers during the summer.

WHICH WAY?

Moûtiers is the town at the bottom end of the Three Valleys, so is a perfect base for Val-Thorens, Méribel and Courchevel. The town is itself only 26 kilometres south of Abertville on the N90. In Moûtiers follow signs for the D915 then D91A Courchevel and carry on up the D91A all the way to the top.

 **MOUNTAIN MOMENTS**

➤ Courchevel first hosted a stage finish in 1997, when King of the Mountains record man, Richard Virenque won. The next visit was in 2000 when Marco Pantani was first to the top. The climb as it is now, where they climb all the way to the Altiport airport, wasn't used until 2005, and on that occasion Alejandro Valverde of Spain took the honours.

➤ Courchevel has seen some great performances from Lance Armstrong. When Pantani and Valverde won it was Armstrong who made the killing surges that took them both clear. Armstrong was second on both occasions, but stage victory wasn't as important as the time Armstrong gained on his other rivals. He beat Pantani and Valverde in the time trials anyway.

Col de la Forclaz

'THE TOUR VISITS SWITZERLAND'

★★★ 3 STARS

Length: 13.3 km.

Altitude: 1526 metres.

Height gain: 1050 metres.

Average gradient: 7.9%.

Maximum gradient: 9%.

WHAT TO EXPECT

➤ **Sunny weather.** The Vallais is called the California of Switzerland.

➤ **Art work.** The Fondation Pierre Gianadda, which is located in Martigny's Rue du Forum is home to both permanent and occasional expositions of the works of Picasso, Kandinsky, Miro, Van Gogh, Chagal and many others. The foundation also has a sculpture park and an automobile museum.

➤ **Unremitting gradient.** There is nowhere to rest and that can make the Forclaz, and mountains like it such as the Ventoux, both a mentally and physically tough proposition.

➤ **Rhône views.** After three kilometres of the climb you come to a big hairpin bend, where there is a fantastic view up the Rhône valley to the Swiss town of Sion and beyond.

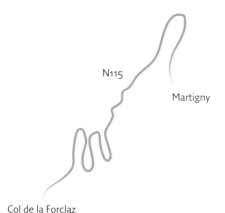

N115

Martigny

Col de la Forclaz

Historically one of the most important high-altitude communication links between France and neighbouring Switzerland, the Col de La Forclaz is a tough unremitting climb that is also steeped in Tour de France history.

The most challenging side is the climb from Martigny in Switzerland, and this is the way that the Tour climbed the Forclaz after a brief visit into Switzerland on one of the most famous stages in its history.

Martigny is a big town with a lovely sunny climate located on a right-angled bend of the river Rhône. The Rhône starts in Switzerland, flows into Lake Leman and reappears on the Geneva shore to become one of the major rivers of France.

The climb starts gently enough, but after three kilometres the road rears up at eight per cent and stays between that figure and nine all the way to the top. The Valais, which is what this part of Switzerland is called, produces good wine and the first part of the Forclaz drifts up between some of the region's finest vineyards.

These soon give way to open grassland and rocks. Keep your eyes peeled for Chamois up here. They are shy, but there are quite a lot of them in this area of

Left: Swiss climber   **Above left:** Alpine dawn   **Above right:** The Mont Blanc massif

Switzerland. They are well worth watching as they make their sure-footed way up and down the steep craggy hillsides.

After the first steep bend the road is straight for about five kilometres, then a series of lacets take you up to the last two straight kilometres and the summit. From there France is nine kilometres away, down a descent that has no particular difficulties and isn't as steep as the road you've just climbed.

Chamonix is the nearest French town, and as you descend to it more and more of the Mont Blanc massif becomes visible on your left. At the French border you can take time out to admire the Aiguile du Tour (3450 metres) that rises in all its glory on your left.

WHICH WAY?

Martigny can be reached on the N5 or E62 from Geneva, it's about 40 kilometres south-east of Montreux. You can get there from Chamonix on the N506. The climb starts in Martigny and is clearly signposted, and the road up it is the N115.

MOUNTAIN MOMENTS

➤ The Forclaz is a regular in the Tour de France. It was first climbed in the 1948 Tour, and first over the top was 'Apo' Lazarides, a tiny French climber with Greek parents who during the Second World War used the cover of being a pro racer to ferry supplies to the Resistance fighters in the hills around his home in Nice.

➤ In 1963 a stage was run from Val d'Isere to Chamonix through Switzerland that was one of the best in Tour history. The ace climber Frederico Bahamontes tried to win the race on this big day in the mountains, but the first five times winner of the Tour, Jacques Anquetil wouldn't let him. He matched Bahamontes as the Spaniard threw everything at him on the Forclaz, leaving everyone minutes behind by the top, except Anquetil. He doggedly hung on and passed Bahamontes on the descent to win the stage and take the yellow jersey.

Col de l'Iseran 'UP IN THE THIN AIR'

⭐⭐⭐⭐ 4 STARS

Length: 16 km.

Altitude: 2764 metres.

Height gain: 960 metres.

Average gradient: 6%.

Maximum gradient: 8%.

WHAT TO EXPECT

➤ **Wind.** Above 2000 metres you are really exposed to the elements , and the peaks around the upper Isere valley tend to channel wind down into it. Once there the wind tends to swirl around and is quite unpredictable.

➤ **Cool conditions.** Height means that even on hot days there is a certain chill to the air. It's not usually a problem going up, but you will feel it on the descent. Always keep a light windproof in your pocket to wear when descending from these heights.

➤ **Steep descent.** The other valley of the Iseran descends into the Maurienne. The road initially goes down at an average of 7 percent, with one stretch of eleven percent about two kilometres before Bonneval-sur-Arc. It's flatter after that with a slight climb coming before the start of Mont-Cenis.

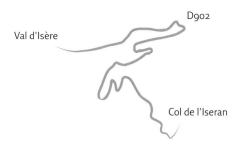

Val d'Isère

D902

Col de l'Iseran

Strictly speaking the Col de l'Iseran starts in Bourg St Maurice, making it a 48-kilometre trek to the top. However, that trek involves negotiating eight tunnels between Tignes and Val d'Isère – and they are long, dark and scary with very little room for cyclists when mixed with other traffic.

The tunnels are an experience to be avoided, so I've split the climb into two, starting the Iseran in Val d'Isère and creating a new climb from Bourg St Maurice to Tignes. There is a precedent though, the Tour de France used the Tignes climb for a stage finish in the 2007 race.

At 1847 metres, Val d'Isère is high. That's why it is a popular ski resort, although the last few years have seen the winter starting later and later even at this the high altitude. The resort is built on an area of flat land between towering peaks like the Rocher de Bellevarde (2827 metres), created by the confluence of two mountain streams, one of which is the youthful river Isère.

The first kilometre is easy, only three percent, giving you a chance to admire the huge circle of mountains that rear up in front of you. You are in real high-altitude territory, the evidence is all around you. At well over 2000 metres the tree line far behind you, and as you climb the Iseran you will see signposts

Above: Information boards tell you how high you are and how far to go

Above left: Ski pistes cross the Iseran road   **Above right:** Out of the saddle effort at altitude

pointing along and across the road. They are the signs for the winter ski runs, several of which use the road you are climbing up.

This wilderness is part of the Vanoise, the first national park ever created in France. The climb continues steadily until the Pont St-Charles, where the road dramatically switches right over the Isere and after two hairpin bends you begin a long inexorable slog up the face of the Signal d'Iseran (3237 metres). The scree on your left is produced by two huge glaciers that run down from the top of the Signal.

More hairpins take you to the Belvedere de la Tarentaise, where the road straightens to run along the base of the Crêtes de Lessieres to the top of the pass. This is a really wild place of cliffs, shattered rock and glaciers. Not entirely hospitable, but a great experience and a nice place to consider that there are only a handful of roads in Europe that take you higher than you are now.

WHICH WAY?

Val d'Isère is 24 kilometres south-east of Bourg-St Maurice on the D902. This road goes straight through the centre of the ski resort and the Col de l'Iseran starts alongside the last building in Val d'Isère.

MOUNTAIN MOMENTS

➤ The Iseran was first climbed in the 1938 Tour by an early Belgian King of the Mountains, Felicien Vervaecke. Vervaecke was a Brussels-based rider who later opened a bike shop in the same suburb as a teenage Eddy Merckx lived. The old Tour rider was Merckx's first coach.
➤ The climb has featured in seven Tour routes, but in 1996 the race didn't get to it because the stage was annulled on account of unseasonable snow. The race organisers were wary of this high climb after that incident, but the Iseran made it back in 2007. There were no incidents and a Ukrainian, Yaroslav Popovich was first to the top.

Col de Joux-Plane 'HARD AS NAILS'

⦿⦿⦿⦿ **4 STARS**

Length: 11.8 km.
Altitude: 1691 metres.
Height gain: 988 metres.
Average gradient: 8.4%.
Maximum gradient: 13.5%.

WHAT TO EXPECT

➤ **Narrow road.** Not a problem going up, but be careful going down. The road is steep and other road users sometimes cut the corners. Don't be tempted to do the same.

➤ **Heat.** The climb is sheltered by high ground, which cuts down the cooling effect of the wind. The patches of forest do give some protection from the sun, but the climb can still be hot.

➤ **Keep something back.** The Joux-Plane is tough all the way to the top, don't give everything on the thirteen-percent stretch. Gear low, keeping something back for later.

➤ **Difficult bends.** No matter what the average gradient of each straight bit is, the road kicks up sharply coming out of each hairpin. It's only for a few metres, but the sharp gradient changes have a cumulative effect on your legs.

Col de Joux- Plane

D354

Samoens

They don't come much harder than the Joux-Plane. The first two kilometres do nothing but lull you into a false sense of security as you leave the town of Samoens. At the first hairpin the climb gets tough, and by the top you will feel brutalised by the savagery of its slopes. The compensation though is the view. The top of the Joux-Plane is an open, grassy place dominated by Mont Blanc – its image reflected eerily in a summit lake.

This climb is more difficult than Alpe d'Huez. The great Tour climber Lucien Van Impe rates it as one of the hardest he's seen, and you can't get a better recommendation than that. The road travels upwards by twisting and turning to seek out the natural lines of least resistance up it's fearsome slope, but cannot avoid a terrible stretch of over thirteen percent at just over six kilometres.

After that comes a short stretch of eight percent, but don't get carried away here because it's not time to celebrate. Save something for the final three kilometres of nine and ten percent to the top, the last two of which is dead straight and a little bit soul destroying.

The Joux-Plane is hard, but don't let that put you off. The climb flits in and out of a gorgeous scented pine forest, through which you will snatch tantalizing views of the white flanks of Mont Blanc. Joux is a Savoie-Jura dialect word meaning high forest. There is a Joux-Vert close to the Morzine-Avoriaz climb.

The summit is worth exploring if you have time. It's a bowl surrounded by gentle slopes that in winter forms a playground for cross-country skiers. There is a chalet and a restaurant there, and at it's western edge there is a short climb over the Col du Ranfloy. After that comes the descent of the Joux-Plane, which plummets down into Morzine at similar gradients to those you have just climbed. Take care.

WHICH WAY?

Samoens is about 40 kilometres east of Geneva along the D907. It's also 21 kilometres north-east of Cluses, which is on the A40 Geneva to St Gervais Autoroute. Take the N205, D902 and D907 to Samoens. Once in Samoens look for signs to the Col de Joux- Plane and Morzine and take the D354 for the climb to the top.

MOUNTAIN MOMENTS

➤ The Joux-Plane is relatively new to the Tour de France. It first appeared in the 1978 race when a stick-thin Breton called Christian Seznec was first up, on his way to a stage victory in Morzine. Seznec was alone at the head of the race for 200 kilometres that day and after it he was heralded as a big hope for French cycling. Despite winning another stage in 1979 Seznec didn't quite to live up to those high expectations. However, he still takes part in all-comers cyclo-sportif events in France.

➤ Marco Pantani and Lance Armstrong are much more famous than Seznec and both, in different ways, stand testament to how tough the Joux-Plane is. In 1997 super-climber Pantani dropped everyone and romped up the climb to win in Morzine, whereas in 2000 Armstrong had a rare moment of weakness when he was in difficulty on these steep slopes.

Above left: A rare easy bit   **Above right:** Descending the Joux-Plane

Col de la Madeleine 'THE SERPENT OF THE ALPS'

⭐⭐⭐⭐ **4 STARS**

Length: 19.3 km.

Altitude: 1993 metres.

Height gain: 1523 metres.

Average gradient: 7.9%.

Maximum gradient: 12.5%.

WHAT TO EXPECT

➤ **Broken rhythm.** Not only are there 40 of them, but every type of bend that Alpine road builders have ever used can be found on the Madeleine. What that means for a cyclist is that you can't get a rhythm going like you can on Alpe d'Huez for example, where most of the bends are the same.

➤ **Back to back climbs.** The Madeleine and Glandon start across the two Maurienne main roads from each other, the Autoroute and N6. Put together they make an extra challenging bike ride.

➤ **Group bonding.** The Madeleine is such an important link between the Maurienne and Tarentaise that at the end of July each year people from both valleys gather at the top to celebrate with a festival of dancing and traditional games.

This serpentine climb writhes and twists its way over the western shoulder of the Vanoise Massif, and like all serpents it bites. After the first two kilometres there is very little respite all the way to the top, making the Madeleine a real challenge for cyclists.

But it was a challenge for the road engineers who built it too. The road you ride on today represents 20 years of hard work that began in the 1940s to make the climb usable. This fact means that the Madeleine is a relative newcomer to the Tour de France and is not quite forty years old in Tour terms, even though it has already appeared in 22 editions of the race.

That says it all really. The Tour loves a tough challenge and the Madeleine is one of the toughest. Like many climbs it starts with a couple of easy kilometres, but the next seven climb at nine and ten per cent. After that there is 500 metres of five percent followed by 500 at 12.5 percent, the steepest pitch of the climb. Apart from a short descent at 14.5 kilometres the rest of the climb is eight per cent all the way to the top. A tough challenge indeed.

While you are climbing the Madeleine it might cross your mind as to why they built a road up here in the first place – but the route is an old one, and along with the Col de l'Iseran is still the only way over the Vanoise from the Maurienne to the Tarentaise valley. However, the result was also worth it just for the feat itself – one of those things that people do just because they can. The road builders used no less than forty bends of every type imaginable to take the road to the col.

The top of the col sits in an open valley between the Cheval Noir (2832 metres) on the right and the Lauzière chain with several peaks over 2500 metres on the left. The top is famed for its views over several mountain ranges

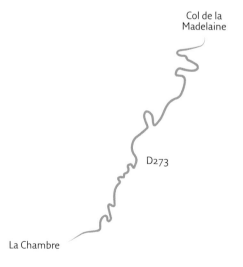

Col de la Madelaine

D273

La Chambre

➤ First Tour rider to the top of the Madeleine was a Spaniard, Andres Gandarias in 1969, and after that the race has visited the Madeleine almost every other year.

➤ The best climbers can change the rhythm they ride at more easily than other cyclists can, because of their light weight and the physical make up of their muscles – so the best have always excelled on the Madeleine. Lucien Van Impe was first up three times and Richard Virenque four. Van Impe and Virenque weren't competitors as their eras didn't overlap, but there is no love lost between them. One reason is that Van Impe says he stopped trying to win the King of the Mountains after six titles was because his boyhood hero, Frederico Bahamontes had won six. He really resented the fact that Virenque went on to win seven.

Left: Alpine excitement   **Above:** Descending Tour riders take a hairpin bend

and for a lush display of Alpine Gentian violets. The other side of the Madeleine isn't nearly as twisty, but it's still steep and the road is narrow, so it demands respect.

WHICH WAY?

The Madeleine starts in a village called La Chambre, which can be accessed from the A43 at junction 26. The village is right next to the N6 about 12 kilometres north-west of St Jean-de-Maurienne and 50 kilometres south of Albertville. The climb uses the D273 and is signposted in La Chambre.

Méribel 'QUEEN OF THE THREE VALLEYS'

☆☆☆☆ 4 STARS

Length: 21 km.

Altitude: 1775 metres.

Height gain: 1305 metres.

Average gradient: 6.2%.

Maximum gradient: 8.5%.

WHAT TO EXPECT

➤ **Headwinds:** Conditions are often still, but if it is windy then the wind tends to come down each of the three valleys from the tops of the mountains. This isn't all bad news as a nice breeze does help you keep cool in summer.

➤ **First-half shelter.** There are plenty of trees during the first part of the climb, but they disappear shortly before the main resort to leave you a little exposed.

➤ **Break it up.** Méribel resort has loads of cafes for a pit-stop on the way up or the way down.

➤ Low flying. Méribel has one of those mad, short-runway Alpine air fields. This one is at 1770 metres and it's use is restricted, although local pilots reckon that it's not a scary as the one at Courchevel.

Brides-les-Bains

D90

Méribel

The most attractive of the Three Valleys ski resort climbs, Méribel starts in St Brides le Bains, the same place as the Courchevel climb. But the road up to Méribel is much quieter than that to its sister resort.

It's well constructed too, with a nice series of lacets taking you up the first few kilometres. You then pass through the hamlet of Les Allues, which was the original settlement in this valley and takes its name from the Allues river that splashes and tumbles its boisterous way down.

The idea for creating a ski resort in the Allues valley came from a British ski enthusiast, Colonel Peter Lindsay, who began developing Méribel in 1938. His descendents still ski their today, and his and his wife's ashes were scattered on the mountains at the top of the valley.

From Les Allues the road twists and turns to take advantage of natural upward lines until the main Méribel resort, where the road flattens for a while. This specially created wooden village of apartment blocks, hotels and chalets is today becoming famous in the advertising world for its annual Ad Festival convention.

The end of the climb is at the highest of the ski resorts, Méribel-Mottaret, and it's a tough pull up to the summit, although you get fantastic views of the

Left: The Moutier road splits, one part goes to Corchevel and the other to Meribel **Above:** The resort of Meribel

Vanoise mountains as you climb. This part of the climb is in nice contrast to the bustle of the resorts. Nature is harder to tame up here and you really feel that you are at last up in the high mountains.

The top is surrounded by peaks of around the 3000-metre mark, which in the Northern Alps means there is always some snow at the very top. On the others side of these peaks there are several huge glaciers that hang in a threatening way above the Maurienne valley.

WHICH WAY?

Brides-les-Bains is on the D915 about five kilometres south-east of Moûtiers, which in turn is 26 kilometres south-east of Albertville on the N90. The road to Méribel is accessed by a slip road from the main D915. It's signposted Les Allues-Méribel and the road to the top is the D90. Climb to Méribel and continue on this main road to Méribel -Mottaret. After Méribel the road gets quite narrow but it's ok, there is only one way up and one way down.

MOUNTAIN MOMENTS

➤ Méribel has only been used once in the Tour, as a stage finish in 1973, but it is the winner that day who made Méribel famous in cycling. It was a Frenchman, Bernard Thevenet, the man who would end the reign of Eddy Merckx in the Tour de France in 1975. Thevenet was a super-strong farmer's son from Burgundy, who was a natural for the Tour de France. He turned professional in 1970 and immediately won a stage. He won another, on Mont Ventoux this time, in 1972 before taking second place overall in the 1973 tour. His Ventoux win was remarkable because a few days earlier he had crashed, banging his head so badly that he didn't know who or where he was. Only when he looked down and saw his racing clothes did things start to become clear and he asked a spectator, "Am I in the Tour de France?"

La Plagne   'THE PROFESSOR'S MOUNTAIN'

✪✪✪ 3 STARS

Length: 21.4 km.

Altitude: 2080 metres.

Height gain: 1419 metres.

Average gradient: 6.6%.

Maximum gradient: 10.4%.

WHAT TO EXPECT

➤ **Three tops.** you've actually got the choice of three ways of ending this climb. About one kilometre short of La Plagne resort you can turn left on the D224 to Belle-Plagne, or just as you enter the resort you can take another left to Plagne-Villages, or you can go to Aimé 2000. Why not try all three?

➤ **Mountains headquarters.** The starts of five Tour de France climbs are within a 20 kilometre radius of Aimé and La Plagne, making it a great base for mountain climbing operations.

➤ **Exploration.** They've never been used by the Tour, but there are a few very steep climbs on narrow and less travelled roads that start in Aimé and climb up the other side of the valley.

➤ **Speed demons.** The bobsleigh events of the 1992 Winter Olympics were held in La Plagne.

Aimé

D221

La Plagne

Another ski resort, this time sitting above the Tarentaise valley, La Plagne has plenty of Tour de France history having hosted four stage finishes and two starts. However, almost every time the stage has finished here it has done so at a higher altitude than the time before, reflecting the growth of the resort and the search for earlier snow.

The top of the climb is even higher now than when the last stage finished here in 2002. As the resort diversifies to add more summer and winter activities, the road builders could still add a bit more to the 1419 metres of climbing that faces you today.

Development started at La Plagne in 1961, based on the village of Mâcot-La Plagne that you encounter at the end of the first upward leg of the climb. The climb starts in Aimé, a pleasant place with some traditional restaurants and hotels. It's a good place to sample an Alpine delicacy, *raclette*, which is a kind of cheese stew. Be warned, it has such a formidable calorie count that you will need to have done some serious riding on the day you try it for dinner.

The first half of the climb uses a series of lacets to gain height. The overall gradient is fairly constant all the way up, but after 11 kilometres the road tips up at 10.4 percent for about 600 metres. There is a good covering of trees on this first part.

During the second half the road follows more natural lines with sweeping left- and right-hand bends taking you up to the main resort of La Plagne. Continue through the holiday village and two lacets take you to Aimé 2000 and the top of the climb.

Beyond the road the ski runs start from a circle of mountains that run from the Roc du Bécoin (2592 metres) in the west to the Sommet de Bellecôte (3416 metres) in the east. The snows of these mountains are the sources of the many streams that run down this side of the valley into the river Isère. Each one has carved the topography to provide an easier way up the steep valley side, which allowed the building of ski resorts on this side of the valley. The other side has less streams and is so steep that it's an almost impenetrable wall of rock, with very few, but very interesting, roads.

Above: La Plagne from the bottom of the Isere valley

WHICH WAY?

Aimé is by the side of the N90, with Bourg-St Maurice 13 kilometres to the east and Moutiers just a little further to the west. From the N90 follow signposts to La Plagne and the D221, which necessitates a slip road and passing under the N90. Follow the D221 to go through La Plagne to Aimé 2000 and the top of the climb.

MOUNTAIN MOMENTS

➤ Frenchman Laurent Fignon didn't fit the traditional image of a cycling champion. He came from Paris, he was an intellectual, wore glasses and tied his long blond hair back into a pony tail. He was nicknamed the Professor, but there was nothing sedate or reserved about the way Fignon raced. He won the Tour de France in 1983 and 1984, when he also won five stages including one to La Plagne. Fignon won again at La Plagne in 1987 after a knee injury had left him with two relatively barren years. He looked certain of another Tour victory in 1989. The final time trial into Fignon's home city celebrated 200 years since the storming of the Bastille, but it was Fignon who was stormed by an American, Greg Lemond, who ran out the winner of the Tour that year by the narrowest margin ever, eight seconds.

Col de la Ramaz 'THE NEW ARRIVAL'

✪✪✪ 3 STARS

Length: 14 km.
Altitude: 1610 metres.
Height gain: 960 metres.
Average gradient: 6.9%
Maximum gradient: 10.2%

WHAT TO EXPECT

➤ **Good access.** The snow doesn't cut off lower climbs like the Ramaz as quickly as it does the high-altitude passes.

➤ **Other cyclists.** Being close to some sizeable centres of population, the Ramaz is a popular destination for local riders.

➤ **Time trials.** Like they do on many other Tour de France climbs, the local bike organisations give you a chance to tackle the Ramaz in anger and set a time for climbing it in the annual Grimpée de la Ramaz. Look on www.ffc.rhonealpes.com and click on *calendrier* for more details.

➤ **Climbing neighbours.** The starts of Morzine-Avoriaz and the Col de Joux Plane are about ten kilometres away from the descent of the Ramaz in Morzine. Turn left after descending onto the D902 and follow signs to Morzine. Both climbs start in the town centre.

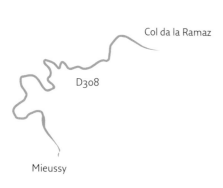

A new climb, but still an Alpine classic – the Col de la Ramaz has many of the features that have made other climbs the mainstays of the Tour de France. The road up the Ramaz is tough and sinuous with serious gradients and hardly any opportunity to ease off.

The climb starts in the pretty village of Mieussy, which is one of the birthplaces of paragliding in France. The first six kilometres rise at less than seven percent, but after that the climb bites hard, with a four-kilometre pitch of between nine and ten percent. The steepest bits are on a long straight at eight kilometres, and on another long one a little bit further up the road after a series of lacets and two rock arches.

If you get a clear day to climb the Ramaz, you can enjoy watching the paragliders swoop over you at this point, as even the beginners make their 1000-metre downward flight to a field near Mieussy. The more experienced flyers go up before they come down, and it isn't unusual to see some circling on thermal air currents thousands of metres above the mountain peaks.

The character of the climb changes as the terrain levels at ten kilometres. Now the road follows the easier contours of the hillside, giving you an opportunity to catch your breath before the last kilometre of 7.2 percent.

Left: The church in Mieussy   **Above:** Paragliding on the Ramaz

At the top of the col you are among the ski runs of the Le Pra-de-Lys resort. There is a nice example of a high-altitude tarn in the form of the Lac de Roy up here, sitting in a big basin surrounded by 2000-metre peaks.

The descent passes through Le Pra-de-Lys before a series of technical hairpin bends that are fun to ride through. Be careful of the straight going into the last hairpin though, it slopes down at eleven percent and you could arrive into the hairpin going faster than you'd like. Remember to do your breaking in the straights, not in the bends.

WHICH WAY?

Mieussy is on the D907, 20 kilometres east of Geneva and ten kilometres north-west of Cluses on the D902 and D907. The Col de la Ramaz is clearly signposted on the D907 roundabout at the edge of the village. The road to the top of the Col de la Ramaz is the D308.

MOUNTAIN MOMENTS

➤ The first Tour de France rider to climb the Ramaz was Richard Virenque in 2003. He won the stage that day, repeating Eddy Merckx's feat of 1971 by taking the yellow and the King of the Mountains jersey at the same time. Virenque's performance sealed his rehabilitation in the French public's eyes. He had been the darling of French cycling fans, especially female ones, but then was deeply involved in the 1998 Festina team drugs scandal. Virenque compounded his guilt by denying his involvement until his position was untenable. He came back to the sport saying that he was a changed man and slowly put together a number of brilliant performances, presumably clean ones this time. Whatever, the French forgave him. Virenque was a hero again.

Le Mont Revard 'START OF THE ALPS'

⭐⭐⭐ 3 STARS

Length: 21.3 km.
Altitude: 1537 metres.
Height gain: 1295 metres.
Average gradient: 6.1%.
Maximum gradient: 8.3%.

WHAT TO EXPECT

➤ **Geological features.** Rainfall has eroded the limestone of Mont Revard into weird and wonderful shapes in many places.

➤ **Mountain bikes.** Mont Revard is a great place for downhill and cross-country mountain biking, with numerous runs and tracks set aside specifically for off-road bikes.

➤ **Warm weather.** Aix-les-Bains is blessed with a Mediteranean micro-climate, which can mean that Mont Revard gets very hot in the summer. If it does, take the exposed parts steadily and remember that nearly all of the second half of the ride is through thick pine forest, so there will be shade coming up.

➤ **Round trip.** Continue after the summit and descend on the D913 towards Chambery, but turn right just before you get there to St Alban-Leysse. Go straight through the village and head for Sonnaz for a back roads route to Aix-les-Bains.

Aix-les-Bains sits on the shores of Lake Bourget in a gap between the Jura to the north and Chartreuse to the south, the two mountain ranges that act as stepping stones to the high Alps. West of the town are a few foothills, outliers of the two guardian ranges. East of it is Mont Revard, part of the Bauges Massif, and east of that the really big stuff starts.

Mont Revard is a perfect introduction to the big climbs. It is long and although it only rises to just above 1500 metres, it starts in the streets of Aix-les-Bains at 243 metres so gains as much height as many an Alpine giant does.

Aix-le-Bains is a great place to visit. Even though it is a gateway to the Alps its low altitude and southerly position means that it has a warm climate. The lake never freezes for example, and in summer the water temperature regularly reaches 25 degrees, despite the fact that it is 145 metres deep in places.

The climb starts near to the railway station and the first part, still in the town's streets, rises at a very gentle three percent. After three kilometres the gradient starts to bite and for the next 16 it fluctuates steadily between seven and eight percent.

You are compensated for your hard work with wonderful views across the lake, especially after the road abruptly changes direction at Trévignan.

D913

Aix-les-Bains   Le Revard

Left: Racing in the Northern Alps   **Above:** Enjoying it   **Below:** Desirable residences

MOUNTAIN MOMENTS

➤ Mont Revard was first used in 1965 when it was a time-trial stage. The winner was a relatively unknown 23-year-old Italian called Felice Gimondi. Gimondi had won the amateur Tour de France the previous year, but was only picked by his professional team for the big race a few days before it started. Gimondi won the Tour de France in 1965 and a great many other races in the coming years, but he had the misfortune for his career to run concurrently with that of the greatest cyclist ever, Eddy Merckx. Many pundits say that if it hadn't been for Merckx, Gimondi would have been the greatest bike rider ever. Gimondi still won many cycling classics, a world title and the Tours of Italy and Spain, and on several occasions he managed to get the better of a Merckx on top form to do it.

After ten kilometres though you lose the view as you enter the Corset forest for the next five kilometres.

The road twists and turns through the forest until it breaks clear at a gap called the Col de la Cluse before entering the forest again for the push to the top. The slope relents a bit before you get there, progressively easing until the summit and the chalets of Le Revard.

The view form the top is amazing. You can see Aix-les-Bains, and the lake and the Jura, Chartreuse and Belledonne ranges are all easy to pick out. If you are lucky and get a clear day you can even see Mont Blanc.

WHICH WAY

Aix-les-Bains is only 14 kilometres north of Chambery on the N201. You can also reach the town by taking junctions 13 or 14 off the A41 Autoroute. Follow the N201 to the centre of Aix-les-Bains looking for signs to Mont Revard or Le Revard and take the D913 nearly to the top and turn right to Le Revard.

Le Cormet de Roselend

'ROCKING UP THE LAKE'

⭐⭐⭐ 3 STARS

Length: 22.5 km.
Altitude: 1697 metres.
Height gain: 1154 metres.
Average gradient: 5.1%.
Maximum gradient: 9%.

WHAT TO EXPECT

➤ **Company.** The Northern Alps aren't as well frequented as the central Alps, but the Cormet de Roselend a gem. It is in the middle of a number of equally beautiful and famous Tour de France mountains, so there will probably be other riders climbing at the same time as you. The climb is also quite popular with motorcyclists, although motor-powered and muscle-powered two-wheelers mix very well.

➤ **Snow.** The Cormet de Roselend is in an area of the Alps that has quite high rainfall, much of which falls as snow, and it's not uncommon to get a little bit of fresh snow up here even in mid-summer. The road usually stays clear, in summer at least.

At the risk of pushing the mountains and cheese connection too far this is another climb that starts in the heart of an area renowned for one of France's most famous products. Gruyère from the Beaufort area has been christened the prince of gruyères, mostly by the locals it has to be said, but they do take it very seriously and it is well worth sampling a piece or two of 'creamy delight'. Their words, not mine.

Don't eat too much cheese though, because the Roselend is a very demanding but spectacularly beautiful climb. The first part is straight, but then come some serious lacets that take you to the Lac de Roselend, a huge turquoise stretch of water that is surrounded by the curiously curved and overhanging rock formations that line the top part of the climb.

You descend for 1500 metres to the lakeside, where a chapel has been rescued from the valley floor before it was flooded when the lake was constructed. This is a pleasant interlude and gives you chance to look at the lake and, if they are in flower, the wild rhododendrons that grow beside it.

Soon though the flat part is over and the road rears up again for the final six kilometres of climbing. This is the most spectacular part of the climb as you steadily rise above the lake with the pale rocks overhanging you.

As you round the Roc de Biolley you leave the lake behind and the scenery becomes increasingly rugged until the summit is reached. The descent to Bourg St Maurice requires great care as the first part is quite steep and twisty. In 1996 a Belgian called Johan Bruyneel, who was a Tour stage winner but who is more famous now as the team manager behind Lance Armstrong's seven Tour wins, crashed over the edge of this road and fell many metres down the mountain side. Look for writing in Flemish on the road that says 'Johan was hier'.

WHICH WAY?

Beaufort is 20 kilometres north east of Albertville on the D925. Continue straight through Beaufort on this road to climb the Cormet de Roselend. Over the summit the D925 becomes the D902.

Beaufort

D902

Cormet
de Roselend

MOUNTAIN MOMENTS

➤ The Cormet de Roselend was first used in the 1979 Tour de France when Henk Lubberding of the legendary TI Raleigh team was first to the top. The Raleigh team was one of the best pro cycling has ever seen. It was backed by British money, although mostly Dutch cyclists provided the leg power, and their aim was to make Raleigh bikes a household name in Europe. They achieved that goal by winning the biggest races in the world, including the Tour de France in 1980 with Joop Zoetemelk, and Raleigh bikes had unprecedented sales in the European heartland of bike racing. Throughout all their reign Lubberding was one of TI Raleigh's best team workers. A talented rider, who could win in his own right, Lubberding seemed to take more pleasure from the success of others.

Above: The Lac de Roselend   **Above right:** Johan Bruyneel crashed here.

Col des Saisies 'ON THE SHOULDER OF MONT BLANC'

✪✪✪ 3 STARS

Length: 15 km.
Altitude: 1107 metres.
Height gain: 1957 metres.
Average gradient: 7.4%.
Maximum gradient: 11%.

WHAT TO EXPECT

➤ **A popular place.** Beaufort is a cycling Mecca with two Tour climbs, the Saisies and Cormet de Roseland, starting there, so there can be a lot of cyclists about. There are also several other challenging climbs in the area that haven't been used by the Tour yet. The best is one that climbs the south side of the Bisanne mountain, and joins the Saisies almost at its top. This is a peach of a climb, somewhat undiscovered and on a narrow road. The start is at Villard-sur-Doron, just one-and-half kilometres west along the D925 from the start of the Saisies.

➤ **Daring descent.** Going down either side of the Saisies is a breathtaking experience with some really testing bends and incredible views over the surrounding mountains, including the whole of the Aravis chain on the north descent. Take care and concentrate on the road. Stop if you want to look at the view.

The Col de Saisies is quite a popular climb in the Tour de France. The race has been there nine times since 1979, but with no preference for a particular side. The Saisies is like a bridge to be crossed one way if the stage is going north, and the opposite way if it is going south. I've chosen the south side, simply because it is the steepest, but both sides have played their part in Tour de France history and of course there's nothing stopping you doing both if you've got time.

The climb starts at the junction of the D925 and D218, the latter road being the one that climbs the col – and it's definitely a climb of two halves. The first uses a set of regular lacets to climb at between seven and eight percent for eight kilometres to a short descent. This part of the climb is steep but it is very regular so you can get a good rhythm going.

The surroundings you ride through are pleasant too. Plenty of trees of all descriptions, and a number of noisy waterfalls crash down from the edge of the Mont Blanc Massif, over which the pass climbs.

The descent lasts for less than one kilometre before the road heads upwards again, but this time it does so in a wide left-hand sweep towards the gap that is the top of the climb. Gradients here are between seven and eight percent again, with one short steeper stretch of eleven percent five kilometres from the top.

Col de Saisies

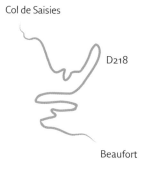

D218

Beaufort

Left: The Route des Grands Alpes uses the Col des Saisies   **Above:** These slopes are ski runs in winter

The Col des Saisies is on the Routes des Grandes Alpes, a tourist itinerary that starts in Geneva and goes down to the French Riviera. As you explore the French Alps you will become familiar with its signposts, because many of the most famous Tour de France climbs, such as the Galibier and Iseran, are included along this more or less north-to-south route.

WHICH WAY?

The nearest place to the start of the Col des Saisies is Beaufort, which is on the D925, 20 kilometres east of Albertville. The road up the climb is the D218 and it's a right turn if you are coming from Albertville and right from Beaufort.

MOUNTAIN MOMENTS

➤ The Col de Saisies first appeared in the 1979 Tour when Henk Lubberding was first.
➤ Best on the Saisies in 1984 was Pedro Delgado, the man who heralded a golden era for Spanish cycling. In 1959 Frederico Bahamontes became the first Spaniard to win the Tour de France. Luis Ocana was next in 1973. Delgado won in 1988, but in 1991 Miguel Indurain began his run of five consecutive victories in the race, the first man ever to do that. Indurain was in the same team as Delgado and learned his trade helping him.
➤ Mario Aerts from Belgium was first over the Saisies in 2002. A team workhorse, Aerts gets through a lot of racing kilometres in a year, but never more than in 2007 when he completed all three major Tours; Italy, France and Spain.

Le Bettex

Length: 9 km.

Altitude: 1400 metres.

Height gain: 500 metres.

Average gradient: 5.5%.

Maximum gradient: 10%.

A short climb right under the nose of Mont Blanc. It's not long or too difficult but you can't help but get a feeling of big mountains in this area, the highest peak in Europe towers over you. Le Bettex has only been used once, for a stage finish in 1990 when Thierry Claveyrolat won.

WHICH WAY? The climb starts on the D909 about two kilometres to the west of St Gervais-les-Bains, which is ten kilometres east of Sallanches and seventeen west of Chamonix. Follow signs in St Gervais for Megève. Turn left onto the D43 to start the climb and follow that road to the top.

Col du Corbier

Length: 6 km.

Altitude: 1237 metres.

Height gain: 517 metres.

Average gradient: 8.6%.

Maximum gradient: 11.1%.

About as far north as you can go in the Northern Alps without getting wet in Lake Leman, this col is quite steep, so it's lucky that it's not long as well. It was first used in 1974 when a Belgian school teacher turned pro rider, Paul Wellens was the first to climb it on his way to winning a stage in Morzine. It's a nice twisty, turny climb and you get a good view of the lake from the top of it.

WHICH WAY? The climb starts in the village of Seytroux, about halfway along the D902 Thonon-les-Bains to Cluses road. The climb is signposted in the village. Head for Le Biot on the D332, then fork right on the D32 for the top of the climb.

Sallanches-Cordon

Length: 4 km.

Altitude: 957 metres.

Height gain: 442 metres.

Average gradient: 11%.

Maximum gradient: 15%.

Very often the shortest climbs are the steepest. This little brute has only been used once by the Tour, for a stage finish in 1968 when a British rider, Barry Hoban won. It was Hoban's only mountain stage among the eight he won in the Tour. He was better known as a sprinter, but not withstanding that he was still sixth in the 1968 King of the Mountains competition.

WHICH WAY? Sallanches sits directly under the majestic Mont Blanc and can be accessed from the A40 Autoroute Blanche by junction 20. The N205 passes straight through the town . The climb to Cordon is on the southern edge of Sallanches and starts where the N212 splits off from the N205. The road to Cordon is the D113.

Col de la Croix Fry

Length: 12.8 km.

Altitude: 1467 metres.

Height gain: 842 metres.

Average gradient: 6.6%.

Maximum gradient: 9.3%.

The Croix Fry must have been created long ago as some secret back way between Thônes and La Clusaz, probably by the farmers who were keeping milk back from their landlords for Reblochon cheese. It's much easier to get between the two places using the D909 main road, but the Croix Fry is there so the Tour used it in 1997. Laurent Jalabert took the maximum points at the summit. Jalabert retired from bike racing in 2002, but has recently taken up triathlon and finished 22nd in the 2007 Swiss Ironman race.

WHICH WAY? Thônes is 21 kilometres east of Annecy along the D909. Turn right off the main road onto the D12 for Thônes and continue through the village. Fork left after one kilometre on the D16 and follow that road to the top of the Croix Fry. From there you can either descend to La Clusaz or a right split in the road will take you to three quarters of the way up the Aravis.

Col de la Forclaz de Montmin

Length: 10.2 km.

Altitude: 1303 metres.

Height gain: 702 metres.

Average gradient: 6.2%.

Maximum gradient: 12%.

First climbed in the Tour by Swiss rider Rolf Graf in 1959, this climb has been visited two further times, the most recent in 2002 when Richard Virenque triumphed. It's a real gem that runs almost parallel to Annecy lake in the western foothills of the Chaine des Aravis. The climb has a bit of everything the Alps have to offer; nice hairpin bends, short tunnels but no snowy peaks in the summer. You have to look from the top to the Aravis and beyond for those.

WHICH WAY? The climb starts in Menthon-St Bernard, five kilometres south along the D909 from Annecy. Turn right off the D909 onto the D909A for the village and follow this road through it. Turn left after 2 kilometres onto the D42 and follow this road to the top of the climb.

Col de l'Epine

Length: 8 km.

Altitude: 987 metres.

Height gain: 552 metres.

Average gradient: 6.9%.

Maximum gradient: 10%.

This is a short climb up to a gap between the Mont du Chat and Montagne de l'Epine, which stand guard on the western approach to Chambéry. The climb has been used by the Tour de France three times and the riders have climbed it from both sides.

The Chambéry side is a bit busy so I've chosen the west side, which starts in a village called Novalaise. The road is quite narrow and very twisty. It's also quite steep with three stretches of ten percent on the natural bends of the first half of the climb. Towards the top some carefully constructed lacets make upward progress a little easier. You get a great view from the top over Chambéry and of the Alps behind the town.

The first Tour rider to climb the Col de l'Epine was 'Apo' Lazarides in 1947. First to the top in 1965 was a 22-year-old Italian called Gianni Motta. He turned pro the previous year and started winning straightaway. He finished third overall in the 1965 Tour de France and won the Tour of Italy in 1966, but was never the same after it. Motta just seemed to burn out. He raced on until 1971 and he is a bike manufacturer today.

WHICH WAY? Novalaise is four kilometres north-west of junction 12 of the A43 Autoroute on the D921. Turn right in the village onto the D916 and continue to the top of the climb.

Montée de Hauteville

Length: 30.6 km.

Altitude: 2469 metres.

Height gain: 1752 metres.

Average gradient: 5.7%.

Maximum gradient: 9.7%.

Col du Grand St Bernard.

Length: 15.3 km.

Altitude: 1639 metres.

Height gain: 799 metres.

Average gradient: 5.1%.

Maximum gradient: 8.1%.

Col de la Joux Vert

Length: 15.2 km.

Altitude: 1760 metres.

Height gain: 876 metres.

Average gradient: 5.8%.

Maximum gradient: 8.9%.

One of the most famous passes in Alpine transport history, the Grand St Bernard has been visited four times by the Tour de France, the first in 1949 when Gino Bartali was the best. The last time it was used though was in 1966, because the Grand St Bernard has become too important to road traffic to close it. It is a part of Tour de France history, as it's roll call of winners testifies. But because of the heavy traffic on it nowadays, the best way to sample it is by just doing the top part, the stretch that comes after Bourg St Bernard and the entry to the Tunnel du Grand St Bernard. Both sides have been climbed by the Tour

WHICH WAY? The north side of the full climbs starts in Sembrancher in Switzerland which is 10 kilometres south-east of Martigny along the E27. Martigny is at the foot of the Col de La Forclaz on the Swiss side. Follow the E27 to Bourg-St-Bernard, where the new road goes through the tunnel and the old one goes over the col. It's a wild, desolate place and the road is usually only open from June to September. The Italian side starts in Aosta and is 32 kilometres long.

A brand new climb in the 2007 Tour de France, when Denmark's Michael Rasmussen was first to the top, the Montée de Hauteville is actually just a crafty way of using the first part of the very long Petit St Bernard pass. It climbs the main N90 route from France into Italy up a series of brilliantly engineered lacets, but then turns off to descend on a minor road to St Foy-Tarentaise to begin the climb up to Tignes. It's very worthwhile though because the lacets up to La Rosière 1850 are the best part of the climb.

WHICH WAY? From Bourg-St Maurice follow directions for the N90, Col du Petit St Bernard, Italy and Aosta. The climb begins at the junction of the N90 with the D902. Follow the N90 until a right turn for the D84, which signifies the end of the climb. The Tour route descends the D84 to St Foy-Tarentaise.

The Joux Vert starts one kilometre from Morzine and ends just short of the top of the Morzine-Avoriaz climb. It was first used in 1981 when the winner was Robert Alban, a French rider with incredibly long legs and a hooked nose. The climb is on a narrow road that passes an attractive lake at the halfway point, and goes through a short tunnel. A nice companion climb to Morzine-Avoriaz.

WHICH WAY? The climb starts in the village of Montriond, one kilometre north-west of Morzine on the D228. Turn right in Montriond and follow the D228 to the top of the climb.

Col de la Marocaz

Length: 9.3 km.

Altitude: 960 metres.

Height gain: 648 metres.

Average gradient: 7.0%.

Maximum gradient: 10%.

This climb over the southern tip of the Bauges massif has only been used once by the Tour de France, but it's difficult to see why they haven't been back. It's a real little toughie that would provide great racing as it's near to towns like Chambéry and Aix-les-Bains, where Tour stages have finished in the past.

There are three stretches of ten percent climbing along its winding route, and French climber Jean Dotto was able to use them to leave the others behind when he romped over this climb in 1954 on his way to winning stage 19 from Briançon to Aix-les-Bains.

WHICH WAY? Start in Arbin, which is just off the N6, 18 kilometres south-east of Chambéry. Head north-east on the D201 and turn left at Cruet onto the D11. Follow this road to the top of the climb.

Les Menuires

Length: 26 km.

Altitude: 1810 metres.

Height gain: 1331 metres.

Average gradient: 5.1%.

Maximum gradient: 8.3%.

This is two climbs in one. Les Menuires is a village on the way to the third of the Three Valleys ski resorts, Val Thorens. Les Menuires was first used as a Tour stage finish in 1979 when Lucien Van Impe won, and Val Thorens made it into the Tour in 1994 when the Colombian Nelson Rodriguez triumphed. The extra bit to Val Thorens adds six kilometres distance and 465 metres in height to the climb. At 2275 metres Val Thorens is the second-highest stage finish in Tour de France history.

WHICH WAY? Both climbs start in Moutiers, which is 26 kilometres south east of Albertville. Les Menuires and Val Thorens are clearly signposted in Moutiers. The road to both is the D117. Once you get to Les Menuires carry straight on up the same road for Val Thorens.

Pas-de-Morgins

Length: 14 km.

Altitude: 1369 metres.

Height gain: 459 metres.

Average gradient: 3.3%.

Maximum gradient: 7.9%.

This climb is another that the Tour has used to get between France and Switzerland. Belgian Paul Wellens was the first Tour rider to climb it in 1977. The climb has been used twice since. It isn't a very difficult climb from the French side, although it is a little more challenging from the Swiss. Colombian double King of the Mountains 'Lucho' Herrera is the most famous rider to have lead over this climb.

WHICH WAY? The French side of the climb starts in Abondance, which is 31 kilometres south east of Thonon-les-Bains along the D902 and D22. Carry straight on the D22 in Abondance to the top of the climb. The Swiss side starts in Monthey, follow signs to Champéry, and turn right to Morgins after four kilometres.

Mont du Chat

Length: 8.7 km.

Altitude: 1504 metres.

Height gain: 905 metres.

Average gradient: 10.4%.

Maximum gradient: 11%.

This climb has only been used once by the Tour de France, in 1970 when Gonzalo Aja from Spain was first to the top, but some French cycling enthusiasts think that the Mont du Chat is the hardest climb in the whole of the country, and they've got a point.

The Mont-du-Chat is an unrelenting slog to the top of a mountain that stands across the southern end of the Bourget Lake, to the east of Aix-les-Bains. Its average and maximum gradients are so close together that they should tell you something about how hard it is. There isn't one metre of respite up the sweeping hairpins of a road that seams to have been constructed with the sole purpose of climbing to the summit of the mountain.

The climb starts in Le-Bourget-du-Lac, quite close to Chambéry airport, and after 500 metres or so of three-percent climbing the road rears up and doesn't let go until the top. But when you get there you can bask in the knowledge that you have just conquered eight kilometres of the most intense climbing in France.

WHICH WAY? Le Bourget is six kilometres north of Chambéry on the N504. From the centre of Le Bourget find the D42, which heads west from the town centre, and follow that road to the top of the climb. If you turn left after the descent onto the D42a you will arrive at the foot of the Côte de l'Epine and can climb that before descending to Chambéry.

Col des Mosses

Length: 18.8 km.

Altitude: 1445 metres.

Height gain: 1028 metres.

Average gradient: 5.5%.

Maximum gradient: 7.5%.

Totally in Switzerland and used on two occasions when stages have finished in Lausanne, the Col des Mosses starts in Aigle where the governing body of cycle racing, the UCI, have their World Cycling Centre. This is a huge, modern complex consisting of an indoor race track, sports halls, conference facilities and exhibitions. It wasn't there when Jean Robic was the first Tour rider to the top of the col in 1949, but it was when Italian Massimiliano Lelli shot by in the 2000 Tour. The Mosses is quite a long climb that starts in a picturesque gorge.

WHICH WAY? Aigle is just off the A9/E27 Autoroute that runs from Geneva on the north side of Lake Léman. Once in town you access the climb by following directions for Château-d'Oex. The Swiss road number is 11.

Col du Petit St-Bernard

Length: 30 km.

Altitude: 2188 metres.

Height gain: 1282 metres.

Average gradient: 4.6%.

Maximum gradient: 8.2%.

A classic climb but also an important transport route so there is usually plenty of other traffic on it. The first part, which is also the new Tour climb of Montée de Hauteville, climbs up an amazing set of lacets. At La Rosiere 1850 the lacets end and the road heads straight for the summit.

This is an amazing wild place, but one that has long been familiar to man. There is an enormous Iron Age stone circle measuring 72 metres in diameter through which the road passes straight. St Bernard dogs are named after the St Bernard passes, the dogs size is said to have evolved from the strength needed to get them through the deep snow that falls here.

WHICH WAY? The climb starts three kilometres north east of Bourg-St-Maurice at the junction of the N90 and D902. Stay on the N90 following signs to the pass, Italy and Aosta.

Col de Plainpalais

Length: 16.5 km.

Altitude: 1173 metres.

Height gain: 903 metres.

Average gradient: 5.6%.

Maximum gradient: 10.4%.

This climb sits right next to and a little below Mont Revard on the Bauges Massif. It has been climbed from both sides in Tour history, the first time by Frenchman Jean Dotto in 1954. The climb from Chambery is the most interesting and scenic, because you get great views over the Bourget Lake and Chambery and Aix-les-Bains as you climb.

The climb is actually part of the descent of Mont Revard, you only turn off that road for a few hundred metres before you reach the top of the Plainpalais. The two mountains make a great challenge by starting in Chambery, climbing the Plainpalais and descending to Lescheraines, then using the D911 to Aix-les-Bains and an assault on Mont Revard.

WHICH WAY? Chambery is 43 kilometres north of Grenoble on the A41 Autoroute or the N90/N6, and 15 kilometres south of Aix-les-Bains on the N201 or D991. From the le Villaret suburb of Chambery take the D912 to the village of Plainpalais and continue through the village on the D912 past the junction with the D913 to the top of the col.

Mont Salève

Length: 15.3 km.
Altitude: 1307 metres.
Height gain: 877 metres.
Average gradient: 5.7%.
Maximum gradient: 17.7%.

Le Semnoz.

Length: 18.5 km.
Altitude: 1699 metres.
Height gain: 1281 metres.
Average gradient: 6.9%.
Maximum gradient: 10%.

This climb has an incredibly tough one kilometre stretch of 17.7 percent gradient in the middle of it. It's a very popular climb with cyclists because of it's proximity to Geneva, and there are four different ways to the top. Of course I've chosen the one with the steep bit in it for you, not out of sadism but for the fact that it starts in Annemasse, which is part of the Geneva conurbation and the climb is very easy to find from there.

Mont Salève was first used in the 1973 Tour, when the overall winner that year, Luis Ocaña was the best man on the climb. The mountain is popular with tourists visiting Geneva and a cable car runs from just over the French border, which rings the southern edge of the city, to the top.

WHICH WAY? Annemasse is virtually joined to the eastern edge of Geneva, but is on the French side of the border. Follow the D906A south out of town to the village of Mornex, where the climb is signposted. The road to the top is the D41A. The other three ways up the Salève start in Cruseilles, Collonges sous Salève and La Muraz.

At the north end of the Bauges Massif, the Montagne du Semnoz stands guard over the southern approaches to Annecy. Locally this climb is sometimes called the Col du Crêt de Châtillon and it's a classic that would merit a page on its own except for its strange Tour de France history. It was included for the first time in the 1998 Tour, but that stage was annulled.

The race must come back soon though because the road follows a beautiful natural line up the spine of the mountain. The descent to Leschaux is a cracker too. After it you can go down the Col de Leschaux, which has never been listed in the Tour, for a round trip back to Annecy.

WHICH WAY? The climb starts at the southern edge of Annecy, which is 34 kilometres south of Geneva on the N201. Look for signs for the D41 to Crêt de Châtillon and follow that road to the top. The descent follows the same road to Leschaux, turn left onto the D912 for the round trip back to Annecy.

Tignes

Length: 18 km.

Altitude: 2068 metres.

Height gain: 1142 metres.

Average gradient: 6%.

Maximum gradient: 10%.

New to the Tour in 2007, when the Tignes ski resort was a stage finish and Michael Rasmussen won, the climb to Tignes starts at Sainte-Foy-Tarentaise, right where the Montée de Hauteville descent ends. The steepest part of this climb come soon after the start.

You follow the D902 in the direction of Val-d'Isère, climbing what some regard as the first part of the Col d'Iseran. The route then turns off to Tignes before the awful Iseran tunnels. You cross the dam wall of the huge Lake Chevril, then climb up to the resort, passing under some rock arches. The finish is right next to the end of a lake, which will be on your left.

WHICH WAY? Sainte-Foy-Tarentaise is 12 kilometres south east of Bourg-St-Maurice on the D902. Stay on this road until you see the huge sign indicating where Tignes is. Turn right onto the D87A and cross the dam wall and continue on this road for another six kilometres to the top of the climb.

Central Alps

This is where the big names are. The central Alps are stuffed with some of the most iconic climbs in cycling, and consequently the place buzzes with bike riders determined to emulate the pass-storming epics they read about in magazines or see on the TV. The Galibier, Alpe d'Huez, the Croix de Fer and many more, whose names ring with tales of triumph and defeat, are all here in the Central Alps.

Some of the most spectacular mountain scenery in France is also to be found in the Central Alps. Snow packed peaks tower above you, glaciers frown on the deep valleys they carved out millions of years ago, and craggy outcrops of bare rock thrust skywards. Riding a bike in the Central Alps is a visual feast.

The Central Alps stretch south from the climbs of the Maurienne valley, to Briançon in the south-east and Gap in the south-west. I've also included the climbs of the Chartreuse, Belledonne and Vercours in the Central Alps. These ranges surround the city of Grenoble, which is a great base for exploring them indeed for the whole of the western part of the Central Alps.

Briançon is a good place to stay for discovering the western part of this area, as is Bourg d'Oisan for the Romanche valley climbs like Alpe d'Huez. St-Jean-de-Maurienne makes a good base for the Maurienne valley climbs, which include the most often used side of the Col du Galibier.

Alpe d'Huez *'THE DUTCH MOUNTAIN'*

★★★★★ **5 STARS**

Length: 14.5 km.

Altitude: 1850 metres.

Height gain: 1150 metres.

Average gradient: 8%.

Maximum gradient: 13%.

WHAT TO EXPECT

➤ **Seasonal weather.** The climb usually is passable from March until November, but spring and autumn can be wet. Early summer is best, as mid-summer can be scalding hot.

➤ **Record attempts.** Someone is always doing something on the Alpe, from seeing how fast they can get up it to seeing how many time they can climb it in a day. If you want to record an official time there is a time trial that anyone can do every Monday evening during the summer. The tourist office in Bourg d'Oisans will give you details.

➤ **Dutch courage.** If you want cheering all the way to the top, take advantage of the Dutch party that starts three days before the Tour stage.

➤ **Coming down.** With the same road being used by cyclists going up and down, take care not to cut the bends whichever direction you are going.

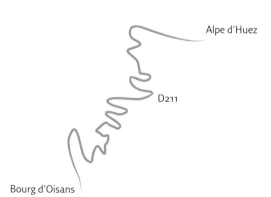

Alpe d'Huez

D211

Bourg d'Oisans

Perhaps the most glamorous mountain of the Tour de France, Alpe d'Huez is a ski station that sits on the lip of a bowl of jagged peaks, and the only reason the road goes up there is to get to it. There is another way down but it's not obvious, so the Alpe is always a stage finish, and a crucial stage finish right in the heart of the Alps. That is why the Alpe d'Huez stage is famous – because it is always won by a Tour contender or a great climber. No one flukes the Alpe.

The winners have given Alpe d'Huez its glamour, and on every one of the 21 hairpin bends that zig-zag up to the top, a winner's name is commemorated along with the year of his victory on a specially erected sign. Look for them and count them off; each is numbered, from number 21 at the bottom on the first bend, to number one on the last bend, close to the top.

The bends provide a regularity that you can use to your advantage, you always know how far you have to go and because of that it is easier to ration your effort evenly along the entire route. Taking in the ever growing views across the deep Romanche valley helps dull the pain in your legs too.

Left page: The village of Alpe d'Huez

Above left: Descending Alpe d'Huez   **Above right:** Memorial to a cyclist who is part of the Alpe d'Huez story

Another thing that helps is the knowledge that the first part of the climb is the steepest, from bend 21 until just after bend 17, and it includes a section at thirteen percent. After that, the worst is over as the gradient lessens, except for one or two short steeper stretches. The distance between bends gradually shortens too, until near the top where the last two bends are quite far apart, but by then the gradient has eased off still further.

The name Dutch mountain comes both from the number of riders from the Netherlands who have won on the Alpe, and from the consequent number of fans who travel from Holland each year in their camper vans to set up a big party beside the road, sometimes many days before the race is due. At one time Alpe d'Huez even had a Dutch parish priest.

WHICH WAY?

From Bourg d'Oisans town centre follow the main N91 east towards Briançon, then take the D211 signposted Alpe d'Huez, which will be on your left. The climb starts about 500 metres along this road. The finish is almost all the way through the ski station. There are plenty of cafes at the top.

 **MOUNTAIN MOMENTS**

➤ First appeared in the Tour de France in 1952, when Italian Tour winner Fautso Coppi was first to the top.
➤ George Rajon, a local hotel owner brought the Tour to the Alpe, but it was 20 years before he persuaded the race to return. By then Rajon's village was a big commercial success, and the Tour has hardly missed a year since.
➤ The record for the climb is 37 minutes 35 seconds, set by Marco Pantani in 1995.
➤ In 1986 America's first Tour winner, Greg Lemond and five times winner, Frenchman Bernard Hinault rode side by side up the last part of the climb and crossed the line together.

Deux-Alpes 'IN THE SHADOW OF ALPE D'HUEZ'

⭐⭐⭐ 3 STARS

Length: 12 km.

Altitude: 1650 metres.

Height gain: 930 metres.

Average gradient: 7.75%

Maximum gradient: 10%

WHAT TO EXPECT

➤ **Bikes going downhill.** It's nowhere near as busy as Alpe d'Huez, but there's always a danger on one-road-up-and-down climbs from riders descending in the opposite direction. Keep well in when climbing, and ride within you ability going down.

➤ **Downhill bikes.** If you've got the time it's definitely worth hiring a downhill mountain bike from one of the many places that offer them in Deux-Alpes and having a go. Just like ski runs, downhill bike runs are designated with colours according to gradient and difficulty. There's a hire place on your right just as you enter the resort.

➤ **Plenty of accommodation.** It might be new to cycling, but Deux-Alpes' ski history means it's a big place with plenty of hotel beds, making it an ideal base for an Alpine bike holiday.

After Chamonix, Deux-Alpes is the second oldest ski resort in France, but it's new to the world of cycling, where it sits uncomfortably in the shadow of Alpe d'Huez. The Dutch Mountain, and all the cycling history that goes with it, is just across the Romanche valley and looks down on Deux-Alpes, both literally and in a figurative sense.

However, that hasn't stopped Deux-Alpes getting wholeheartedly involved in cycling. Summer trade in the resort thrives on downhill mountain biking, and in 1998 they landed their first Tour de France stage finish. That stage saw a virtuoso performance from the Italian climbing genius, Marco Pantani.

The climb starts at the Barrage du Chambon, a dam that is another link in the green credentials of France's hydro-electric power network. It was built in the late 1920s and holds back the waters of the Romanche, creating a huge lake to the east of it. The Barrage is about one-eighth of the way up the Col du Lautaret, so the lake is on your right as you climb the Lautaret from the Romanche side.

The similarities with Alpe d'Huez start as soon as you begin to climb. Deux-Alpes is one road up and down a steep valley side to a ski station, so it climbs by a series of hairpin bends, each one with a numbered sign. However, perhaps not wanting to be accused of plagiarism, Deux-Alpes' signs start with number one at the bottom, and no winners' names have been added yet.

The road is wide, well surfaced and well constructed, so the gradient tends to be fairly constant. Three short stretches of ten percent come one-third, halfway, and two-thirds of the way up the climb.

Barrage
de Chambon

D213

Deux-Alpes

Left page: Deux Alpes village Above: Tackling Deux-Alpes Below: Signs tick off the corners one by one, just like Alpe d'Huez

Initially there are lots of trees, so shade is plentiful on hot days, unless the sun is directly overhead, and the wind is never a problem on Deux-Alpes. Eventually, the trees peter out, but by then it's not far to the top. As you get there you get a great view of the mountains behind the resort, in particular the Roche de la Muzelle (3465 metres)

WHICH WAY?

Access to the climb is from the main Romanche Valley road, the N91. The climb starts 16 kilometres east of Bourg d'Oisans and 25 kilometres west of the summit of the Col du Lautaret. Deux Alpes is well signposted at the Barrage de Chambon turn, right if you've come from Bourg d'Oisans and left from the Col du Lautaret. The road to the top is the D213.

MOUNTAIN MOMENTS

➤ The German rider, Jan Ullrich won the 1997 Tour de France when he was only 23. He was expected to dominate for years, and in 1998 he led the race before the stage from Grenoble to Deux-Alpes. It was a stage full of mountains and it was raining. Marco Pantani attacked early on the Galibier and turned the race upside down as only a true climber can. He won alone in Deux-Alpes, where Ullrich had lost nine minutes and the Tour de France to Pantani.
➤ The Tour visited Deux-Alpes again in 2002. This time the stage was won by a Colombian, Santiago Botero, who attacked a small breakaway group at the foot of the climb and won alone. Botero, the son of a wealthy Colombian family, was subject to kidnap threats, so had to train at home with an armed escort.

Col Bayard *'AN ALPINE FIRST'*

⊛⊛ 2 STARS

Length: 7.5 km.

Altitude: 1246 metres.

Height gain: 513 metres.

Average gradient: 6.8%.

Maximum gradient: 10%.

WHAT TO EXPECT

➤ **Traffic.** The N85 is busy, especially at peak times and during holidays.

➤ **Good engineering.** The road is built to take traffic, so it's wide, well maintained and the gradient is very regular.

➤ **City views.** Gap is a real jewel and worth exploring. It's a city nestling in the lap of huge mountains.

➤ **Sports cars.** The Route Napoleon is on the Grand Tour list for all sorts of sports car clubs, and the Bayard's slopes often echo with the roar of a classic Aston Martin or Ferrari.

➤ **Museum.** La Laiterie is a restaurant and museum in Laye on the north side of the climb.

Col Bayard

N85

Gap

One of the first mountain climbs ever to be used in the Tour de France, the Col de Bayard keeps its status today because of that. It's not particularly long or the height gain as impressive as many of the climbs that surround it, but you are following in the wheel tracks of true pioneers when you climb the Bayard.

The Tour de France had only been going for two years when the organisers first dared to route the race into the Alps. And when they did they climbed the Bayard from its easier north side, after starting out from Grenoble and tracing the Route Napolean over the Côte de Laffrey, then the Bayard, before descending into Gap.

The Route Napoleon, or N85 to give it its road designation, traces the route taken by the French Emperor on his return from exile on the Island of Elba in 1815. That route was inaugurated in 1935 and runs from Antibes on the Côte d'Azur to Grenoble. The way is marked by signs bearing a flying eagle symbol.

The col's south side is far more interesting and challenging than the north. It starts almost in the streets of Gap and twists and turns up the N85, affording ever widening views of the city behind you. There are plenty of places to stop and take in the vista of Gap.

The road rises in a series of hairpin bends that are all quite steep, although the straights between them aren't, until three-quarters of the way up when there is a stretch of a about one kilometre of ten-percent gradient.

Left: An Alpine gateway   **Above:** The Bayard was part of the first Tour de France day in the Alps

The Bayard is well surfaced but busy with people going to and coming from Gap, so it's best not to climb it at rush hour. The Tour de France still uses the climb in its itinerary, climbing it in either direction, but it is not one of the race's decisive climbs.

WHICH WAY?

From Gap just follow the N85 north in the direction of Grenoble. About halfway up the climb there is an interesting deviation over the Col de Manse on your right. This takes you over to the Drac valley from where you can turn left on the D114 and then left again onto the N85 and climb the Bayard the way the first Tour riders did, or you can turn right and take on the much bigger Alpine climb of Orcières-Merlette.

MOUNTAIN MOMENTS

➤ The Bayard was first climbed in 1905. First to the top was Julien Maintron, who had broken away with fellow Frenchman Hippolyte Aucouturier. The whole stage was a marathon trek from Grenoble to Toulon, but interest centred on the leg from Grenoble to Gap, the first time the Tour visited the Alpine mountains. In those day it took a coach pulled by six horses, aided by four more on the hills, 12 hours to cover the 103 kilometres. Maintron and Aucoutourier made the headlines next day because they did it four.

➤ Hannibal, a Spaniard who waged war on the Roman Empire by taking the fight to them in Italy, marched an army, including several elephants recruited for their carrying capacity, over many Tour de France mountain climbs. One of the first was the Bayard.

Col de la Croix de Fer

'PYRENEES MEET THE ALPS'

⊕⊕⊕⊕ 4 STARS

Length: 31.6 km.
Altitude: 2067 metres.
Height gain: 1502 metres.
Average gradient: 5%.
Maximum gradient: 12%.

WHAT TO EXPECT

➤ **Gradient changes.** They interrupt your climbing rhythm and you need to change gear constantly to keep the same cadence. The descents are particularly disruptive, and you should use a lower gear than normal when you start climbing again after each one. Find your rhythm again while you are in the lower gear, then shift up if you want to.

➤ **Rock sheep.** All of the big valleys of the Alps were gouged out by the huge glaciers that existed during the Ice Age. The glaciers did their work through a number of processes including the abrasive action of the rocks that the glaciers carried within them. Near the top of the Croix de la Fer you can see evidence of how the ice worked in the form of rock formations on the valley floor called Roches Moutonées. These are areas of rock that are harder than their surrounds. The side of the rock that the ice was flowing from is marked by deep scratches, caused by abrasion. Their leeward sides are rough and truncated, caused by the glacier plucking great lumps off them. Roches Moutonées means rock sheep, because the formations look like sleeping sheep.

The Croix de Fer climb is a little taste of the Pyrenees dropped right into the heart of the Alps. It runs from the Romanche valley, more or less north to the Maurienne, climbing in erratic steps up the course of the Eau d'Oie, which has been dammed to create two spectacular turquoise lakes.

It's a climb like no other in the Alps, it goes up then down, then up and down again, with its gradient constantly changing just like many climbs in the Pyrenees do. It starts about seven kilometres north-west of Bourg d'Oisans, and there are two kilometres of flat road before two switchback ramps take you up the Barrage du Verney, the first dam.

The road then climbs steadily past a big hydro-electric station, which also houses a museum charting the history of hydro-electric power production in France. From here the going gets tough with six kilometres of climbing during which the gradient builds slowly from seven to ten percent.

The road descends after the village of Rivier-d'Allemond, where the direction of the climb changes dramatically for a few kilometres and so does the gradient. A cruel stretch of twelve percent begins just after the descent, and you need to really gear down for this part.

The forests of the early part of the climb now give way to wide open views, with another six kilometres of fairly straight road of varying pitch, then a couple of steep hairpins, taking you level with the dam that holds back the waters of the Lac de Grand Maison. There are 140 million cubic metres of water in the lake, which are steadily piped to feed the hydro-electric station lower down the valley.

Another descent loses you some of the height you've just fought so hard to gain, but at least it gives you time to enjoy the view of the numerous waterfalls tumbling down the faces of the mountains on your right, and take in

Col de la Croix de Fer

D526

N91

Left: An Alpine mountain village   **Above left:** It's very steep in places early on   **Above right:** The wide open top of the Croix de la Fer

the majesty of the Aiguilles de l'Argentière range on your left. All too soon you are climbing again, past the exit of the Col du Glandon, then on to the top of the Croix de la Fer.

WHICH WAY?

From Bourg d'Oisans take the N91 north west, and from Grenoble take the N85 to Vizille then the N91 east. About five kilometres from Bourg d'Oisans, in Rochetaille, the Col de la Croix de Fer is signposted. Follow the signposts on the D526. This road splits soon after the climb starts so that lorries go up the D44 to avoid the Barrage du Verney, but you carry straight on the D526. After the Barrage the roads join up and you follow the D526 to the summit.

MOUNTAIN MOMENTS

➤ The first Tour de France rider over the Croix de la Fer was Fermo Camellini of Italy in 1947.
The Tour doesn't visit the Croix de la Fer as frequently as some other major climbs in the Alps, and when it does it favours neither side. I picked the southern ascent because I think it represents an unusual challenge, and the two lakes are spectacular.
➤ The climb has been the scene of some incredible mountain efforts, including a 130-kilometre solo breakaway in 1989 by Gert-Jan Theunisse while wearing the King of the Mountains Jersey. Theunisse, a Dutch rider whose long flowing locks and pointed nose made him look like he'd jumped out of a Breughel painting, crossed the Croix de la Fer alone and continued to the top of Alpe d'Huez to take the stage and the mountains title.

Above: Lake in the Defile de Maupas

Col du Galibier 'GIANT OF THE ALPS'

⭐⭐⭐⭐⭐ **5 STARS**

Length: 18 km.
Altitude: 2646 metres.
Height gain: 1216 metres.
Average gradient: 7%.
Maximum gradient: 10%.

WHAT TO EXPECT

➤ **No cover.** There are no trees on the Galibier and even the grass starts to get pretty threadbare as you approach the top.

➤ **Side valleys.** Two beguiling off-shoot valleys from the climb, the Combe des Aiguilles and Combe de Mortavielle beg to be explored later on foot.

➤ **Feeling of space.** Few cars and huge views give a real sense of freedom on the Galibier. You can really breath deeply up here, which comes in handy ... because you need to.

➤ **Father Tour.** Just after you descend from the summit, on a flat piece of ground before the plunge down to the top of the Lautaret, there is a statue commemorating the life of the founder of the Tour de France, Henri Desgrange. A great journalist, he loved the Galibier and once wrote: "In front of this giant we can do nothing but take our hats off and bow."

Valloire

D902

Col du Galibier

This is one of the most celebrated climbs of the Tour de France. It's long, it's quite steep, especially towards the top, and it often comes close to the end of a stage. The best riders always make a race of it when the Tour climbs the Galibier.

It begins fairly gently with a stretch of what French cyclists call false flat. What they mean is it looks flat but your legs tell you that you are climbing. Soon though the gradient racks up as you ride into a huge valley that seems to have no way out.

The road runs straight, between huge grey scree slopes, but you can't see how it will take you over the giant wall of mountains you are riding towards. The way is finally revealed at a place called Plan Lachat. A hairpin bend takes you right, and above you see the road wriggling over a gap between the peaks.

The gradient really bites here and it won't let go until you reach the top. The road turns this way and that, trying to find the easiest way up, but the gradient doesn't slip below 7.5 percent and some of the corners are ferociously steep.

There have been several roads built and abandoned to take people over this part of the mountain, you can see evidence of older ones snaking around below you as you ride. The newest road is the top part that goes right over the summit. It was

Left: The Henri Desgrange memorial stone   **Above left:** Descending the Galibier

built when they closed the summit tunnel in 1976. The tunnel, which can be closed off by its huge wooden doors, is open again now, but cyclists aren't allowed through it and must ride right over the top.

The first Tour de France rider to cross the Col du Galibier was Émile Georget in 1911. Georget, Paul Duboc and Gustave Garrigou were the only three riders who didn't have to dismount and walk the last part of the climb.

WHICH WAY?

From Valloire, which is on the D902 that links the Maurienne valley with the Romanche and Guisanne, follow the signs in the town for Grenoble and Briançon, paying attention that you are going the right way around Valloire's one-way system. Once you are out of Valloire and heading uphill and south, there are no other roads until the top. Remember though, you can't go through the summit tunnel, it's only for motors. The big mountain peak above you at the top is the Grand Galibier (3229 metres)

MOUNTAIN MOMENTS

➤ In 1966 the final act of one of cycling's most intense rivalries was played out on the Galibier. Jacques Anquetil and Raymond Poulidor split France at a time when the countryside in particular was undergoing social change. Traditional France supported the strong but shy and tongue-tied farmer's boy Poulidor. Modern France admired the elegant and sophisticated Anquetil.
Anquetil was older and by 1966 had won the Tour de France five times, but he knew by then that Poulidor could beat him, a prospect that appalled him. Earlier in the race Anquetil's team mate, Lucien Aimar took the lead. Poulidor attacked on the Galibier to gain time back, but Anquetil rode alongside Poulidor matching him pedal turn for pedal turn. Poulidor became discouraged that he still could not break his old rival, and Aimar won the Tour. Anquetil never rode another Tour de France, but Poulidor raced on until 1978, although he still never managed to win the race.

Col du Glandon 'THE SIAMESE TWIN'

⊛⊛⊛ 3 STARS

Length: 22 km.

Altitude: 1924 metres.

Height gain: 1475 metres.

Average gradient: 6.9%.

Maximum gradient: 13%.

WHAT TO EXPECT

➤ **Tough at the top.** There are fearsome gradients as you approach the summit, keep something in reserve.

➤ **Being watched.** Para-gliders leap off the top of the Glandon and people stop in the summit car park to watch them. They can also study your progress up the agonizing last part of the climb, which is another reason for keeping something in reserve. You want to look cool don't you?

➤ **War memorials.** There's one on the summit dedicated to the activities of the Maquis, the Guerrilla branch of the French resistance that operated in rural areas against the occupying German forces, and in particular against the collaborators of the Milice. Maquis is the word for the vegetation found on high ground in south-eastern France.

La Chambre

D927

Col du Glandon

The Glandon is attached to its twin, the Croix de La Fer – lying some three kilometres from the latter's summit. It's another fairly straight climb, so it has some of the Croix de la Fer's flavour, but there are no descents during the climb to confuse your legs and break your rhythm.

Quite the opposite in fact – the Glandon starts relatively gently but its top section presents one of the steepest pitches in the whole of the Alps. The last two kilometres rack up to ten percent, then twelve and thirteen in the last few hundred metres.

The final bit is made even harder by the fact that there is a car park at the top that acts as a gallery for people looking down the mountain. They can watch every gasping pedal turn you make up the final bit. And don't people enjoy watching other people suffer?

The climb starts after you cross a bridge over the A43 autoroute that runs almost the length of the Maurienne valley, taking people either to the Fréjus tunnel at Modane or the Col du Mont-Cenis, and into Italy.

The Glandon is named after a stream, and the road follows its valley for the first half of the climb. This part of the climb is quite gentle, and after eight kilometres it even flattens out for a bit, but that is the calm before the storm. At St Colomban the road rears up again, but don't attack it all out yet, save something for the last bit.

The Glandon valley is left behind on your right now, the big mountains coming into view are the edges of the Aiguilles de l'Argentiãre. The summit of the Glandon is marked by the usual sign posts, but there is also a couple of metres of small slabs set into the road, cycling's own brick yard of Indianapolis 500 fame.

If you stop at the top and look back down where you've just ridden, you can see directly across to the Col de La Madeleine on the other side of the Maurienne. Look the other way and the last part of the Croix de La Fer is laid out below you.

WHICH WAY?

La Chambre, which is on the N6 at junction 26 of the A43 in the Maurienne valley, is where the climb starts. Follow directions in town for the col and for the D927, which is the road that goes over it. If you turn left after climbing the Glandon onto the D926 you can climb the last part of the Croix de la Fer and descend to St Jean de Maurienne, then take the N6 for 7.5 kilometres back to La Chambre for a nice circuit.

Above: Last few metres of the Glandon   **Below:** Remembering the heroism of the Maquis

 **MOUNTAIN MOMENTS**

➤ In 1990 the American Greg Lemond sealed his last Tour victory on the Glandon when he dug in and hung on to a breakaway on one of the key stages of the Tour. Lemond was in a class of his own when he won his first Tour in 1986, but after a near fatal hunting accident he had to rely as much on character and bravery as athletic ability to win in 1989 and 1990

➤ In 2006 the race leader, another American, Floyd Landis, was in trouble from the start of the Glandon, and eventually lost ten minutes and his Yellow Jersey to Spain's Oscar Pereiro. Next day Landis staged a remarkable comeback and went on to win the Tour, but he also provided a positive drugs test and has since been stripped of the title.

Col du Lautaret

'GUARDIAN OF THE GUISANNE VALLEY'

⊛⊛ 2 STARS

Length: 40 km.

Altitude: 2058 metres.

Height gain: 1400 metres.

Average gradient: 3.8%.

Maximum gradient: 9%.

WHAT TO EXPECT

➤ **Mountain views.** Two big mountains, Le Râteau (3669 metres) and La Meije (3983 metres) dominate the Lautaret. At La Grave you are level with La Meije, which is directly on your right.

➤ **Geomorphic action.** The Massif des Ecrins, of which Le Râteau and La Meije are part, is a living demonstration of how ice moulds the scenery. You can see glaciers scooping out great bowl-like corries high up where they start near the mountain tops. Then where the glaciers flow they gouge U-shaped declivities into the rock, ending in melt-water streams, which cut a V-shaped notch as they splash down to the two bigger rivers below. The Romanche which flows west and the Guisanne flowing east

➤ **Botanical gardens.** On the summit, at the Station Alpine de Lautaret, is a botanical gardens where 2000 species of flowers from all over the world grow. Peak blooming season is in June and July.

The Lautaret is a pass that is more often used to get somewhere else, and the Tour de France has climbed it in both directions. It is the main road between Grenoble and Briançon and an important route into Italy, so it's fairly busy with traffic. Cyclists are more likely to use it as a descent into Briançon or Bourg d'Oisan after climbing the Galibier. The short descent of that monster climb ends on the top of the Lautaret.

Having said all that, on a sunny day the Lautaret can be a glorious experience because of the superb views it gives you of the glaciers clinging onto the rugged slopes of the Massif des Écrins. The views west into the Romanche valley and east into the Guisianne are two of the most beautiful in France.

The south western ascent from Briançon is just as attractive, but with an average gradient of three percent and a maximum of six, nowhere near as challenging. One of the deciding factors in which way you climb the Lautaret is the wind. They are both very long rides, and 40 kilometres up hill into a headwind is no joke, no matter how gentle the slope.

The climb from the Romanche valley starts at Les Clapiers and twists and turns for the first nine kilometres, passing through a couple of short tunnels. After the

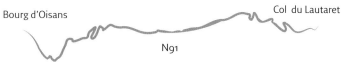

Bourg d'Oisans   Col du Lautaret

N91

Left: The Lautaret is long but not steep   **Above left:** Glaciers above the Romanche valley   **Above right:** July snow on top of the Lautaret

entrance to the road up to les Deux Alpes the route straightens for 14 kilometres and takes in the (aptly named for cycling nuts) Tunnel du Grand Clot, before La Grave, where the hairpin bends begin – and take you to the top.

There's a cluster of building at the summit that include a café and a hotel. On your left, if you've come up the west side, is the short road to the top of Galibier. The descent to Briançon is straight on and sweeps through an avalanche tunnel before continuing down straight for most of the way.

WHICH WAY?

The road that climbs the Lautaret is the N91, and Bourg d'Oisans at the foot of the Alpe d'Huez is a good place to start. There's plenty of parking spaces there for a start. Les Clapiers, where the climb starts, is 5 kilometres east of Bourg d'Oisans. Follow signs for Briançon. If you are climbing from the Briançon side look for signs directing you to the N91 and Grenoble.

MOUNTAIN MOMENTS

➤ Not really a major climb in the Tour, the Lautaret is usually given a second category rating. It becomes a major climb when the south side of the Galibier are added to it, like they were in the 2006 Tour. That adds 8 kilometres of near nine-percent gradient to the Lautaret.

➤ The short descent from the top of the Galibier onto the Lautaret was the scene of the first of only three fatalities in Tour de France history. In 1935 the Spanish rider, Francesco Cepeda crashed there and suffered head injuries. He died three days later. The Tour last climbed this side in 2008.

Col du Mont-Cenis

'HOME OF NAPOLEON'S PYRAMID'

⊛⊛ 2 STARS

Length: 9.84 km.

Altitude: 2083 metres.

Height gain: 682 metres.

Average gradient: 6.9%.

Maximum gradient: 10.6%.

WHAT TO EXPECT

➤ **A pyramid.** Yes, a pyramid. When he passed though here on some campaign or other, Napoleon thought it would be a splendid idea to build a pyramid at the top of the climb to mark his Egyptian campaigns. It took until 1968 for someone to grant the Emperor's wish. Electricité de France (EDF) eventually built Napoleon's pyramid, right next to the lake. It's a museum now.

➤ **Ice.** The lake up here freezes each winter until May, but don't test it by standing on it. Even at this altitude winter's aren't what they used to be.

➤ **A border crossing.** It's worth descending the ten kilometres between the top and Italy, just to impress your friends by telling them you went there by bike.

➤ **Vanoise views.** While you are climbing each westerly hairpin, glance to your right and take in the views over the Vanoise Alps.

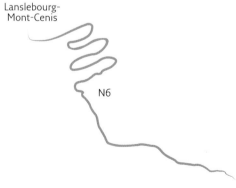

Lanslebourg-Mont-Cenis

N6

Plan des Fontainettes

This climb is worth doing just to marvel at the equally spaced hairpins and straights that take you up the first few kilometres. Their construction is a fine example of the road engineer's art, especially as they had to be sturdily built to take a lot of heavy goods traffic from France into Italy before the Fréjus tunnel opened.

The climb is a continuation of the N6 that runs the length of the Maurienne valley. It starts as soon as you leave the village of Lanselbourg-Mont-Cenis, and the first part is definitely the hardest.

The wide hairpins give you a breather, but the straights between them are steep, especially the fifth one, where the steepest gradients of the whole climb lie in wait for you. There is a satisfying regularity about this part of the climb, that allows you to get a good rhythm going. Also, once you've done this bit you can take heart that the worst is over.

The road straightens for the second part of the climb, past the blue waters of the Lac du Mont Cenis. Botanists have recorded over 700 species of flower in the fields surrounding the lake.

Approaching the top, you emerge into a vista of big mountain peaks. The biggest being the Pointe de Ronce (3610 metres) on your left, and Mont Lamet (3478 metres) dead ahead. It is a stark and barren but incredibly beautiful place. Evidence has been found here, in pastures up to 2800 metres, of human habitation thought to date to 3000 BC.

Most compelling are the huge engraved rocks, each marked with hundreds of deeply cut hemispheric gouges that archaeologists have called cupules. They are remarkably symmetrical and skilfully formed. The cupules point in slightly different directions, causing some to suggest they are early star charts, although nothing is known for certain about them.

WHICH WAY?

Any Maurienne valley town is a good base for Mont Cenis. Lots of interesting side roads mean that you don't have to use the N6 to get everywhere on your bike, although it's perfect for transporting them by car. You could also stop in Val d'Isere and include Mont Cenis after an attack on the Col d'Iseran. From the Maurienne, follow the N6 east and Mont Cenis starts in Lanslebourg. From Val d'Isere take the D902 over the Iseran and turn left onto the N6 just before Lanslebourg.

MOUNTAIN MOMENTS

➤ Mont Cenis first appeared in the Tour de France in 1949. An Italian, Giuseppe Tacca was first rider over it.

➤ In 1961 Mont Cenis featured on a stage from Grenoble to Turin. It was hot, so the race was lethargic. Two non-favourites, Frenchmen Guy Ignolin and Manuel Busto, built a huge lead of 27 minutes by the start of the climb. They still had 25 minutes at the top, so Busto jumped in the lake to cool down. Ignolin waited for him, which was nice, and the pair carried on to Turin, where Ignolin won in a sprint.

➤ The Tour sometimes climbs Mont Cenis from the Italian side. In 1999, the year of Lance Armstrong's first Tour victory, it was the first climb in a stage that started in Sestrières. A Russian, Dimitry Konyshev was first to the top.

Left: Sometimes it's cold on top **Above:** Mont Cenis starts in the Maurienne Valley

Col de Montgenèvre

'GATEWAY TO ITALY'

⭐⭐ 2 STARS

Length: 7.73 km.
Altitude: 1850 metres.
Height gain: 494 metres.
Average gradient: 6.4%.
Maximum gradient: 8%.

WHAT TO EXPECT

➤ **Some traffic.** It's not too bad though, and the road is wide, barring recent big road works.

➤ **Fortifications.** A brilliant-looking fort overlooks the pass in Briançon, built on what is called the Rock of Briançon. It was started by the Romans, reinforced by the Gauls and built on further by subsequent rulers of the region.

➤ **Coloured rocks.** On the hairpins you can see the mountains on the left side of the Clairée valley, which spears off north of the N94 just before the climb starts in La Vachette. These mountains are streaked with reds and pinks due to the minerals within them.

➤ **Mountain bikers.** A high altitude off-road track over Mont Chaberton from Italy into France descends to Montgenèvre. It descends the climb then continues up the Clairée valley.

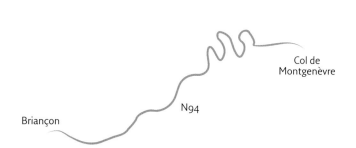

Its other name, Passo di Montginevro, should give you some indication of where this one goes. At the top you are just three kilometres west from the Italian border. Because of that the road can be busy, although nowadays most traffic goes through the Maurienne valley and then the Fréjus Tunnel, only joining this road well after the Col de Montgenèvre.

In any case it's a good wide road, although road works to correct some landslips have been going on there recently. But the main reason for climbing Montgenèvre are the wide open views you get to your right as you climb. The view into Italy at the top is well worth the climb too.

The climb starts at La Vachette and is straight for the first part. Then comes a series of hairpins. The gradient is steepest at the beginning and end of these bends. On your right you look across at the Sommet des Anges on whose slopes one of France's biggest rivers, the Durance begins.

The top of Montgenèvre is a really nice place to be. There is a large area of flat ground, surrounded by peaks, on which the village of Montgenèvre is situated. Because the top isn't too high, it's the lowest crossing into Italy from France, there are plenty of trees and in season, lots of mountain flowers in the gently undulating meadows. To the west there are some great views over Briançon.

Left page: Wild flowers near the summit

Above left: A top French amateur team training on the Montgenevre **Above right:** Pink stained rocks above the Clairee valley

Given its low altitude its not surprising that the pass was attractive to the Romans. Pompey first recorded its use in 77 BC, when he mounted his campaigns to Spain. It was later used by Julius Caesar when travelling to Gaul and became the most important crossing of what are called the Cottian Alps, the mountains between France and Italy.

WHICH WAY?

From Briançon follow directions on the N94 to Grenoble and Italy. At the point where the N91 forks left off the N94 to Grenoble take the right fork, still on the N94, signposted Col de Montgenèvre. Follow the N94 to the top of the climb. This road is re-named the S24 at the border with Italy, which is on the descent from the Montgenèvre in Clavière.

MOUNTAIN MOMENTS

➤ First rider to top the Col de Montgenèvre in the Tour de France in 1949 was the Italian, Gino Bartali in 1949. Bartali was the great rival of Fausto Coppi. Their rivalry was another that split a country. Bartali, known as Pious Gino, was very religious and he represented old Italy. Coppi married a divorcee, he was excommunicated from the church, he liked the good life and he was a hero to the young and to modern Italy.

➤ The Montgenèvre descent ruined the homecoming of another charismatic Italian in 1999 when Mario Cipollini crashed on it. He was a sprinter who won lots of Tour stages but never finished the race. He won four stages in 1999, and was going to stop when the race reached Italy that day to do the thing he did best next to sprinting, and that was partying. Instead Cipollini ended up in hospital having stitches put in his head.

Orcières-Merlette '_OCAÑA'S MASTERPIECE_'

✪✪✪ 3 STARS

Length: 11 km.

Altitude: 1838 metres.

Height gain: 828 metres.

Average gradient: 7.5%

Maximum gradient: 10%

WHAT TO EXPECT

➤ **Outdoor activities.** The Drac valley is a haven for rock climbers, paragliders, kayakers and mountain bikers.

➤ **Side roads.** There are loads of them up the valley sides, but for a real mountain experience try the point where the Drac is formed from two torrents, the Drac Blanc and the Drac Noir. A narrow lonely road follows the Drac Blanc right up to near its source in the mountains at the heart of the Écrins national park.

➤ **Team it up.** The Col de Noyer isn't too far away. It starts just eight kilometres north from where the D14 joins the N85 and makes a great double with Orcières-Merlette

This climb up to a ski station has only been visited four times by the Tour de France, but it is a legend in the race because of a Spanish climbing genius called Luis Ocaña. In 1971 Ocaña destroyed the great Eddy Merckx on an Alpine stage that started in Grenoble and finished here. Ocaña later crashed out of the Tour while leading by what looked like an unassailable margin, and Merckx won.

Merckx was shaken by the experience and when Ocaña got back to form in 1973, Merckx avoided the Tour de France that year and Ocaña won with hardly a challenge. Unfortunately Ocaña was never able to recover his climbing legs after 1973 and his career slowly wound to a close.

Tour de France mountain climbers have often been controversial, mercurial characters, and for a few their lives were coloured by tragedy. Luis Ocaña was one of them. After he stopped racing he invested heavily in producing Armagnac, but was hit by bad harvests and ran into money difficulties. A proud man, Ocaña also began to suffer from an enfeebling illness and in 1994 he committed suicide. He was 48.

The climb of Orcières-Merlette begins at a bridge over the river Drac. The road is well surfaced, quite wide and fairly straight at first, as it climbs to the

Orcières-Merlette

D76

Pont-du-Fossè

Above A welcome sign

Above left: On the climb   **Above right:** Time to offer a prayer

head of a steep sided valley and the village of Orcières.

The ski station is actually called Merlette, and the steepest part of the whole climb begins in Orcières and ends in Merlette. The road is narrower now, as it wiggles up the Drouvet mountain in a series of hairpins and short straights. The road stops just where the ski lifts start.

WHICH WAY?

From Gap you can either climb the N85 Col de Bayard to halfway, turn right on the D944 and go over the Col de Manse, or you can cross the summit of the Bayard, descend and turn right on the D114. Both roads join the D944 and the climb begins around eight kilometres along that road. Once you arrive in Orcières, just follow the signs to Merlette. The road that climbs the last bit is the D76.

MOUNTAIN MOMENTS

➤ Ocaña's 1971 victory was the first visit by the Tour to Orcières-Merlette. It was a hot day, so one that suited a Spaniard born in Castile. Ocaña and his team had attacked Merckx for two days, and by the time they arrived at the Côte de Laffrey the Belgian had nothing left. Ocaña romped away and by the finish line he had taken his Tour lead to over eight minutes. He was so good that only 38 riders finished inside the time limit for the stage, and the Tour organisers were forced to raise it, or the spectacle of the race would have gone

➤ In 1989 there was a time trial from Gap over the Col Bayard and up to Orcières-Merlette. It was won by the Dutchman Steven Rooks, who had been King of the Mountains the previous year. Greg Lemond of America finished fifth at 57 seconds, but he was 47 seconds ahead of his French rival, Laurent Fignon and he took over the yellow jersey. Fignon later won it back, but Lemond beat him in a time trial on the last day to take the Tour by eight seconds, the narrowest margin ever.

Sestrières 'AN ADVENTURE INTO ITALY'

✪✪✪ 3 STARS

Length: 11 km.

Altitude: 2035 metres.

Height gain: 691 metres.

Average gradient: 6.2%.

Maximum gradient: 10%.

WHAT TO EXPECT

➤ **Border crossing.** Sestrières is in Italy, so take your passport if you are riding from France. Actually you should always carry recognized identification when out and about in France. Either a passport, driving licence or national identity card.

➤ **Sporting types.** Sestrières is a mecca for all kinds of sports, summer and winter. The town is busy with people playing everything from Golf to Football. It's also a big mountain bike centre. The town is also a high-altitude training centre for Italian athletes.

➤ **Tourism.** The non-seasonal population of Sestrières numbers 908, but there are 6000 hotel beds, so nearly everyone works at catering for the temporary needs of others. That makes it a good base for cycling in the Italian Alps though.

Sestrières is an Italian ski resort that sits on top of a mountain pass. Understandably the Tour de France climbs the pass from the French side, but the Tour of Italy uses Sestrières as well, and more often they ride up the opposite side of the pass.

The Italian Tour climb starts in Pinerolo, and it is 55 kilometres long with a height gain of 1600 metres. Not steep, but a stiff test when it was a time trial in the 1993 Tour of Italy and the Spanish winner of five Tours de France, Miguel Indurain went up in a little over 90 minutes.

The pass represents another important route between France and Italy, one that was forged by the Romans and was engineered, like so many Alpine roads were, by Napoleon. The name Sestrières comes from Petra Sextreria, Latin for sixth stone, because the Romans measured distances with evenly placed stones and Sestrières was where the sixth equidistant stone from Turin was placed.

The Tour de France climb starts in Cesana and begins with a big sweeping left and right hairpin bend. The first steep section of the climb comes straight after the first bends, but the gradient slackens as the road straightens. The next set of hairpins, at Champlas du Col, signals more steep stretches that this time continue to the top.

Sestrières has always been an important place in the sport of skiing. The first World Cup ski race held there was in 1967, when the French ski legend, and an avid

Cesana-Torinese   Sestrières

R23

Left: An Italian peak   **Above:** The road to Sestrieres

cyclist who was president of the Tour de France organisation from 1992 until 2001, Jean-Claude Killy won. Sestrières skiing credentials were sealed when they hosted the sport for the 2006 Turin Winter Olympic Games.

WHICH WAY?

Briançon is a good base for an attack on Sestrieres, but you have to climb the Col de Montgenèvre first. Follow signs in town for Turin, then take the N94 north-west, over the Montgenèvre, then descend into Italy. At the border the road turns into the S24, and the descent is fairly straight and very fast. It's fun but take care through the two tunnels. It ends with two big hairpins that take you to Cesana-Torinese and the start of the climb. Turn right onto the R23 and continue to the top of the climb.

MOUNTAIN MOMENTS

➤ Fausto Coppi won the first Tour de France stage to finish in Sestrieres. That was in 1952 and it was his second consecutive stage win in the race. The previous day 'Il Campionissimo' had won at Alpe d'Huez, another first visit. The Italian was unstoppable that year, winning the Tour by 28 minutes.

➤ Another Italian star, Claudio Chiappucci won here forty years after Coppi. But where Coppi was an elegant athlete who made his superiority count, Chiappucci was a feisty battler given to huge efforts that often brought him very little. He attacked on the first mountain and stayed away on his own in tremendous heat over the following three, ruining the chances of several favourites, but only gaining a little over a minute on Miguel Indurain. Ciappucci won the stage, but Indurain won the Tour.

Col du Télégraphe '*STEPPING STONE TO A GIANT*'

●● 2 STARS

Length: 12 km.

Altitude: 1566 metres.

Height gain: 878 metres.

Average gradient: 7%.

Maximum gradient: 8.2%.

WHAT TO EXPECT

➤ **Great views**. The Maurienne valley is really beautiful and there's a great feeling of exposure as you look down into it while climbing the Télégraphe

➤ **A few lorries**. Valloire is a busy holiday place all year round, so they need a lot of deliveries making there. Don't be put off, the road is wide and French drivers usually take plenty of care when overtaking cyclists.

➤ **Lots of Shelter**. The trees keep the wind and the worst of the summer sun off you. A big contrast to what you will find on the Galibier.

➤ **A garden**. There is an attractive little garden and planters hung from the guard rail at the top. Not your usual mountain top at all.

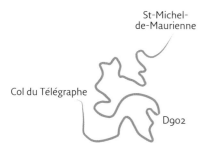

St-Michel-de-Maurienne

Col du Télégraphe

D902

Most people climbing the Télégraphe are doing so to get to the start of Col de Galibier, which is one of the most famous climbs of the Tour de France. The Télégraphe is also quite busy with road traffic, as it is the only way to the resort of Valloire that sits between the two climbs. However, the Télégraphe is still worth climbing in its own right. You don't have to do the Galibier, which is a big undertaking. You could just turn around at the summit and ride back down the Télégraphe.

The climb got its name from the TV and radio aerials at its summit. The way up is on a well-engineered Alpine road with a steady gradient that never gets super steep, so it isn't too demanding. The atmospheric forests it climbs through, plus the ever widening glimpses of the Maurienne valley below you, make the Télégraphe a very attractive prospect.

The pass has played its part in history too, as the various fortifications you see on the way up testify. Towards the top a huge fort overlooks the Maurienne valley. You need no more evidence that this climb has always been an important link between the northern and southern Alps.

The road twists and turns up what is essentially quite a steep face, the hardest part coming just above a collection of chalet's at Seignieres, which is also where the best views are to be had. Close to this point you will also find some of the best road art of the Tour, where many rider's names have been picked out on the road in a rainbow of coloured paints.

There is a café at the top called the Relais du Télégraphe, and from here it is just a short four-kilometre, shallow (three percent) descent to Valloire and the start of the Galibier. The total length of the Télégraphe and Galibier is 34.8 kilometres and the height gain is 2096 metres.

WHICH WAY?

The Maurienne valley is a main route between France and Italy that contains the N6 and A43 highways. The Télégraphe starts in St Michel de Maurienne, a town that became famous by producing aluminium machinery. Follow signs for the Col du Télégraphe and D902. The climbing starts as soon as you make the right hand turn out of the town centre.

 **MOUNTAIN MOMENTS**

➤ The first Tour de France rider to cross the summit of the Télégraphe was Emile Georget in 1911. While you are climbing on your modern bike, think what it must have been like for those ancient 'Convicts of the Road' as writers covering the first Tours de France called them. Their bikes weighed more than 20 kilos, they had one gear ratio for climbing and another for descending. And in those days Tour de France stages were often between 300 and 400 kilometres long.

➤ The climb isn't always categorized by the Tour de France, often it is just seen as part of the Galibier, and they have a point, there being only four kilometres of descent between the two.

Above left: Take it easy if you are climbing the Galibier as well   **Above**: Road art

Col de Chaillolet

Length: 9 km.

Altitude: 1560 metres.

Height gain: 621 metres.

Average gradient: 6.9%.

Maximum gradient: 8%.

A climb with a metronomic gradient that provides another way into the Drac Valley, and access to the much more famous Orcières-Merlette climb, from the N85 north of Gap. The Col de Chaillolet has only been climbed once by the Tour de France.

That was in 1982 and the man who went over was Pascal Simon, who also won the stage at the top of the Drac valley in Orcières-Merlette that day. Simon led over each of six climbs on the 15th stage of the 1982 Tour, a classy ride that served as an aperitif for his 1983 performance in the big race, when he spent seven days in the yellow jersey. For several of them Simon nursed a broken shoulder, until eventually the pain became too much and he had to leave the Tour with tears soaking his yellow jersey.

Simon is the oldest of five brothers who were all professional bike racers, and all except one won stages in the Tour de France. The one who didn't, François, who was also the youngest, at least had the pleasure of wearing the yellow jersey himself for three days in the 2001 Tour de France.

The Col de Chaillolet is a stiff climb with no easy bits at all. It starts in St-Bonnet-de-Champsaur, which is just off the N85, and climbs at a steady seven percent in a straightish line for most of the way to the top in the village of Chaillolet. The descent drops you into the Drac valley, and is a wriggly and quite technical contrast to the way up.

WHICH WAY? The nearest big place to stay is Gap. If you want to stay faithful to the way the Tour climbed the Chaillolet head north on the N85 up the Col Bayard. Turn right after the descent onto the D43 and follow that road to the top of the climb. After the descent you can either turn left on the D944 and tackle Orcieres-Merlette or right and climb the Col de Manse back to Gap.

Chamrousse

Length: 19 km.

Altitude: 1650 metres.

Height gain: 1235 metres.

Average gradient: 6.5%.

Maximum gradient: 11%.

This ski resort just outside Grenoble was created for the 1968 Winter Olympics. The Tour de France first used the climb in 2001, when it was the last part of a 32-kilometre time trial that started in the streets of Grenoble.

Lance Armstrong won the time trial with an average speed of 28.4 kilometres per hour, beating arch rival Jan Ullrich by exactly one minute. Armstrong went on to win the Tour, the third of his seven victories. The Tour hasn't visited Chamrousse since.

It's a very good climb though. A well-surfaced, interesting and twisty road leads you up to the top, where there are splendid views over Grenoble. The climb is in the Belledonne range that overlooks the city.

WHICH WAY? From Uriage-les-Bains, 11 kilometres east of Grenoble along the D524, follow the signs for D111 Chamrousse to the top. You can descend the same way you came up, or go down the Col du Luitel and back to Uriage.

Col du Coq

Length: 12 km.

Altitude: 1738 metres.

Height gain: 780 metres.

Average gradient: 6.5%.

Maximum gradient: 16%.

Situated in another range that you can see from Grenoble, the Chartreuse, which lies to the north of the city, the Col du Coq has a tough average gradient and one fearsome pitch of 16 percent about halfway up. The gradient is made worse because you can see the road rearing up ahead of you at the end of a long straight.

The Tour has only climbed the Col du Coq twice, the first time in 1984 when the Spaniard with a perfect climber's name, Angel Arroyo was first to the top. The other time was in 1987 when Frenchman Denis Roux, who now works as a coach for a French pro team, was first.

You can have a very nice day out on your bike in the Chartreuse, as it's not a large area but contains three other Tour climbs, the Porte, Cucheron and Granier, as well as a few others that the race hasn't visited. The Gorges du Guiers Mort and Guiers Vif are worth visiting too.

WHICH WAY? The Col du Coq starts on the southern side of St Pierre de la Chartreuse, which is 26 kilometres north of Grenoble on the D512. Look for signs on that road pointing in the direction of the col. The road up is the D30E, but it's not clearly signposted, luckily the col is.

Col du Cucheron

Length: 8.5 km.

Altitude: 1139 metres.

Height gain: 501 metres.

Average gradient: 5.9%.

Maximum gradient: 8%.

This is the middle climb of the Chartreuse Massif, the Tour usually attacks the Cucheron from St Pierre-d'Entremont, which makes it a fairly straight climb with one long bend towards the Malissard forest. The climb is situated between the Gorge du Guiers Mort and Gorge du Guiers Vif.

The first Tour de France rider to the top of the Cucheron was Jean Robic in 1947. A Breton rider who won the Tour that year without once wearing the yellow jersey, Robic was quite a character and had more nicknames than any other cyclist in history.

Tête de Cuir, or Leather Head in English, was one. The name was given to Robic on account of the leather crash hat he wore after an early career full of accidents in which he broke nearly every bone in his body. Not the tallest or best looking bike rider, one French journalist dubbed Robic as "a goblin from the bogs of Brittany".

Robic loved cycling and raced as a pro until well into his forties. He carried on as an amateur after that, racing whenever he could. Robic died in a car accident in 1980 after competing in a race for ex-pro riders. French cycling still misses little 'Biquet'.

WHICH WAY? The climb is on the D512, south out of St Pierre-d'Entremont. If you turn right after the descent you can go down the Gorge du Guiers Mort. Then go right on the D520 and right again on the D102, and another right on the D520 to ride up the Gorge du Guiers Vif and back to St Pierre-d'Entremont.

Côte des Engins

Length: 13 km.
Altitude: 860 metres.
Height gain: 654 metres.
Average gradient: 5%.
Maximum gradient: 8%.

This climb starts almost in the streets of Grenoble and has been used twice in the Tour de France as part of time-trial stages between the city and Villard de Lans in the Vercours. Both times the stage was won by a Dutch rider: Steven Rooks in 1988 and Erik Breukink in 1990. Rooks, who won the 1988 Tour King of the mountains, is still fairly competitive on his bike and finished quite high in the 2007 Etape du Tour cyclo-sportive event.

The climb starts on the western bank of the river Isère, across from the main part of Grenoble in a village called Sassenage. A series of hairpins take you up the steeper first part of the climb. Then it becomes a straight run on the top, which is in the village of Engins.

WHICH WAY? Head for the main boulevard road in Grenoble and follow that to junction 3 of the A480 and cross the Autoroute onto the N532. Turn left just after Sassenge onto the D531 and follow that road to the top of the climb.

Col du Festre

Length: 14.4 km.
Altitude: 1441 metres.
Height gain: 584 metres.
Average gradient: 4.1%.
Maximum gradient: 7%.

A very straightforward climb that is to the west of Gap. The Col du Festre is quite long at 14-plus kilometres but isn't steep and doesn't have many twists or turns. You get some lovely open views of the Crête des Aiguilles on your left as you climb. It has been climbed twice in Tour de France history. The first occasion was in 1970 when an Italian, Primo Mori was first to the top.

WHICH WAY? Start in La Madeleine, which is about 18 kilometres west of Gap on the D994. Turn right in the village onto the D937 and follow that road north to the top of the climb. If you go down the others side it's possible to climb the Col de Noyer, then the Col de Chaillolet and Col de Manse for a nice round trip back to Gap.

Col du Granier

Length: 11.5 km.
Altitude: 1134 metres.
Height gain: 823 metres.
Average gradient: 7.2%.
Maximum gradient: 10.3%.

A tough climb, the most northerly of those in the Chartreuse, the Granier's most famous Tour moment was in 1958 when it was the final climb in an epic day during which Luxembourg's Charly Gaul took back 12 minutes on the leaders to win the stage, and lay the foundations for winning the Tour de France.

The Granier is a pretty climb – a classic twisting Alpine route with a fairly constant gradient. But there is one hard stretch right in the middle. If you carry on down the straight descent you come out in St Pierre-d'Entremont at the foot of the Cucheron.

WHICH WAY? The climb starts in St Badolph about two kilometres south of Chambery on the D912. Follow this road to the top. You can descend to Entremont for the Cucheron or take a left at the summit and the D201 back to Chambery.

Col du Granon

Length: 16.77 km.

Altitude: 2404 metres.

Height gain: 1000 metres.

Average gradient: 7.2%.

Maximum gradient: 10.8%.

This is a big one, but it's not used often in the Tour as the road up is very narrow and is unpaved over the summit. It's also quite hard to find, and you must be careful at the top because the whole place is a military training area.

Don't let any of this put you off though, the Granon is a very interesting challenge. If you are riding a mountain bike, or have big tyres on your road bike, try crossing the top and descending to Val-des-Prés, which eventually brings you to the foot of the Col de Montgenèvre.

First Tour de France rider to conquer the Granon was the Spaniard, Eduardo Chozas in 1986. In what was the highest ever stage finish in Tour history.

WHICH WAY? Take the N91 north out of Briançon in the direction of Grenoble. There are no signs to the Granon, so just after St Chaffrey turn right to Villard-Laté. Continue through the village and eventually you will be climbing the Granon.

Côte de Laffrey

Length: 8.7 km.

Altitude: 904 metres.

Height gain: 540 metres.

Average gradient: 6.2%.

Maximum gradient: 11.2%.

Not a high climb, and often used early on in Tour stages because of its proximity to Grenoble, the Laffrey is famous because it was one of the first mountains ever to be used in the Tour. It was the first climb in the legendary 1905 stage that was the first in the Alps – starting in Grenoble and finishing in Toulon on the southern French coast. Hyppolyte Aucouturier was first to the top.

WHICH WAY? The climb starts in Séchilliene, a village just north of the N91 and 17 kilometres south -east of Grenoble. Take the D114 south for one kilometre, then turn right where the col is indicated and follow the D113 to the top. There is a labyrinth of quiet roads around Laffrey village, where the climb ends, so you can make up a round trip. Alternatively descend the Laffrey, turn right and climb to La Morte.

Col des Limouches

Length: 10.7 km.

Altitude: 1068 metres.

Height gain: 670 metres.

Average gradient: 6.7%.

Maximum gradient: 7%.

This climb is a very attractive way of entering the Vercous from the west. It starts in Peyrus and follows lovely natural lines over the first chain of the Vercours mountains. The descent of the Limouches takes you to the foot of the Col de la Bataille, which is a Tour de France climb but failed to make the 400-metre height gain cut off point for this book by the narrowest of margins.

Richard Virenque is the only Tour rider to have led the race over the Col des Limouches. He did it 2004 on the way to winning his seventh King of the Mountains title. After his retirement that year Virenque carried on winning by taking first place in the French version if 'I'm a Celebrity Get Me Out of Here'.

WHICH WAY? Peyrus is 19 kilometres east of Valence on the D68. Continue on that road for the top of the Col des Limouches.

Col du Luitel

Length: 10.9 km.

Altitude: 1265 metres.

Height gain: 855 metres.

Average gradient: 7.8%.

Maximum gradient: 10.2%.

The Luitel starts only one kilometre from the base of Chamrousse in the Belledonne. It's a nice twisty climb through the Premol pine forest, with impressive views over Grenoble during the first few kilometres.

The climb has seen several Tour de France battles since Charly Gaul was the first man to the top in 1956, one of which was when Giancarlo Bellini of Italy won the King of the Mountains in 1976. Bellini wasn't a super climber, but that year the best of them all, Lucien Van Impe of Belgium, was trying to win the Tour, so Bellini set out on day one to chase every point the could.

He took first place on the Luitel, but was nowhere near the leaders when battle raged later that day on Alpe d'Huez. Bellini carried on with his tactics until the last day of the Tour, prompting a journalist to write: "Many have suffered more to win the King of the Mountains, but no one has suffered longer than Bellini."

WHICH WAY? The climb starts in Vaulnaveys-le-Haut on the D524, which is three kilometres south of Uriage-les-Bains and fourteen from Grenoble. Go north on the D524 and after two kilometres turn right on the D111 and follow to the top of the Luitel. You can also climb the Luitel from Séchillienne.

Col de Menée

Length: 15.2 km.

Altitude: 1447 metres.

Height gain: 821 metres.

Average gradient: 5.4%.

Maximum gradient: 7%.

The top of this climb marks the border between the Isere and Vercours. It also ends in a short tunnel, and has only been included in one Tour de France. That was the 1994 event when Ronan Pensec was first to the top.

The climb starts in the village of Menée and lazily follows natural lines to the top, with just one stretch of seven percent following sharp left and right hairpins after two kilometres.

WHICH WAY? Menée is 20 kilometres south of Die, the nearest big town, on the D93, D539 and D120. Once in Menée keep going on the D120 to the top of the climb.

Col du Mollard

Length: 5.9 km.

Altitude: 1630 metres.

Height gain: 403 metres.

Average gradient: 6.8%.

Maximum gradient: 10%.

This is another climb that starts on the descent of the Croix de Fer, and was first used in the 2006 Tour de France on the stage to La Toussuire that Michael Rasmussen won. The Dane was first over the Col du Mollard that day too.

The climb starts in a tiny village called Belleville, just after the point where the Croix de Fer descent switches from going north-east to due north. Look for a right turn over a bridge over the baby river Arvette, which grows up later on the Croix de Fer descent to become the river Arven.

Once over the bridge the first part of the climb is relatively easy, but nearer the summit you get two quite lengthy stretches of ten percent for your money. The top of the climb comes just after the village of Le Mollet.

There are a choice of descents. Turn right shortly after the summit to descend to the Villargondran, which is just to the east of St-Jean-de-Maurienne. Or turn left to descend to the foot of the La Toussuire climb. You can also turn right at the foot of La Toussuire and go directly into St-Jean.

WHICH WAY? If you are descending the Croix de Fer on the D926 turn right and if climbing from St- Jean-de-Maurienne turn left onto the D80 in Belleville. Continue on the D80 to the top of the climb.

Col de la Morte

Length: 15.3 km.

Altitude: 1360 metres.

Height gain: 996 metres.

Average gradient: 6.5%.

Maximum gradient: 8%.

Col de Noyer

Length: 7.5 km.

Altitude: 1664 metres.

Height gain: 616 metres.

Average gradient: 8.2%.

Maximum gradient: 9.8%.

Another climb that has only been used once by the Tour, in 1979 when Mariano Martinez from France won the climbing points on it. The race must surely return again one day because the first part of this climb is a spectacular experience.

Its starts in Séchillienne, which is on the north side of the Romanche river and the N91. You ride over both on a bridge then start a series of natural bends, with a section of eight percent coming after the third bend. This section is followed by a series of lacets with a more constructed and symmetrical look. The mountain you can see on your left as you climb is the Taillefer (2857 metres)

Towards the top of the lacets there are two viewing points which afford great views over the lower Romanche valley, the western part of Grenoble and southern Belledonne climbs. Once you turn your back and continue climbing it is only a couple of kilometres of easy climbing to the summit in La Blache.

WHICH WAY? Séchellienne is 24 kilometres south-east of Grenoble on the N85 and N91. From the centre of the village take the D114 south over the N91 and follow that road to the top of the climb.

An ideal aperitif for an assault on Orcieres-Merlette, the Noyer is a short climb with an almost uniform gradient that was first used in the Tour in 1970, when Frenchman Raymond Delisle led over the summit.

If you base yourself at Gap you can turn this climb into a nice round trip by descending the way you came up it and turning left on the D14 to Orcieres. After that climb, retrace again until the start of the Col de Manse and use that to get back to Gap.

WHICH WAY? From Gap go over the Col de Bayard north on the N85. Turn left at Poligny and follow the D171 to Le Noyer, then continue to the top.

Le Pleynet-
les-Sept-Laux

Length: 22.7 km.

Altitude: 1450 metres.

Height gain: 985 metres.

Average gradient: 4.3%.

Maximum gradient: 7.1%.

Le Pleynet is a ski resort located towards the northern end of the Belledonne chain. It's a long but gradual climb with no really steep sections, so is ideal for anyone new to cycling, but who wants to have a go at an Alpine climb.

The last part is particularly good for beginners as the road climbs in a series of lacets that are so typical of Alpine climbs. There are lovely mountain views at the top over high lakes and some near-3000-metre peaks.

The first Tour rider to conquer Le Pleynet was the five times winner, and the last Frenchman to take victory in the Tour de France, Bernard Hinault. Nowadays Hinault works on the Tour de France organising the podium, in between being a very successful Breton farmer.

WHICH WAY? The climb starts in Allevard, which is a quite large town and a nice base for climbing the Belledonne. There's a signpost to Le Pleynet in the town centre. The climb is on the D525A. Don't confuse it with another climb which starts where the D109 splits from the D525A. The road you want is the right hand split.

Col de Porte

Length: 8.3 km.

Altitude: 1326 metres.

Height gain: 521 metres.

Average gradient: 6.3%.

Maximum gradient: 8.7%.

The most southerly of the Tour de France climbs in the Chartreuse Massif, the Col de Porte has been climbed from both sides by the race. It's closeness to Grenoble, the southern ascent starts almost in the city streets, mean that the Col de Porte has been the first or last climb in the many stages involving the Alpine gateway city.

The best side is undoubtedly the northern one, starting in La Diat at the foot of the Col de Cucheron. It starts fairly steadily but steepens after five kilometres for a couple of kilometres, then the gradient slowly relents all the way to the top. Emile Georget in 1907 was the first Tour de France rider to get there.

You can make a nice Tour stage of your own with the Col de Porte by stringing together the three Chartreuse climbs that lie between Chambery and Grenoble. The total distance is around 70 kilometres and by climbing the Granier, Cucheron and Porte in quick succession, you get the feel of what a Tour de France stage is like – except Tour stages are usually at least twice as long.

WHICH WAY? La Diat lies just south of St Pierre-de-Chartreuse on the D512. After a few hundred metres the road splits and one fork is the D520 going right into the Gorge du Guiers Mort, you continue straight on the D512 to the top of the col.

Prapoutel-
les-Sept-Laux

Length: 16.5 km.

Altitude: 1355 metres.

Height gain: 1115 metres.

Average gradient: 6.8%.

Maximum gradient: 7.8%.

Another Belledonne ski station, Parpoutel has been visited only once by the Tour de France. That was in 1980, when the climb was also the stage finish and a Belgian rider, Ludo Loos won.

The climb starts in the village of Tencin on the D523, about five kilometres north-west of Grenoble. It follows the natural contours of the hillside at first, but just after Les Ayes the road makes its final assault on the summit with a series of hairpin bends.

WHICH WAY? From the southern edge of Tencin on the D523, follow directions for the D30 and Prapoutel-les-Sept-Laux. Turn left straight after Les Ayes and take a right onto the D281 for the final part of the climb. There are lots of similar climbs that start between Domène and Tencin along the D 523, none of which have been visited by the Tour but you can spend a very pleasant day exploring them.

Col du Rousset

Length: 20.6 km.

Altitude: 1254 metres.

Height gain: 852 metres.

Average gradient: 4.2%.

Maximum gradient: 6%.

The Vercours climbs are a bit difficult to categorise. They have a southern feel, but Grenoble is on the north-eastern edge of the Vercours, so I've included them in the Central Alpine climbs.

Situated at the southern end of the Vercours regional park, the Col du Rousset was first included in the 1984 Tour de France when the Frenchman, Jean-Rene Bernaudeau was first to the top. The climb starts in Die, which lies on the river Drôme, and after an easy couple of kilometres the road begins to twist gently upwards before a short descent after four kilometres. The road then steepens as tight hairpins and long straights take you to the top.

WHICH WAY? Die is quite a sizable town, so it's a good base for the Vercours. It's on the D93 which you can access from the A7 Autoroute du Soleil about 16 kilometres south of Valence. The road to the top of the Rousset is the D518, which runs north, off the D93, on the eastern edge of Die.

Col de Romeyère

Length: 20.4 km.

Altitude: 1069 metres.

Height gain: 854 metres.

Average gradient: 4.2%.

Maximum gradient: 7.2%.

The most northerly of the Vercours climbs, the Romeyère is a delightful one without any particularly steep gradients that starts in the meandering Gorge de la Bourne. First Tour rider on the Romeyère was the great Federico Bahamontes on his way to winning the first of his six King of the Mountains titles in 1954.

WHICH WAY? The climb starts in Pont-en-Royans 10 kilometres south of junction nine of the A49 Autoroute on the D518. Just before the village turn left onto the D531, and follow this road through the T- junction at the eastern end of the village following directions to Villard de Lans. After 12.5 kilometres turn left out of the Gorge de la Bourne onto the D35, which is sometimes referred to as the Route des Ecourges.

Col de Tourniol

Length: 17 km.
Altitude: 1145 metres.
Height gain: 990 metres.
Average gradient: 5.8%.
Maximum gradient: 7.7%.

La Toussuire

Length: 17.6 km.
Altitude: 1705 metres.
Height gain: 1145 metres.
Average gradient: 6.5%.
Maximum gradient: 8%.

Starting in Barbières right on the edge of the regional park, the Tourniol is another climb that starts easy but gets progressively harder. It's a very attractive climb that twists and turns up a narrow road and provides fantastic views of the wide open lower Rhone Valley and the city of Valence.

The Tour has only used the Tourniol once, in 1987 when a Dutchman called Teun Van Vliet was first to the top. That stage also climbed the Col de La Bataille, which starts just a short way down the Tourniol descent. But with just under 400 metres of height gain from the Tourniol side, La Bataille is below the cut off point for inclusion in this book.

La Bataille is worth riding though, as are many other climbs and gorges in the Vercours, which is an excellent place for cycling.

WHICH WAY? Romans-sur-Isère is a good place to stay, if you want to be faithful to the Tour route and climb the Col from the Barbières side. From Romans take the D149 south-east out of town following directions for Marches. Go through Marches and pick up the D101 where it joins the D149 and continue through Barbières to start the climb. Switch to the D70 at the top if you want to descend and climb La Bataille.

A newcomer to the Tour in 2006, when this ski resort hosted the stage and finish Denmark's Michael Rasmussen won. La Toussuire has all the making of a Tour de France classic climb when it aquires a bit more history.

It starts in the town of St-Jean-de-Maurienne and it is steep from the off, especially just before the right turn to St Panacre. After that the gradient eases a bit but there are a lot of twists and turns and some of the hairpins are pretty steep as you climb out of them.

WHICH WAY? Take the D926 south-west out of St Jean-de-Maurienne. Turn right onto the D78C to St Panacre, then turn left after the village onto the D78 and continue to the top of the climb. The start of this climb is the end of the Col de la Croix de Fer, so a trip up to La Toussuire would round off a climb of the Croix de Fer nicely.

Southern Alps

Dividing the Alps into northern and central regions is a question of drawing an almost arbitrary line between similar regions, but the Southern Alps have an entirely different feel to the rest off the range. They are drier, often warmer, so less affected by snow. Most of it is gone by summer and falls in the winter are lighter.

Consequently, winter sports tourism isn't as important here, and it hasn't taken the place of older ways of making a living, like working on the land or producing wool and textiles. This means that the mountains of this region are less populated than those further north, and the whole region is quieter.

The Southern Alps are a hard place to live, but are heaven for cyclists with some amazing sights to take in. Sights such as the gorges of the Alpe Maritimes, or the lofty heights of the Cime de la Bonnette, or the simple loneliness of the country around the Col d'Allos. This is my favourite region of the Alps.

The remoteness of the Southern Alps means that are a bit short of base towns from which you can explore several mountains in one stay. So you need to be fairly mobile if you want to visit a lot of climbs in this region. Barcelonette is handy for the Cime de la Bonette, Allos, Cayolle, Pra Loup and Vars. Nice or any of the towns around it makes a great base for the Alpes-Maritimes and the other southerly climbs of this area.

Col d'Allos 'AT THE HEART OF TOUR TRADITION'

✪✪✪ 3 STARS

Length: 21 km.

Altitude: 2240 metres.

Height gain: 1090 metres.

Average gradient: 5.2%.

Maximum gradient: 10%.

WHAT TO EXPECT

➤ **Wilderness.** The southern Alps are the quietest of all three Alpine sections. The scenery has a wilder feel to it and there aren't the number of ski resorts that you find in the rest of the Alps.

➤ **Warm weather.** The southerly position and sparse vegetation means that the sun is strong on the southern climbs, plus many of them are at quite high altitudes, so put on plenty of sunscreen and unless it is all-day stuff, don't forget to keep reapplying it.

➤ **Careful descent.** The road up the Allos is quite narrow and very twisty, so take care if you descend the way you went up.

➤ **Ride into town.** The village of Allos is quite large and well worth a visit. You descend seven kilometres down the other side of the col to reach it, and there is a really nice climb that starts in the village and goes up to Lake Allos (2229 metres) that has a stretch of 15 percent gradient in it.

Barcelonnette

D908

Col d'Allos

This pass connects the valleys of the Ubaye and Verdon, and is one of the most attractive and unspoilt climbs that the Tour de France uses. It shares its start with the bottom of two other Tour climbs, the Col de la Cayolle and Pra-Loup.

If you start from the town of Barcelonnette, a nice place with plenty of amenities that doesn't feel like the outpost its location suggests, you have three kilometres of flat riding to complete before starting the climb up the side of the Bachelard Gorge.

The first part of the climb is a delightful passage through the Bachelard forest, where you'll be accompanied by the sound of the river tumbling through the bottom of the gorge below you. A stone bridge at six kilometres, the Pont du Fau, takes you over one of its tributary torrents.

The gradient eases after the bridge, but then the road direction swings sharply right and the hardest part of the climb begins. It follows the valley of another tributary of the Bachelard, climbing at around nine percent average with two short bits of ten percent around the 12-kilometre mark, where the Agneliers ski station is located.

Here the gradient eases a bit as a series of twists, turns and lacets take you upwards out of the forest for a short stretch then back along the top edge of it before reaching the summit. This is typical of the Southern Alps, the vegetation is much more sparse and dry-looking than you find on the northern summits of equivalent height.

Left: Twists and turns near the top   **Above:** Valley of the Alleux

The name Allos is a derivation of the French word *alleux*, which dates from the Middle Ages when most farmers were tenants on the land they farmed and had to give part of their crop to their landlords. The term 'alleux' was used to describe people who didn't recognise this right of landlords and were independent of them. Many of the high-altitude farmers of the Southern Alps were Alleux, and it seems that the people of the Col d'Allos were certainly not prepared to bend their collective knee to the aristocracy.

WHICH WAY?

Barcelonnette is on the D900 Ubaye valley road that runs between Gap and Italy. It's a great base for several Southern Alps climbs. To get to the start of the Col d'Allos you need to find the D902 road at the western edge of Barcelonnette. Turn right towards Pra-Loup, but at the first lacet of that climb carry straight on the D908 to the top of the Col d'Allos.

MOUNTAIN MOMENTS

➤ The Allos is an old climb in Tour terms. It was first climbed in 1911 by the Luxembourg rider, and 1910 race winner, Francois Faber.
First to the top of the Allos in 1934, on his way to becoming best climber that year, was a really strange character called Rene Vietto. His best cycling years coincided with the Second World War, so he never won the Tour de France. Whether that made him a bit cranky is anyone's guess, but there are some weird tales about Vietto. The strangest was when he had an aching toe in the 1947 race and he told his doctor to cut it off. "I'll be lighter in the mountains," he said. He also ordered his protégé 'Apo' Lazarides to have his toe removed as well. Vietto's toe is preserved in formaldehyde in a bar in Marseille.

Col de Braus   *'ENGINEERING MARVEL'*

★★☆ 3 STARS

Length: 11.2 km.

Altitude: 1002 metres.

Height gain: 639 metres.

Average gradient: 5.7%.

Maximum gradient: 9%.

WHAT TO EXPECT

➤ **Perfect climate.** Never too cold, never too hot, you can climb the Col de Braus all year round.

➤ **Tall storeys.** This part of the Alpes-Maritime is all gorges and deeply dissected valleys. There isn't much flat space to build long ... so they build tall here, and some of the villages are amazing feats of engineering ingenuity.

➤ **Memory of the king.** There is a memorial stone at the top of the Col de Braus in memory of Tour rider René Vietto, the man who had an infected toe cut off to make him lighter in the mountains and who 1930s bike fans called 'King René'.

➤ **Warm weather trainers.** A lot of pro riders live in this area all year round, but in January and February many northern-based cyclists come here for early season training camps.

I felt I had to include at least one of the mountains around the back of the Côte d'Azur as a major climb in this book, and in my opinion there isn't one that better represents this part of France than the Col de Braus. From either side, Sospel or l'Escarène, the climb uses beautiful natural lines or precision-built lacets to scale the maquis covered mountainside. It is a real peach.

The Col de Braus is also a good climb for spotting off-duty Tour de France racers. A lot of them live in Monaco and in Nice, especially Australians, who have made this part of France their home in Europe. They regularly use the Col de Braus to train.

The climb isn't particularly steep and the gradient is fairly uniform, only towards the top does it get anything like taxing. The Col de Braus is therefore a great climb for beginners as a one-off, and for the more experienced it's a great one to start a day of exploring the Alpes-Maritime. The Col de Turini, which as well as being a Tour de France climb is also a special stage in the Monte-Carlo rally, is close by. So are several other well-known climbs, although not all of them have had mountains points ratings in the Tour de France.

The climate in this area is particularly pleasant. There is very little snow in winter and when the coastal resorts get a bit muggy at the height of summer, the Alpes-Maritimes always make a pleasant change. You don't get the clogging traffic of the coastal strip up here either.

From Sospel the road heads south, wriggling its way up a valley then swings west to climb some of the most precisely built lacets you will ever see. Once you have climbed them the road follows a more natural line until another set of steep hairpins take you to the top.

It's 22 kilometres from Sospel over the top of the col and down to l'Escarine, but deep below ground the Nice-Cuneo railways trains go through the Sospel tunnel, which is bored straight through the mountain, in less than eleven.

WHICH WAY?

Sospel is on the crossroads of the D2204 and D2566. The former road is part of an old route called the salt road that runs from Turin to Nice, and the D2566 runs north from Menton. Follow signs to l'Escarine south on the D2204 for the Col de Braus. During the first set of lacets the road is joined by the D54. This is the Col de St Jean. Carry straight on the D2204 for the top of the Col de Braus.

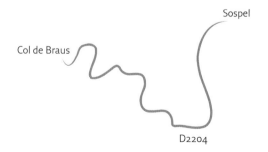

Sospel

Col de Braus

D2204

Above: One of the most amazing roads in Europe

 **MOUNTAIN MOMENTS**

➤ The Tour de France doesn't visit this area much nowadays. But it was very popular in races before the Second World War. Émile Georget in 1911 was the first Tour rider to the top.

➤ Benoit Fauré was the best on the Braus in 1929 and 1930. He was the last of a breed of racers called Touriste-Routiers, men who were outside of the main teams and ranged from rank amateurs who just wanted to have a go at the Tour, to talented individuals like Fauré who were good racers but who didn't want to be part of a team because they didn't want to be obliged to help their team mates. Fauré won the stage that climbed the Braus in 1929, and his individual approach took him to Eighth place overall in the 1930 Tour.

Cime de la Bonette 'THE TOP OF THE TOUR'

✪✪✪✪ **4 STARS**

Length: 23.8 km.
Altitude: 2802 metres.
Height gain: 1582 metres.
Average gradient: 6.7%.
Maximum gradient: 12%.

WHAT TO EXPECT

➤ **Thin air.** You can feel the effects of less oxygen in the air as you reach the top of the Bonette. The length of the climb and the difficult sections make this climb a real challenge. Gear down and treat it with respect.

➤ **Tale of two cols.** You sometimes hear of this climb being called the Col de Restefond, but today the Restefond is a pass you reach at 2656 metres, from which old tracks dating back to the days before motor vehicles lead down into two valleys on either side of it. The new road continues to the Col de la Bonette, which you can just go straight over, or you can go around the Cime de la Bonette purely for the highest road in France experience.

➤ **Gun emplacements.** The Bonette is very close to the Italian border today, and was even closer years ago. You will pass several concrete gun emplacements on the way up, and a whole deserted fort close to the Col de Restefond.

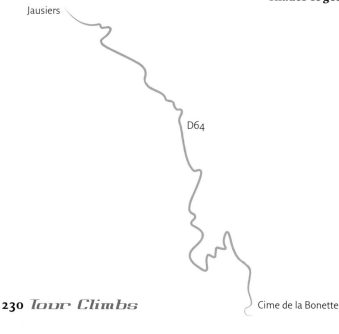

Jausiers

D64

Cime de la Bonette

This is the second highest road in Europe, although you'll see signs at the bottom that claim it to be the highest. They're wrong, unfortunately for local pride there is a road in Spain's Sierra Nevada that is reckoned to climb to more than 3000 metres. The Bonette is definitely the highest road that the Tour de France has ever climbed though, and riders who've done it in the race testify to feeling the oxygen thinning as they climb.

Actually it took a little local ingenuity to make the Bonette even the highest road in France. The Col de la Bonette is the natural pass that the road used for centuries to get between the Ubaye and Tinée valleys, but at 2731 metres that was fractionally lower than the Col d'Iseran. So in 1961 the local council's engineering department added 1700 metres of higher road starting at the Col de la Bonette, going up and around the Bonette's mountain peak, called the Cime de la Bonette, before returning to the level of the col.

Civic chicanery or not, the quest to be the highest takes nothing away from the majesty and unspoilt loneliness of the Bonette. The remoteness of the place is reinforced when you begin the climb and see that there are signs telling you this is a wild place and to be very careful.

They mean it too. The Bonette once had quite a few people living on it, but there is hardly anyone up there now. You'll see lots of ruined farm houses and smaller buildings as you ride up. There is even a deserted village on the descent. Today the Bonette is home to a few shepherds and lots of sheep.

The climb starts in Jausiers. The first part uses the valley of a small river, the Arbriès to gain height. Then it switches out into the open and you find yourself amid some of the most stunning high-altitude scenery in France. The colours here are amazing, rich shades of gold set against jet black rock, all enhanced by the crystal clear air.

Above left: Way above the tree line   **Above right:** Do they count cyclists?

Left: Descending the Bonette   **Above:** This was once the Italian border

![Mountain icon] **MOUNTAIN MOMENTS**

➤ Even though it has only been used three times by the Tour, only the best have shone on the Bonette. Frederico Bahamontes was the first Tour rider to cross the roof of the Tour. He did it in 1962, then repeated the feat in 1964, adding it to the 50 climbs he crossed in first place during his career.

➤ In 1993 Britain's only King of the Mountains, Robert Millar was first over the climb. Millar climbed the Bonette in solitary splendour but was caught on the descent by a group that included Miguel Indurain. He attacked again on the climb to the finish in Isola 2000, but was captured once more by Indurain and couldn't add to the three Tour stage wins the Scot took in his career.

The Bonette is a real treasure, a treasure protected by being part of the Mercatour National Park, whose rules at first appear quite draconian. But if they are what is required to keep this place like it is, then they are worth obeying to the letter.

WHICH WAY?

The climb starts in Jausiers, nine kilometres north east of Barcelonnette on the D900. The way to the climb is clearly indicated in the village. The D64 is the road up to Cime de la Bonette. It changes into the D2205 on the descent. The Bonette is part of a traditional high altitude route between Briançon and Nice that has been travelled for years.

Col de la Cayolle 'SOURCE OF THE VAR'

✪✪✪ 3 STARS

Length: 20.5 km.

Altitude: 2326 metres.

Height gain: 1291 metres.

Average gradient: 6.3%.

Maximum gradient: 10%.

WHAT TO EXPECT

➤ **Peace**. Not many people live around here and most holiday makers go north from the Côte d'Azur by using the N85 Route Napoleon.

➤ **Exposure**. There are some pretty scary drops going up the south side of the Cayolle. Take care.

➤ **Round trips**. The fit and keen might like to ride the Gorge de Daluis, climb the Cayolle, then climb the Col d'Allos and descend to Annot. It's just over a 100-mile round trip in glorious scenery with plenty of nice villages to stop and eat something.

➤ **Gorge circuit**. Another brilliant round trip is to ride up the Gorge de Daluis from the N202, then turn right at Guillaumes on the D28, head over the Col du Vasson for Beuil and descend the Gorge du Cians

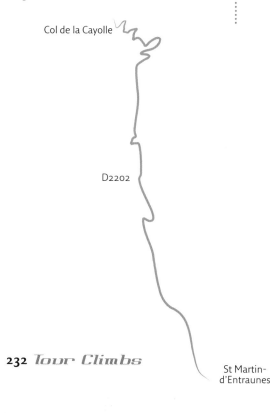

Col de la Cayolle

D2202

St Martin-
d'Entraunes

Both sides of the Col de la Cayolle have been climbed by the Tour, but the most attractive is the southern side from St Martin d'Entraunes, especially if you precede it with a ride up the Gorges de Daluis, which is like a mini version of America's Grand Canyon.

The Gorge is incredible. It's a deep meandering rift carved out by the river Var, which has its source close to the top of the Cayolle, and the rock sculpture that the river has left behind is truly amazing. The road clings to the vertical side of the gorge and you pass through several arches and tunnels cut into the sandstone by the road builders. Riding the gorge is unforgettable, and very little other traffic uses it.

You emerge from the Gorge about ten kilometres south of St Martin d'Entraunes, but pass through several medieval villages to keep your interest going before you get there. St Martin is also the start of the Col des Champs. You turn off the main road for that and keep going straight on for the Cayolle.

The road quickly narrows once you start climbing the first steep part of the Cayolle. The gradient lessens at halfway, but increases again after a couple of kilometres. The steepest two sections are in the second half of the climb, but neither of them are more than a few hundred metres long.

Left: Summit marker   **Above left:** Looking down the ascent   **Above right:** "We had Lance Armstrong up here last week, you know"

Just after the hamlet of Estenc you pass the source of the river Var, before pushing for the summit up a set of lacets. Be careful on this bit, the local white cattle tend to wander carelessly out into the road, or simply stand in it, blocking your way.

The summit of the Cayolle is the border between the Alpes-Maritimes and Alpes-Haute Provence departments, and is dominated by Mont Pelat (3501 metres), the first 3000-metre peak heading north from the Côte d'Azur. In a bit of natural symmetry, the descent of the Cayolle ends in the Gorge de Bachelard.

WHICH WAY?

There are no big centres of population near the Col de la Cayolle. The Gorge de Daluis starts on the N202, 13 kilometres west of Puget Théniers and seven kilometres east of Annot, which are the two biggest places in the area. Follow the D902 then D2202 north through the gorge, turning left, still following the D2202, at the junction with the D28 at Guillaumes. Continue to St Martin-d'Entraunes where you carry straight on to the top of the Cayolle.

MOUNTAIN MOMENTS

➤ Jean Robic in 1950 was the first Tour rider over the Col de la Cayolle, but I've chosen the Cayolle as a major climb because of its beauty rather than its Tour de France history. The climb has only been used twice since Robic had his day. Charly Gaul was first over in 1955, and a Spaniard Vincente Lopez-Carril proved to be best in 1973.

➤ Climbers tend to be one-offs, people the French call 'originals', but marginal is probably a better word. After Gaul stopped racing he opened a bar in Luxembourg, but closed it six months later and went to live in the Ardennes as a recluse. He lived without running water or electricity, and wouldn't talk to anyone. He emerged back into normal life 20 years later, saying he couldn't cope with everyday life after he stopped racing.

Col des Champs '*VAULTING THE VERDON AND VAR*'

⭐⭐ 2 STARS

Length: 16.3 km.

Altitude: 2087 metres.

Height gain: 1052 metres.

Average gradient: 6.5%.

Maximum gradient: 10.7%.

WHAT TO EXPECT

➤ **Mountain bikes.** The land either side of the Col des Champs is laced with mountain bike trails, and some of them include bits of the road in them too. Don't be surprised if a descending cross-country mountain bike clatters out of the bushes in front of you. One of the tracks they use is called the Col des Champs Muletier, which crosses the summit of the climb at right angles to the metalled road.

➤ **Butterflies.** The abundant and varied wild flowers that grow on the Cold des Champs attract one of the most varied collections of butterflies in France. One of them, the Candide, has bright yellow wings that are edged with pink and a striking pink body.

➤ **Tricky descent.** The road narrows on the descent to Colmars, and there are some tricky bends just before you reach the town.

The Col des Champs only features once in Tour de France history, but it is nevertheless an incredible feeling to climb it. It starts from the same place as the Col de la Cayolle, St Martin-d'Entraunes, but leaps up the valley side aiming for a low point in the continuous mountain crest that separates the Var and Verdon valleys.

This is another Alpine climb with a Pyrenean character. It starts with a tough 500 metres of 9.5 percent, which is as unusual start in the Alps, but after that the gradient is rarely the same for very long.

After the initial shock, the climb eases for three-and-a-half kilometres, but after that it bites again for the next four, and then goes flat. This lasts for one-and-a-half kilometres, but after that the gradients increase all the way to the toughest part of the climb at 14 kilometres, which is a one-kilometre stretch of just over ten percent. All the time the road writhes from left to right to seek out the easiest route up the valley side.

Nature is the compensation for all your efforts. There are an abundant supply of Alpine flowers and a large colony of marmots live up here. They are curious looking creatures with big buck teeth and this lot are very tame, often playing by the side of the road. You don't get many cars venturing up the Col des Champs.

Col des Champs

D78

St Martin-d'Entraunes

Above left: Looking down the ascent   **Above middle:** Erosion in soft sandstone approaching the climb   **Above right:** St Martin-d'Entraunes

The gradient eases for the last two kilometres, and the summit affords you fantastic views over the two valleys. The descent to Colmars is just as tortuous and unpredictable as the road you've climbed up. It's also narrower, so if you are not going back down the way you came, take care.

In the Verdon valley you can turn right and climb the south side of the Col d'Allos. A ride starting in Barcelonnette and including the Allos' north side, the west side of the Col des Champs and the Col de La Cayolle is just over 120 kilometres long, and a good test for any legs.

WHICH WAY?

The Col des Champs starts in St Martin-d'Entraunes, close to a bridge. On the main D2202 going through the village look for signs on your left to the Col de Champs and D78, the road that goes over it. Continue on the D78 to the top of the climb. This road turns into the D2 at the summit.

MOUNTAIN MOMENTS

➤ The Col des Champs has only been used once in the Tour de France, and it's inclusion as a major climb in this book is due more to its attractiveness and the abundant wildlife on it. However, the one time it was used was a momentous day in the history of the Tour de France. Eddy Merckx passed over the top of the climb in the lead wearing the yellow jersey of overall race leadership. He could have stayed with his rivals and watched them, but that wasn't the Merckx way. Just as he had done many times before he attacked when he thought he had the upper hand. He often used to say, "When the wind is favourable you don't stop sailing." This time though the wind died for Merckx, but you need to turn to pages on Pra Loup to find out what happened next.

Left: Gorges de Daluis

Isola 2000 'SKIING INTO ITALY'

★★★ 3 STARS

Length: 16.5 km.

Altitude: 2010 metres.

Height gain: 1137 metres.

Average gradient: 6.9%.

Maximum gradient: 9%.

WHAT TO EXPECT

➤ **Good weather.** Isola 2000 is close enough to the Mediteranean to enjoy lots of sun, although it's certainly high enough for good falls of snow in the winter.

➤ **Rock falls.** The valley sides are prone to them. If you see rocks on the edge of the road give them a wide berth. Where one falls another could follow.

➤ **Ring of mountains.** The Isola resort is surrounded by high peaks, many of which trace the border of France and Italy.

➤ **Southern edge.** Isola 2000 is the most southerly of the high Alpine Tour climbs.

Starting in the town of Isola, the Isola 2000 climb is one road up and one road down to the ski resort of the same name that is perched almost on the French and Italian border. It's a tough climb that without having any particular steep bits in it is fairly unremitting along its whole length.

It is also very attractive. Isola is a pretty town, the Italian influence in its buildings reflecting that it was part of Italy until the Second World War. Indeed the lands where the ski resort is now used to be a hunting ground for the King Victor Emmanuel of Italy. The climb pushes upwards through the torrents and waterfalls of the Guerche stream, and on to the resort at the top. Isola 2000 is an exciting voyage of unexpected views and experiences.

The climb starts almost in the town square of Isola and gains height rapidly as you enter the steep-sided valley of the Guerche. There are several bridges over this vibrant stream to cross, and it's worth stopping on the first one to take a look back down the valley and up at Mount Mounier (2817 metres) framed between the valley sides.

There are two stretches of nine-percent gradient in the first five kilometres, but after that the climb is still fairly constant around the six-and-a-half percent mark for almost its whole length, only relenting a bit at the very end as you approach the resort.

D97

Isola 2000

Isola

Left: The Guerche stream   **Above:** Nearing Isola 2000

If you have any energy left at the top there is a climb called the Col de la Lombarde that starts just as you reach Isola 2000 itself. This is a narrow twisting climb of five kilometres that takes you over the border and onto an interesting loop of Italian roads under the shadows of the Cime de la Lombarde (2800 metres) and Mont Aver (2745 metres).

The Col de la Lombarde was climbed for the first time in the 2008 Tour de France, but from the Italian side.

WHICH WAY?

Isola town is on the D2205, the road that runs north from the D6202, which is the main artery from Nice into the Alpes Maritime. The road to Isola 2000 is the D97 and you pick it up by leaving the D2205 and entering Isola town centre, the resort is clearly signposted.

MOUNTAIN MOMENTS

➤ Isola 2000 is another climb that I've included with the major ones because of its attractiveness rather than its Tour de France history. It has been used only once, in 1993 when it was the finish of a stage from Serre-Chevalier that was won by Tony Rominger. Rominger, a Swiss rider who was born in Denmark and speaks seven languages fluently, was one of the biggest rival to five times Tour winner Miguel Indurain.

➤ He ran Indurain closest in the 1993 race. Slightly the better climber, Rominger was King of the Mountains that year, but he never managed to take enough time from the Spaniard to win overall.

Col d'Izoard   'WHERE THE GHOSTS OF COPPI AND BOBET LIVE'

✪✪✪✪ 4 STARS

Length: 31.7 km.
Altitude: 2360 metres.
Height gain: 1438 metres.
Average gradient: 4.5%.
Maximum gradient: 7%.

WHAT TO EXPECT

➤ **Allow time.** Thirty-one kilometres is a long way up hill.

➤ **Take supplies.** There's not much commerce up here.

➤ **Easy start, hard finish.** Don't overdo your effort on the easy first bit, the Izoard gets much tougher as you near the summit.

➤ **Loneliness.** The Izoard is a bit off the beaten track

➤ **Tunnels.** You will encounter several early on.

➤ **The Bobet-Coppi memorial.** On the left, about two kilometres from the top, silhouettes of cycling greats Louison Bobet of France and the Italian, Fausto Coppi have been attached to one of the rock pinnacles in the Casse Deserte.

Col d'Izoard

D902

Guillestre

The Izoard is a long trek up into a geological wonderland called the Casse-Deserte, a barren scree slope punctuated by huge rock pillars that change colour with the changing light of the day. Pink at dawn, bleached pale yellow under the afternoon sun, they become eerie dark shadows by evening twilight, standing guard on the top of the col.

This route links the Guil and Cerveyrette valleys, historically an important back way to the outpost town of Briançon from the south of France and Italy. Napoleon's army of the Alps used it a lot, and so did local hunters.

The climbing starts shortly after Guillestre amid a ring of high peaks that surround the town. The first two-and-a-half kilometres are fairly gentle. You can stop at the orientation table by the side of the road that tells you the names of the surrounding mountains.

Then a short steep stretch leads to a descent and the real start of the climb at five kilometres. The mountain torrent beside you is the infant river Guil, which is born out of the snows of Mont Viso, a 3841 metre peak just over the border in Italy.

Eventually the road turns away from the roar of the Guil, climbing in a daunting straight line for seven kilometres up to the settlement of Brunissard. This is the highest of several settlements along the climb where gourmands might like to sample the two local cheeses, Blue Queyras and Tomme d'Izoard.

Left: Entering the most famous part of the climb **Above left:** One of the highst Tour climbs **Above right:** The rock pinnacles of the Casse Deserte

Now the road squirms upwards, doubling on itself to mount the steep top part of the col. A short descent and you are in the Casse Deserte wilderness, where only a sparse few pines and scrubby grass can grow. Look out for marmots, the large bucktoothed rodents that live and forage among this rock jungle.

At the top there is a small museum to the Tour de France, more orientation tables and a long twisting and very well engineered descent through picturesque villages into Briançon.

WHICH WAY?

From Guillestre, which is just off the N94 Gap to Briançon road, take the D902 north-east through a narrow canyon called the Combe du Queyras. Turn left at the junction of the D902 and D947 and continue following the D902 to the summit.

MOUNTAIN MOMENTS

➤ The Izoard first appeared in the Tour de France in 1922. The Belgian Philippe Thys was first to the top.
➤ Fausto Coppi and Louison Bobet were the first charismatic stars of cycling. Great champions had largely been tough farm boys, but Coppi and Bobet added a layer of sophistication to cycling. They were admired by fans from all sorts of backgrounds, they attracted money to the sport and they took cycling to another level. Their racing made them rich, and they had the lifestyles to go with it. Coppi won the Tour de France twice and Bobet three times. Both had some of their greatest racing moments on the slopes of the Col d'Izoard.
➤ Eddy Merckx's grip on the Tour de France ended the day before the race climbed the Izoard in 1975. The man who had ended it, Bernard Thevenet of France, climbed the mountain alone in the lead wearing the yellow jersey. He won the stage and the Tour de France.

Pra Loup 'WHERE WOLVES ROAMED'

●● 2 STARS

Length: 9.4 km.

Altitude: 1630 metres.

Height gain: 494 metres.

Average gradient: 5.3%.

Maximum gradient: 8%.

WHAT TO EXPECT

➤ **Mountain bikes.** Pra-Loup is a big place for downhill and cross-country skiing. The Masters World Championships were held there in 2007.

➤ **Wide roads.** Once you have turned off the first part of the Allos, the road to Pra-Loup is wide and well surfaced. You will really enjoy swooshing back down it.

➤ **Make a day of it.** Pra-Loup is perfect for ending an attack on the Allos, Champs and Cayolle.

➤ **Make a stay of it.** There is lots of accommodation in Pra-Loup.

➤ **Road with a view.** The higher you get the better the view across the Ubaye valley becomes. Stop before the buildings begin at the top to take in the upper valley east towards Italy.

Another climb to a ski resort, Pra Loup played a momentous part in the history of the Tour de France. It was the place where the reign of the great Eddy Merckx ended.

The ski resort started here in 1961 and is said to be one of the best in the Southern Alps, with facilities for many kinds of snow sports and 167 kilometres of runs from 1500 metres to 2600 metre altitude.

The climb starts in Barcelonnette, which is already at just over 1000 metres. The town grew here through the manufacture of woollen clothing, but distribution was always a problem at such an altitude because of the tough winters. By the start of the 19th century trade was in terminal decline.

This prompted the emigration of many young Barcelonnettes and a few ended up in Mexico, where they started up a textiles business that just grew and grew. They got rich, but instead of staying in their adopted country they returned to Barcelonnette, building a number of fine Mexican style mansions that can still be seen in town and in nearby Jausiers today.

They also brought a few Mexicans with them, some of who enlisted and were killed in the Great War. There is a memorial in town bearing their names, and many descendents still live there.

The first part of the climb runs alongside the enthusiastic Ubaye river as it splashes its way down to the lake at Serre Poncon and its confluence with the Durance. This is quickly left behind as you turn into the opening of the Bachelard gorge, the place that leads to the Col d'Allos and Col de la Cayolle.

The route quickly turns off the Allos road and begins a series of lacets that take you to the lower edges of Pra-Loup resort. The steepest part of the climb comes one kilometre before the end, which is the point in the resort where the road splits into three.

WHICH WAY?

Barcelonnette is on the D900 that runs from Gap to Italy. Take the D902 south west out of the centre of town and turn right onto the D908 after 2.5 kilometres and follow the signs to Pra-Loup, turning right again onto the D109.

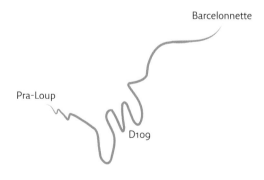

Barcelonnette

Pra-Loup

D109

Above: Looking down on the Ubaye valley and Barcelonnette

MOUNTAIN MOMENTS

➤ By 1975 Eddy Merckx had won almost everything in cycling, and many things more than once. He had won the Tour de France five times and his results so far that year, and so far in that Tour, gave no-one any reason to think that he would not win again. He was already the greatest cyclists ever, and he looked to be getting greater.

➤ When the stage to Pra-Loup started Merckx was leading overall, but he still attacked. Attacking was what he did. He led the race over the Col des Champs then put in a serious attack on Col d'Allos. He got a gap, but it wasn't a convincing one. He gained time on the descent but on the first slopes of Pra-Loup Merckx ran out of power. This had never happened to him before. He was caught and dropped by Bernard Thévenet, then others. In a few kilometres Merckx lost the yellow jersey and was never to wear it again.

Above: Mountains of the east Bachelard valley from Pra-Loup

Col de Vars 'HOME OF THE DAMSELS'

✪✪✪ 3 STARS

Length: 22 km.
Altitude: 2108 metres.
Height gain: 889 metres.
Average gradient: 5%.
Maximum gradient: 10.6%.

WHAT TO EXPECT

➤ **Off-roaders.** The Parpaillon mountain and ridge, and the tracks and passes of the upper Ubaye valley are very popular with cross-country mountain bikers.

➤ **Weather changes.** The Vars is getting to the limit of the benign effects the Mediteranean climate has on the southern Alps. The top is at 2000 metres and surrounding peaks are higher, so be prepared for a variety of conditions.

➤ **Linking up.** Combining the Vars with the Cime de la Bonnette to the south or Izoard to the north gets two high-altitude passes under your belt in one day, but they make 90- and 100-kilometre round trips.

➤ **Exploring.** The upper Ubaye valley has some interesting settlements in it. The road is the GR 5, it starts in St Paul-sur-Ubaye and follows the river up near its source in a high lake.

Col de Vars

Fort de Tournoux

Heavily fortified at its base, this climb is a Tour de France classic that links the Ubaye in the south and Queyras in the north. Its summit is also the border between the departments of Haute Alpes and Alpes Haute de Provence.

It is a north-thrusting side shoot to the Col de Larche, a main route carrying the D900 into Italy. At the beginning of the col you pass the Fort de Tournoux, which clings to a rock face high above the Ubaye valley. This has been a strategically important place since Roman times, but the present fort was built just before the Second World War. The French held out well in it against the invading Italians until Hitler's forces rolled into Paris and France fell.

The climbs starts steadily, but gets steeper just past another fort, the Redoute de Berwick, as it threads its way through the Pas de la Reyssole. This part of the climb uses the steep-sided valley of the upper Ubaye, but just past the village of St Paul sur Ubaye the road begins to climb out of that valley up a series of hairpins.

Just past a tiny track to the hamlet of Le Prat, start looking on your right for the Colonnes Coiffées. They are rock formations where hard stones have been contained within a softer matrix. The matrix is easily eroded by rainwater and the hard stones are not, so the hard stones protect parts of the rock below them and when the matrix around them is washed away they form columns. They look like tall women with piled up hairdos, and similar formations in France are called 'Demoiselles Coiffées', which is why I've called them the damsels of the Vars.

The damsels signal the hardest part of the climb as the road snakes right and left to the summit, which is at the eastern edge of the Parpaillon mountain (2988 metres). The descent is a long one, 27 kilometres down to Guillestre and the foot of the Col d'Izoard.

WHICH WAY?

The start of the climb is 18 kilometres north east of Barcelonnette along the D900. Going east turn left onto the D902 just after the Fort de Tournoux, which is high up on your left. Follow this road to the top of the climb.

Above: Halfway up

➤ The Col de Vars has been used 33 times in the Tour de France. The first time it was climbed was by a Belgian, Philippe Thys in 1922. Thys won the Tour three times; in 1912, 1913 and again after the First World War in 1920. It's fair to say that the war robbed Thys of more victories, even so it took until 1955 for Frenchman Louison Bobet to equal Thys' record of three wins.

➤ Fausto Coppi won the Tour de France in 1949 after a battle with countryman Gino Bartali, but his Tour nearly went wrong on the stage from Cannes to Briançon. Swiss rider Ferdi Kübler crossed the Vars nearly five minute up on the Italians, but punctured three times on the descent. Kübler won the Tour in 1950 and in 2009 was the race's oldest surviving winner.

Above: Mountains of the Mercatour from the Col de Vars

Above: Beginning of the Vars descent

Mont Ventoux '*THE GIANT OF PROVENCE*'

☆☆☆☆☆ 5 STARS

Length: 21 km.
Altitude: 1909 metres.
Height gain: 1610 metres.
Average gradient: 7.6%.
Maximum gradient: 10.7%.

WHAT TO EXPECT

➤ **Weather extremes.** Tends to be hot in the summer, but if the Mistral blows it can be bitterly cold. Go prepared for both.

➤ **Unrelenting gradient.** Use lower gears than you think you need for the first part.

➤ **Altitude effects.** It can be difficult to breath on the Ventoux, especially if it is hot.

➤ **Lots of company.** Despite its fierce reputation, or maybe because of it, the Ventoux is a cyclist's mecca

➤ **A coffee break.** Chalet Reynard is a famous cyclist's watering hole.

➤ **Exotic wildlife.** I've seen a wildcat up here, and I know somebody very believable who claims to have seen a white wolf.

This is a big one, a place for heroics and a place that punishes anyone who underestimates it. With proper preparation it is do-able, but whether you are a first-time big mountain climber or a Tour de France champion, Mont Ventoux demands respect.

There are three ways to the top; from Malaucène, Sault or Bédoin. None of them are easy, but the Tour de France always uses the south side from Bédoin. That way provides the classic Ventoux experience, where you climb an unrelenting road that screws upwards through a huge cedar forest, emerging from it at the Chalet Reynard to begin your drive on the summit.

It's a climb of two halves, of two characters. The forest section is steep but sheltered, a boon on this mountain where climate extremes are normal. Once out of the forest, whatever the weather is doing, the full force of the Ventoux will hit you. It can be bitterly cold, it can be stiflingly hot, and then there is the wind. The record wind speed recorded at the Ventoux summit was 193 mph!

Although the gradient is less, the climb gets really tough after Chalet Reynard. The trees are gone leaving a white, barren scree of rock. The road clings to this like a discarded ribbon, slanting diagonally across the mountain's face, so that when you are riding you can always see the summit. Here the weather is magnified. It's an extreme place, a barren moonscape on earth. The wind will try to blow you back from where you've come, and on a hot day the sun will burn you, bounce off the white rock and burn you again.

This isn't an easy day out on your bike, you must respect the Ventoux and it is really important that you start the climb cautiously and ride the first part well

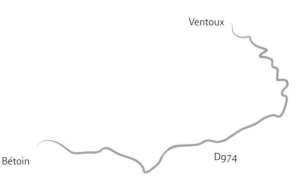

Ventoux

Bétoin   D974

Left page: The Tom Simpson memorial   **Above left:** Mont Ventoux silhouette   **Above right:** A future Tour winner?

within yourself. Even pro riders have come unstuck on the top section. But when you get to the top you will have climbed Mont Ventoux, something that every cyclist who has achieved it will relate to you with pride.

WHICH WAY?

From the centre of Bedoin follow the signposts directing you to 'Le Ventoux'. The road you want is the D974. The climb starts gently just outside Bédoin, but after 3 km, at St Estève, the gradient ramps up and stays almost constant until Chalet Reynard, where there is a short flat stretch. From the Chalet the gradient is slightly less for the remaining 6 km. From the top you can see the valley of the Rhône and the Mediterranean to the south, and the Alps to the east.

 **MOUNTAIN MOMENTS**

➤ **Tragedy.** British cyclist Tom Simpson collapsed and died during the 1967 Tour de France about 2 km from the summit of the Ventoux. You will pass a memorial stone on the right hand side of the road at the point where he fell. It is a tradition to leave something that you have carried up the mountain on the stone; a drinks bottle, an inner tube maybe, or a flower or a stone.

➤ **Grudge match.** In 2000 American Tour legend Lance Armstrong and Italy's Marco Pantani romped up the Ventoux, head and shoulders above the rest. Pantani was one of cycling's climbing greats, and matching his pace that day helped Armstrong to win the Tour, so he gave the stage to Pantani. The proud Italian, who died in 2004, never forgave Armstrong for not fighting him for the stage win, he said that it demeaned his victory.

➤ **First ascent.** The Tour first climbed the Ventoux in 1951, Lucien Lazarides, was first to the top.

Above: There's a sweet shop on top

245

Col de Brouis

Length: 10.5 km.

Altitude: 880 metres.

Height gain: 570 metres.

Average gradient: 5.4%.

Maximum gradient: 7%.

Used twice in the Tour, in 1952 and 1961, this is a main-road climb on the D6204/D2204 route from Turin to Nice. Its starts in La Giandola and winds up to the summit at just under six percent, with one bit of seven percent about three kilometres from the top.

The first Tour rider to the top of the Brouis was a naturalized Frenchman called Jean Dotto, who lived on the Côte d'Azur. He was a good climber who won a stage of the 1954 Tour de France, and the following year he became the first Frenchman to win the Tour of Spain.

WHICH WAY? The Col de Brouis is on the same road as the Col de Tende. You have to descend the way the Tour riders climbed up the Brouis to get to the Tende. Start the Brouis in the village of La Giandola on the D6204 going south. Turn right onto the D2204 after two kilometres and continue on this road to the top. The descent of the Brouis takes you to Sospel and the Col de Braus.

Col de Castillon

Length: 15 km.

Altitude: 707 metres.

Height gain: 697 metres.

Average gradient: 4.6%.

Maximum gradient: 6.8%.

This rarely used but pretty climb is one of the few in the Tour de France that starts virtually from sea level, right in the French Riviera resort of Menton. It's very popular with local cyclists and is ideal for getting to the other climbs that provide the green and white mountain backdrop to the Côte d'Azur. It's descent drops down to Sospel and from there you have the Col de Braus and the Turini and many others within easy riding range.

While you are riding you can marvel at the skills of the men who built the Menton to Sospel tramway, and the viaducts that take it into the hills. The Tour first used this climb in 1911, but the records only say that the riders were grouped together at the top, so we don't know who went over it first.

WHICH WAY? From the centre of Menton take the D2566 north, under the A8 Autoroute and on up to the top of the Castillon. You can descend to Sospel to turn left onto the D2204 and climb the Col de Braus, or take the narrow D54 left turn from the Castillon summit up the Col de St Jean, which joins the Braus halfway up. But if you do you miss the Braus' legendary lacets.

La Colmiane

Length: 8 km.

Altitude: 1504 metres.

Height gain: 513 metres.

Average gradient: 6.4%.

Maximum gradient: 8%.

This attractive and little-known climb to road riders was first used in the 1975 Tour when Spaniard Pedro Torres was first to the top. However, it is well known to local mountain bikers who use it in part of an off road circuit they call La Colmiane that explores the slopes of the Pic de la Colmiane mountain (1795 metres).

The best side to climb is from the medieval fortified town of St Martin-Vesubie, which has a stream called La Gargouille running down its main shopping street that you have to keep jumping over to cross from one side of the street to the other. It must keep the locals fit.

The first part of the climb heads up a steep valley then does a 180 degree turn to climb out of the valley and over the shoulder of the Baus de la Frema (2250 metres) and on to the top of the climb.

WHICH WAY? St Martin-Vesubie is on the D2565 about 55 kilometres north of Nice. Roquebillière is a slightly bigger town than St Martin, about 13 kilometres south of it on the same road, if you want a nearer base than Nice. Continue on the D2565 to cross the climb. The descent ends on the D2205. Turn right and Isola, the start place for Isola 2000, is just 13 kilometres away. La Colmiane is sometimes called the Col St-Martin

Col du Corobin

Length: 8 km.

Altitude: 1230 metres.

Height gain: 547 metres.

Average gradient: 6.8%.

Maximum gradient: 8%.

The Col du Corobin has been used twice in stages ending in Digne-les-Bains, where its descent virtually ends in the town streets. It's a sort of back road into town off the N85 and over a relatively small mountain called the Coupe.

The climb was first used in the 1969 Tour de France when a Spaniard, Gabriel Mascaro, was first to the top. Mascaro raced in three Tours but didn't win any stages. His most famous victory was probably in a hilly Basque Spanish one-day race called the Subida a Urkiola.

WHICH WAY? In Chaudon Norante on the N85, 31 kilometres north-west of La Castellane and 18 kilometres south-east of Digne-les-Bains, turn right from the south and left from the north onto the D20 and continue on that road to the top. If you carry on down the descent you will reach Digne-les-Bains.

Col de l'Espigoulier

Length: 9.6 km.

Altitude: 728 metres.

Height gain: 536 metres.

Average gradient: 5.6%.

Maximum gradient: 7.2%.

Located right on the edge of the Massif de la Sainte-Baume, not far from Marseille, and bordering the Chaine de l'Etoile where Marcel Pagnol's books, Jean de Florette and Manon des Sources were set, the Tour de France has climbed the Espigoulier three times and from both sides.

The first was in 1957 when Jean Stablinski was first to the top. Stablinski was a Frenchman with Polish parents who saw his father shot during the occupation of France. That left the 12 year old as the breadwinner for a large family, so because he wanted to be a racing cyclist rather than work down the mines of northern France, Stablinski advertised for a husband for his mother. A man replied, Stablinski's mother married him and Stablinski eventually married the man's daughter. He always said that it was the advert was best one franc he ever spent.

WHICH WAY? The slightly more attractive side to climb is from Gémenos, but they are both beauties. Gémenos is five kilometres east of Aubagne on the D2, and Aubagne is virtually connected to Marseille, 15 kilometres to the west on the A50 Autoroute. In Gémenos follow the D2 to the top of the climb. The descent to Pujol is on the D45A.

Col de Perty

Length: 12.5 km.

Altitude: 1302 metres.

Height gain: 600 metres.

Average gradient: 4.8%.

Maximum gradient: 9.3%.

Mont Faron

Length: 5.5 km.

Altitude: 508 metres.

Height gain: 494 metres.

Average gradient: 9%.

Maximum gradient: 16%.

A fabulous climb that rises in a series of ever shortening hairpins, like a flicked ribbon, up a little known area of mountains just north of Mont Ventoux called Les Baronnies. Everyone heads south to the Ventoux, and every cyclist should climb the Giant of Provençe once, but if you get the opportunity go and look at this part of France. The area has a micro-climate that is fractionally cooler than Provençe, which can be a blessing in summer, so the vegetation is greener. There are lots of small climbs and less trafficked roads for cyclists, some lovely peaks up to 1600 metres for walkers, and this is great country for mountain bikers.

The Col de Perty starts in La Combe, which is in the upper Ouvèze valley. The gradient is very light at first, but as soon as you hit the hairpins it rises to six and seven percent and increases to just over nine near the top.

Vaison-La-Romaine is a great base for looking at Les Baronnies. It quite a big town further down the Ouvèze valley with some fantastic preserved Roman buildings. It's close to Mont Ventoux as well.

WHICH WAY? From Vaison go south-east on the D938 towards Malaucène, then turn left on the D54, then left again onto the D13 and D5. Follow the D5 to Buis-les-Baronnies and take the D546. At St Auban-sur-Ouvèze turn left onto the D65 and La Combe and the start of the Col de Perty. The D65 goes all the way to the top.

Mont Faron towers above the port of Toulon and has been used for centuries by sailors to navigate their way into the harbour. It has only been climbed once by the Tour, in 1957 when Jean Stablinski was the best on his way to winning the stage from Cannes to Marseille. Stablinski had led for most of that stage, finishing 12 minutes ahead of the next man.

This climb features regularly in the early season Paris-Nice stage race, when there is often a time trial up its slopes, which are quite fearsome. It starts easily enough but the second kilometre has an average gradient of 11.4 percent and a couple of stretches 16 percent. The rest of the climb is at a constant eight to nine percent. The views over Toulon and across the Mediteranean more than compensate for the effort.

WHICH WAY? Start in the old port part of Toulon and follow signs for Super-Toulon, then Mont Faron. The roads are urban unclassified ones.

Col de Murs

Length: 10.4 km.
Altitude: 637 metres.
Height gain: 459 metres.
Average gradient: 4.3%.
Maximum gradient: 8%.

A relative newcomer to the Tour, this Provençal climb has been used twice by the Tour, the first time being in 1998 when Vincente Garcia-Acosta from Spain was first to the top. He climbed the south-east side and descended the north-west side. In 2000 the Tour climbed the north-west side, which is by far the most attractive as it passes first through the Venasque Forest then between a sculpture park of natural rock formations. The climb is on the western edge of the Plateau de Vaucluse, and from the top you can see Mont Ventoux towering above the plateaux to the north.

WHICH WAY? The climb is on the D4 road running between Carpentras and Apt. Carpentras is a great base for trying out the Provençal climbs, as it's also only 15 kilometres from the start of Mont Ventoux. From Carpentras follow the D4 south-east in the direction of Apt. The climb starts at the hamlet of Notre Dame de Vie, just before Venasque. Follow the D4 to the top.

Les Orres

Length: 17.7 km.

Altitude: 1650 metres.

Height gain: 780 metres.

Average gradient: 4.4%.

Maximum gradient: 8%.

Col de Tende

Length: 29 km.

Altitude: 1279 metres.

Height gain: 987 metres.

Average gradient: 3.4%.

Maximum gradient: 9.8%.

Les Orres is a ski station above Embrun, a town situated at the eastern edge of the Serre-Ponçon lake. The station sits in the shadow of the Parpaillon ridge and it runs almost parallel with the descent from the Col de Vars. It's not a very steep climb, but it twists and turns its way up to the ski station giving nice views over Embrun.

The climb has only been used once by the Tour when it was a stage finish in 1973. Luis Ocaña, the Spanish winner of the Tour that year won the stage, one of six he took in the 1973 Tour.

Embrun is a famous place in the sport of triathlon, as it is where the Embrunman race is run. Competitors face a cold 3.8 kilometres swim in the lake at dawn, then a 183 kilometres cycle leg that includes the Col d'Izoard. To end their day they run a marathon.

WHICH WAY? Embrun is on the N94 road that links Gap with Briançon. The road to Les Orres is the D40 and it joins the N94 on the western edge of Embrun. Turn right if approaching from the west and left if approaching from the east. Like many ski resorts Les Orres is a stretch of buildings with different centres, just continue to the end of the mettled road for the top of the climb.

The figures we quote are the official ones for the Col de Tende that now runs from Breil-sur-Roya and through the Tende tunnel, but the road is very busy as it is the main one from the French Riviera into Italy.

I think it's better to start this climb in Tende, which is at 791 metres of altitude, and go over the top on the old road that was the only way before the rail and road tunnels were dug. This makes a climb of 13 kilometres and 1080 metres of height gain up to 1870 metres of altitude, giving an average gradient of 8.3 percent and a real challenge.

You stick with the main road at first, right up until the tunnel mouth, but then the old road spears off to the left and climbs in a series of hairpins to the top of the col. You can descend to the mouth of the tunnel on the Italian side if you like and return to Tende by the same way. It's only a 33 kilometre round trip, but one with some serious climbing in it. If you've energy left there are some lovely climbs up the Minière, Levense and Refrei valleys to explore using Tende as a base.

On its two visit's the Tour de France climbed the old road. Jean Robic was first over in 1952 and an Italian, Imerio Massignan repeated the feat in 1961. Massignan was the Tour's King of the Mountains in 1960 and 1961, when he also finished fourth overall.

WHICH WAY? Tende is on the D6204, which is part of the main route from Nice to Turin. The D2204/D6204 junction is 21 kilometres north of Sospel and is reached from Nice on the D2204. Go north on the D6204 for 19 kilometres to Tende. Continue on this road until just before the Tende tunnel entrance and turn left to cross the Col de Tende.

Col de Turini

Length: 24 km.
Altitude: 1607 metres.
Height gain: 1244 metres.
Average gradient: 5.2%.
Maximum gradient: 9%.

Another of the Riviera climbs, the Col de Turini has been used by the Tour three times, twice climbing from Sospel, where the Col de Braus also starts, and once from La Bollène-Vésubie. The above statistics are from Sospel. From Bollène-Vésubie the climb is 15.3 kilometres at an average gradient of 7.2 percent giving a height gain of 917 metres.

The climb is an interesting engaging and visually satisfying one, the only word of caution being that the Turini is also used as a special stage in the Monte Carlo car rally, so it is of interest to car enthusiasts who sometimes try their skills on it. Unfortunately not all of them are as polished as their pro driver heroes, so keep well in on all bends and use special caution if you hear a powerful motor coming up or down.

The Turini isn't a race track though. Most of the time it is very peaceful, and despite its car connections cyclists do rule the climb. The first Tour riders to cross the Turini was the great Frenchman Louison Bobet. Bobet was the son of a Breton baker who after he stopped racing made a fortune from developing the health and beauty treatment of Thallasotherapy, which is basically a sea therapy but is still a multi million dollar business and very popular in France.

WHICH WAY? From Sospel follow the first 100 metres of the Col de Braus then turn right on the D2566. At the top of the col the D2566 will take you back to the other side of the Col de Braus and you can go over the col back to Sospel. Or you can follow the D70 to La Bollène-Vésubie, then turn around and climb the col de Turini from that side and descend to Sospel for a full Turini experience.

Col du Vasson

Length: 13 km.
Altitude: 1700 metres.
Height gain: 932 metres.
Average gradient: 7.1%.
Maximum gradient: 9%.

This climb is the road up to Valberg, the ski resort that sits on the D2 between the spectacular gorges of Daluis and Cians. The Tour climbed it twice in the fifties, the first rider being a Belgian Armand Baeyens in 1950. It hasn't been back since the fifties, maybe because of the difficulty in getting its whole entourage through the gorges.

It's a tough climb, from the start in Guillaumes the gradient hovers around the seven percent mark all the way to the top. The climb is a great experience when used to link a ride of the two gorges. Do the Daluis first, climb the Vasson, then descend from Valberg and continue east until you turn right at Beuil to enter the Gorge du Cians.

WHICH WAY? Guillaumes is on the D2202, 90 kilometres north east of Nice using the D6202 D902 and D2202. Go south on the D2202 out of Guillaumes and turn first left on the D28 to Valberg for the climb..

Index